Cultural Critique

32

Print and cover design: Nora Pauwels

Cultural Critique

Cultural Critique (ISSN 0882-4371) is published three times a year by Oxford University Press, 2001 Evans Road, Cary, NC 27513, in association with the Society for Cultural Critique, a nonprofit, educational organization.

Manuscript submissions. Contributors should submit three copies of their manuscripts to Abdul R. JanMohamed, *Cultural Critique*, c/o African American Studies Program, 305 HTC, University of California, Irvine, Irvine, CA 92717–6850. Manuscripts should conform to the recommendations of *The MLA Style Manual;* authors should use parenthetical documentation with a list of works cited. Contact the editorial office at the address above for further instructions on style. Manuscripts will be returned if accompanied by a stamped, self-addressed envelope. Please allow a minimum of four months for editorial consideration.

Subscriptions. Subscriptions are available on a calendar-year basis. The annual rates (Issues 32–34, 1996) are £25 (UK & Europe), US$38 for individuals, and £44 (UK & Europe), US $65 for institutions. Single issues are available for £10 (UK & Europe), US$15 (USA and elsewhere) for individuals, and £17 (UK & Europe), US$25 (USA and elsewhere) for institutions.

All prices include postage.

Personal rates apply only when issues of the journal are sent to a private address and payment is made by personal check or credit card. All subscription, single issue, back issue, changes-of-address, and claims for missing issues should be sent to:

NORTH AMERICA: Oxford University Press, Journals Customer Service, 2001 Evans Road, Cary, NC 27513, USA. Toll-free in the USA and Canada 1-800-852-7323 or 919-677-0977. Fax: 919-677-1714. E-mail: jnlorders@oup-usa.org.

ELSEWHERE: Oxford University Press, Journals Customer Service, Walton St., Oxford OX2 6DP, UK. Tel: +44 1865 56767. Fax: +44 1865 267485. E-mail: jnlorders@oup.co.uk.

Advertising. Jane Parker, Oxford University Press, Journals Advertising, Walton St., Oxford OX2 6DP, UK. Fax: +44 1865 267835.

Indexing/abstracting. *Cultural Critique* is indexed/abstracted in *The Left Index, Alternative Press Index, Sociological Abstracts (SA), Social Welfare, Social Planning/Policy and Social Development (SOPODA), International Political Science Abstracts, MLA Directory of Periodicals, MLA International Bibliography,* and *Periodica Islamica.*

Postmaster. Send address changes to Journals Customer Service, Oxford University Press, 2001 Evans Road, Cary, NC 27513. Postage paid at Cary, NC, and additional post offices.

⊗ The journal is printed on acid-free paper that meets the minimum requirements of ANSI Standard Z39.48-1984 (Permanence of Paper), beginning with Number 1.

Can the Postcolonial Critic Speak? Orientalism and the Rushdie Affair

Anouar Majid

Postcoloniality is the condition of what we might ungenerously call a comprador intelligentsia: of a relatively small, Western-style, Western-trained, group of writers and thinkers who mediate the trade in cultural commodities of world capitalism at the periphery. In the West they are known through the Africa they offer; their compatriots know them both through the West they present to Africa and through an Africa they have invented for the world, for each other, and for Africa.
—Kwame Anthony Appiah, *In My Father's House* (149)

Nor defame nor be sarcastic to each other, nor call each other by (offensive) nicknames.
—*The Holy Qur'an* (49: 11)

Let there be no compulsion in religion: Truth stands out clear from error.
—*The Holy Qur'an* (2: 256)

The ascendancy of postcolonial theory in the American academy has had an ambiguous effect at best, for though it has

© 1996 by *Cultural Critique*. Winter 1995–96. 0882-4371/96/$5.00.

brought the concerns of the hitherto marginalized people to the front of intellectual debates, it has also, by the same token, managed to obfuscate some of the enduring legacies of colonialism, including the pauperization of the Third World in the age of late capitalism. For the diverse groups of Islamists who are trying to challenge this unprecedented threat to their cultures and religion, this has meant challenging a rearticulated discourse of orientalism that seeks to portray Islam as an undifferentiated monolith, an Islam whose supposed ultimate goal is the dismantling of the most cherished values of the West, namely, freedom of expression, democracy, and human rights. Islamism is increasingly seen, by both its adherents and its detractors, as the voice of the South in its struggles against the hegemonic aims of the North. More than a mere manifestation of a globalized trend of fundamentalism, the process of Islamization is, as François Burgat has recently argued, the strident voice of God's "once-forgotten sons of the South" (*The Islamic Movement in North Africa* 69). In this context, new theories have emerged to redefine military strategies and redraw the map of the world along cultural lines. Since the Gulf War, Huntington states in his widely read essay "The Clash of Civilizations?," "NATO planning is increasingly directed to potential threats and instability along its 'southern tier'" (31). He acknowledges, like others have done before him, that Turkey is denied membership in the European community because it is Islamic (42) and warns, as the *Economist* had done before him, against the emergence of a Confucian-Islamic alliance to challenge the West (45–47).[1] Just when postmodern theories were thought to have taken us to a new dimension of thinking about ourselves in the world, essentialist views of civilization are being resurrected to account for continuing tensions, without subjecting the culture of capitalism and the lasting effects of colonialism on the shape of the world today to rigorous criticism. The heroic efforts of postcolonial critics such as Edward Said to highlight the nefarious consequences of an orientalist scholarship that is complicitous with the violent enterprise of colonialism has most certainly given a new meaning to cultural criticism in the West, but, as Arif Dirlik has recently argued, "postcolonialism has been silent about its own status as a possible ideological effect of a new world order situation after colonialism"

("The Postcolonial Aura" 331). Not only is "postcoloniality . . . the condition of the intelligentsia of global capitalism" (356) and the discursive power of "new found power" by Third World intellectuals in First World academe (329, 339), but it has also been "designed to *avoid* making sense of the present crisis and, in the process, to cover up the origins of postcolonial intellectuals in a global capitalism in which they are not so much victims as beneficiaries" (353). I would, however, qualify these dubious benefits, for despite the high visibility of a select group of intellectuals (mostly of Indian origin [Dirlik 340]), their sense of alienation and loss can barely be disguised; and although their theories, like all theories, should be subjected to criticism, they must continue to be seen as victims of a larger enterprise whose origins go back to the earliest colonialist phase. For the seemingly liberating discursive power of various "post" theories notwithstanding, one must decide whether the struggle for liberation from the clutches of neocolonial policies that support the transactions of transnational capitalism is, as Frantz Fanon once put it, "a cultural phenomenon or not." Obviously a rhetorical question, Fanon's immediate answer is unequivocal: "We believe that the conscious and organized undertaking by a colonized people to reestablish the sovereignty of that nation constitutes the most complete and obvious cultural manifestation that exists" (*Wretched* 245). But since, according to Dirlik, Third World intellectuals such as Homi Bhabha have been "completely reworked by the language of First World cultural criticism" (n334) and have largely managed to obfuscate realities without a mapping of which no viable struggle can be mounted, it is doubtful, at best, whether their insight on cultural practices can be useful to the struggle of Third World peoples. For, to invoke Fanon once again, "the business of obscuring language is a mask behind which stand out the much greater business of plunder" (189). Because the postcolonial state is more colonial, inasmuch as its culture is more thoroughly infiltrated by the ideologies and culture of former metropolitan centers, the restoration of an indigenous vocabulary is not the nostalgic and sentimental gesture that many of its critics make it out to be, but is the very act of cultural affirmation and political expression needed to reconnect the individual with his or her tradition. Part of the Islamist agenda, then, is to contest the West's absolute certainties, without necessarily rejecting aspects of modernity, although modernism is, in a post-Weberian analysis, "the incorporation of all areas of the world and all areas of even formerly 'private' life into the money economy" (Appiah 145). The commodification of life calls for a high degree of individualism, appropriate for the capitalist conception of art,[2] but which erodes historical continuity and the sense of community that sustains traditional societies (see Appiah 141–46). In other words, many of the categories used by secular(ized) intellectuals to dismiss alternatives rooted in religion can be convincingly critiqued; yet the latter continue to cast a cold eye on Islamic revivalism, especially in the wake of the recent controversy over Rushdie's *The Satanic Verses*. While extremism can take on both secular and religious aspects, it is the unmediated Islamic contestation of the West that has been censored out of prestigious academic journals, often legitimized by the paradigmatic names of a handful of superstars.

Gayatri Spivak, Akeel Bilgrami, and Edward Said were, for example, among the postcolonial critics who strongly protested Khomeini's *fatwa* on Rushdie, exonerated Islam from such "bigoted violence," and reaffirmed their "belief in the universal principles of rational discussion and freedom of expression" in a letter to the editor of the *New York Times* (17 Feb. 1989, A38). Spivak's signature on the letter may have been politically strategic, but when, later that year, *Harper's* published a forum on the canon, she had failed to defend Islam from the orientalist criticisms of scholars such as Roger Shattuck. The latter, at one point during the debate over the canon, fired point blank at the two ends of the political spectrum. "Have you read the Koran [sic]?" he asked Hirsch. "No," answered this most conspicuous defender of cultural literacy in the U.S. Then, after announcing that he had read the Qur'an "three times in two different languages," he turned to Spivak:

> **Shattuck:** [. . .] Gayatri, have you read it?
> **Spivak:** No.
> **Shattuck:** Okay. Look at what you find in the Bible and in the Koran. As classics, these books are not moral equivalents or literary equivalents or equivalents in greatness. [Shattuck goes on to explain how the Bible is superior.] (47–48)

Spivak and Hirsch, however, did not accept this proposition: Spivak because she doesn't believe in hierarchical structures or value binarisms; Hirsch, because to say so (and he agrees with Shattuck on the issue of quality) is not "politically feasible." Although one is hard pressed to know in exactly what two languages Shattuck had read the Qur'an, he succeeded, by this simple gesture, to legitimize the virtues of the classical liberal education challenged by new pedagogical and curricular theories, and to problematize the reliability of postcolonial intellectuals in the West as adequate speakers for theoretical Islam.[3] Spivak, who had defended Islam against intolerance, had not read the most central text of Islamic cultures.

I am writing this essay not to critique Spivak or other leading Third World writers and intellectuals in the West—on the contrary, my intervention would most certainly have been difficult, if not impossible, without their groundbreaking efforts—but rather to question the representation of Islam and Islamic identity in postcolonial studies and to suggest that Islamic alternatives (which cannot be thoroughly examined in this paper) are necessary for the emergence of a new multicultural order based on dialogue, not exploitation. At a time when issues of subjectivity are rigorously debated, many Muslims—whether familiar with Western theory or not—continue to be denied access to mainstream prestigious journals. Thus Edward Said's diagnosis of a self-perpetuating Orientalist tradition of distortion and prejudice is being applied to the U.S. (and perhaps Western) culture at large, since Muslims' inability to represent themselves—in other words, their passive participation in their own orientalizing—is not only related to repressive régimes and inadequate facilities in the Islamic world,[4] but it is also actually hindered by the pervasive proliferation of a few theories (e.g., Orientalism as a discursive gesture or deconstruction as a self-negating technique) that have now become the standards against which all postcolonial theories are tested. Dirlik's suspicion that postcolonial theories are complicitous with the exploitative tendencies of global capitalism will need to be persuasively answered if the postcolonial project is to have legitimacy for the downtrodden; for despite Spivak's and Said's heroic efforts to steer the course of Western cultural criticism away from its historically parochial confines, their excessive familiarity with the most arcane and inaccessible philosophical and literary traditions of the West makes them appear unsettlingly unreliable to many Muslims. Spivak has had to struggle with the issue of her own reliability: regarding theory as a form of Orientalism ("Subaltern" 295–96), she concedes, after a lengthy examination of two French intellectuals' coming to terms with the irreducible problematic of representing Others, that the "subaltern" (the leftovers, *le déchet* of social strata, the Other of the Other, the nameless muted Hindu woman) "cannot speak" (308). The impossibility of representation properly acknowledged, she nevertheless refuses to "disown" her female intellectual's "circumscribed task" with "a flourish" (308). In other words, the pull of the American cultural apparatus (along with the inescapable urge to speak itself) cannot be easily resisted; this apparatus, after all, describes Spivak as "one of *our* best known cultural and literary theorists" (*Postcolonial* [henceforth *PC*], pbk. back cover).[5]

The nameless speaking Subject of this generous evaluation reproblematizes the positionality of the self-consciously acculturated Third World intellectual and pushes us to inquire further into the questionable program of postmodernism as a "final solution" to the crisis of identity. Although Spivak may be more comfortable in the U.S. than she would in India (*PC* 94), and rootlessness may be a virtue (37), she still resists total assimilation—at least symbolically—by refusing to apply for U.S. citizenship or to vote (*PC* 135). She defines her role as that of a scholar who brings metanarratives to a "crisis," a strategy that is useful in "contact politics" (questions of subjectivity), for "the only thing one really deconstructs are things into which one is intimately mired" (135). The Subject of Spivak's evaluation thus transforms a depoliticized (in the grand tradition) scholar, permanently alienated from her homeland since the age of 19, a woman who yearns to be Bengali and Indian again (115) into the mediator of an unequal cultural exchange, a dialogue conducted almost invariably in one of the modern imperialist languages. For while the Western academic conscience is readily assuaged by the symbolic representations of the Other (Third World peoples), it refuses to ask the equally significant if not troubling question: At what price postcoloniality? This aspect of postcoloniality is what Dirlik forgets to address, for if Third World intellectuals in the West are empowered by the insight of their displacement, their trauma is nonetheless real. To forget this is to forget the reality of pain, to reveal a disturbing lack of sentience and the myopic limitations of reified scholarship. If the goal of postcolonial theory is to abolish certainties at the superstructural level, the entire project cannot be completed, as E. M. Forster concluded on friendship between political unequals in *A Passage to India,* without genuine political sovereignty. Only at this moment does displacement lose the coercive power of necessity and become the purely intellectual force it otherwise can and should be.

Edward Said, the prototypical "specular border intellectual" familiar with two cultures but "unable or unwilling" to be in either (JanMohamed 97) not only embodies the harrowing predicament of the Third World critic in the West, but his very presence in the Western academy and the "tense productivity" of his scholarship are expressions of the Palestinian suffering, the people who are condemned to be at home in their homelessness (to use one of JanMohamed's metaphors). In fact, the project of questioning *Orientalism* itself can be seen as an act of protest that aims at unmasking the cultural face of imperialism without necessarily being interested in offering "an alternate positivity" (JanMohamed 105). This is why postcolonial theory transforms itself into a discursive gesture that is simultaneously informed and coopted by the very assumptions of Western humanism it questions in the beginning. If Said once had to defend himself against the surprising charge of Eurocentrism when a black woman historian found his allusion to "white European males" excessive (Said, "Criticism/Self-Criticism" 37–43), it is because he seems to have been severely constrained by a struggle that demands that he first legitimize himself to that nameless Subject that claims and disclaims, the panoptical Western Body whose capricious selectivity finally drains the energies of Third World resources—both human and natural.[6] Said's *"worldliness,"* therefore, while ideal under economic socialism, not only risks displacing struggle as one of the most effective ways to be heard, but it may also evoke images of a utopian cosmopolitanism that is unachievable in the present arrangements. Said is surely aware of all this; what seems problematic, however, is the status he confers on the migrant or the exile as the best situated intellectual and contrapuntal reader of culture in the age of global capitalism. It is, he writes,

> no exaggeration to say that liberation as an intellectual mission, born in the resistance and opposition to the confinements and ravages of imperialism, has now shifted from the settled, established, and domesticated dynamics of culture to its unhoused, decentered, and exilic energies, energies whose incarnation today is the migrant, and whose consciousness is that of the intellectual and artist in exile, the political figure between domains, between forms, and between languages. (*Culture and Imperialism* 332)

If the "specular border intellectual" is equipped to examine the synchronicity of culture in the (post)modern era, exile, as in Said's case, remains the condition of disempowerment whose "salutary" effects are to be decided against "the normal sense of belonging" (Said xxvi, xxvii). A Christian who is culturally a Muslim, Said critiques "the forces of resistance to Islam" but does not address the "major epistemological problems" of "modernity, "heritage," and "authority" that Arab and Muslim scholars are now in the process of examining ("The Phony Islamic Threat" 62–65). Yet Islamic alternatives have been almost unanimously rejected, while making sense of this Islamic phenomenon has been entrusted to scholars whose impressive credentials in Western culture are not enough to disqualify others whose project is precisely to theorize Islamic alternatives to Western hegemony.

Take the case of Akeel Bilgrami's reading of the Islamic identity in a special issue of *Critical Inquiry* about identities, guest edited by Kwame Anthony Appiah and Henry Louis Gates, Jr. (Summer 1992). Here moderate Muslims appear to be besieged by the mounting crescendo of an antihistorical absolutist dogma (read: "fundamentalism"), a belief that has outlived its functional context (since it is decidedly antisecularist), and therefore becomes excessive, much like neurosis. This is the "surplus phenomenology of identity" (833, see 832–35). Bilgrami then proposes that Islam be reduced to "deist core" (840) in a secular modern social arrangement. What Bilgrami does philosophically is precisely what the modern orientalist discourse has been doing and continues to do

to this day: by dismissing the strong revivalist current in much of
the Islamic world to a "neurosis," the author implicitly condemns
serious alternatives (models of social reconstruction erected not on
an absolutist economism and the high individualism to which it
corresponds [postmodern condition], but on a moral order that
defines the role of human existence in radically different terms)
to the pathological wards of insanity.[7] Relying on the discourse of
psychoanalysis, Bilgrami conveniently (mis)diagnoses what is often
a struggle for cultural liberation (in the wider sense implied by
Fanon), and prepares the terrain for anti-Islamic forces to continue their mission of violence and conquest. Edward Said's critical
project of orientalism is precisely, as he emphasizes in *Culture and
Imperialism*, to show the ways in which cultural practices precede,
support, and justify imperialism (see, for instance, 200, 221–22).
Yet his monumental influence notwithstanding, the orientalist discourse continues unabated; for as long as the secular premises of
Western scholarship are not interrogated, it is at best doubtful
whether the discursive interventions of some Third World critics
can effectively contribute to the liberation of Third World peoples.
In other words, the intractable secret to unrelenting cultural imperialism, together with the orientalist discourse it engenders, is the
framework within which political contestations take place. No matter how insightful and liberating Western self-critique can be, it
still partakes of the secular assumptions of the Enlightenment, and
cannot persuasively intervene in any discourse without accepting
the limitations of this condition. Moreover, when radical critiques
of the West are articulated in one of the European languages, they
end up, as John Tomlinson has argued in *Cultural Imperialism* (11),
reproducing the very hegemonic structures they want to eradicate.
An irresolvable paradox borne out of existing power relations, one
that can only be overcome with the emancipation of the entire humanity from the clutches of an anticultural capitalism. But even
within this seemingly inescapable structure, the term postcolonialism is strategically disabling, as its prefix not only seems to relegate
colonialism to a past that no longer is (McClintock, "The Angel of
Progress" 84–98; Shohat, "Notes on the 'Post-Colonial'" 105), but
also suggests a "dubious spatiality" that erases the concreteness of
inequality (Shohat 103). (Besides the dubious claim that countries
such as the U.S. and Australia are postcolonial, Said's contrapuntal

reading does suggest, rather ironically, that the whole world is *post-colonial*, a suggestion that may be totally incomprehensible to the Palestinian people who are still under occupation, for instance).[8] I therefore suggest that if the critical project of Third World critics in the West is to have relevance, we must continue to call ourselves "colonized" intellectuals, despite our desire for equality and mutuality, and despite some of the privileges that have accrued to us in our displacement. The best we can do is try to persuade the master to change his mind, for our rival (Western capitalism) will act at its own discretion until that privilege is substantially diminished. To collapse irreducible differences into an uncritical universalism or to advocate the adherence to regnant Western paradigms would therefore only obfuscate the basic structures of the present global system and complicate the struggle needed for the emancipation of the wretched.[9] The time now is for self-assertion; not to accept this proposition is simply a political position that must be challenged.

The growing concern over Islamic revivalism has reinvigorated the orientalist discourse precisely because Western(ized) academics, including those on the Left, cannot accept and are not willing to learn why certain basic universalist tenets of Western civilization are, in fact, historically and culturally specific. François Burgat, for instance, explains that while it is ready to accept the Other,

> the Left has retrenched to its finicky attachment to secular symbols, and today seems to be a prisoner of its own inability to admit that the universalism of republican thought can be called into question, or that anyone might dare to write history in a vocabulary other than the one that it has forged itself.
>
> But it is precisely the rupture in language and syntax—the discarding of Western political terminology—which is the core of the Islamist recipe. Henceforth, the potential for misunderstandings becomes vast. (*The Islamic Movement* 6)

Since the secular reading of faith as religion "has its origins in the post-Enlightenment West," Western academics, Esposito believes, "have been a major obstacle to understanding Islamic politics and so have contributed to a tendency to reduce Islam to fundamentalism and fundamentalism to extremism" (*The Islamic Threat* 199,

200). Relying on the unshakable tenets of "secular liberalism and relativism," they act as "conservative clerics" when they fail to see Islam as a dynamic "faith-in-history" (200).[10] And this is how a new form of orientalism is disseminated (202). So the question that Said asked in *Covering Islam*, "What is it about 'Islam' that provokes so quick and unrestrained a response [in the West]?" (8) is as valid now as it has always been, for Islam continues to be seen as a "threat to Western civilization" (136).[11] Said suggested that the answer may lie in the insularity and "guild orthodoxy" of Orientalism, especially since meaning depends at least as much on "affiliative" ("related to what other interpreters have said" [154]) configurations as it does on reading alien cultures.[12] But Akbar Ahmed's thesis that, under the tutelage of its dominant Greek heritage, Western culture has erected its foundations on elitism, sexism, impatience with human frailty, and arrogance—a legacy of ruthless humanism that stands in sharp contrast with the semitic (including Christian) insistence on humility and obedience[13]—broadens the argument further and helps shed light on those irreducible cultural differences discursive universalisms cannot mend. While the semitic tradition is predicated on the "fall from [divine] grace" and salvation,[14] the Greek legacy, the most recent expression of which in the academy are current theories of postmodernism, is predicated on a human-bound notion of "progress":

> Consider three of the most important founding fathers of the modern Western mind, Marx, Nietzsche and Freud. Marx's doctoral dissertation (1841) was on the materialist and anti-metaphysical philosophers Democritus and Epicurus; Nietzsche became a professor of classics in 1869 before he was 30; and Freud was fascinated by many aspects of Greek culture—for example, Platonic love and catharsis—long before he coined the term "Oedipus complex" in 1900. (*Postmodernism and Islam* 87)

Westernized African and Asian intellectuals enter this history with varying degrees of assimilation and resistance (their attitude partly reflecting their class origins, determined, in recent history, by colonialism), but Muslims (especially those who have had a fair exposure to Islamic education, such as remembering the Qur'an and praying during childhood) seem to experience the dichotomous pull of the two historical currents much more intensely. Indeed, their very location in the West is itself a monumental challenge to their being, for as Fredric Jameson suggested in another context, the practice of faith needs a relevant context: the monadic experience of the subject in late capitalism commodifies belief and renders its meaning superfluous (see *The Political Unconscious* 252). This may also help explain why the idea of monotheism troubles postmodern writers, for without the anchor of faith, without the ability to transcend the circulation of images, the inevitable instabilities that Lyotard celebrates, and the instant perishability of meaning in the era of the *petit récit* (call it the régime of untruths, if you will),[15] it is, as Harvey has conclusively demonstrated in *The Condition of Postmodernity*, the most apt representation of the increasingly irrational human and social life under the tyrannical flexibility and irresponsibility of transnational capitalism. Like Islam, postmodernism is also "submission," but submission to a mirage, to a condition of extreme alienation, and no Muslim intellectual can convincingly accommodate alienation by espousing European theory. Since, as Spivak admitted, we all have irreducible essences and essentializing, although preferably minimal and perpetually self-critical, is inevitable (*PC* 11–12, 45, 51, 53, 68), alienation will continue to traumatize Muslims unless they reclaim their traditions as the starting point for a suitable model of social reconstruction. Thus, collapsing differences into a (Western-dictated) universalism obliterates the promise of non-Western systems to struggle for cultural equality, without which encounters are condemned to remain one-dimensional and hegemonic. But how does one equalize cultural encounters under the logic of transnational capital and the "corporate takeover of public expression"?[16] How are the estimated 3,500 spoken languages that exist in the world today given an equal status in the family of human languages when more than two-thirds of global communications are produced in five European languages (Tomlinson, *Cultural Imperialism* 11)? This is the insurmountable hurdle that legitimizes the right of alternative emancipatory models to be taken seriously, even supported, as Sartre knew, unconditionally; for only the total liberation of non-Western peoples and the unequivocal defeat of Western imperialism can give birth to a new human consciousness.

The search for universality has led theory to transform the

catastrophe of homelessness, rootlessness, and just plain displacement into a virtue. Hybridity (the cause of so much trauma in the
Third World)[17] and syncretism are proposed as best available models to dismantle the unproductive polarizations inherent in the to-
talizing narratives of difference (and which are necessary for a
gradual emancipation); but since both conditions are also the effect
of unequal global relations, their unthinking propagation risks becoming complicitous with the systemic violence inflicted on billions
of people worldwide. While the salutary effects of contrapuntal or
deconstructionist readings cannot be denied, the darker side of
theory needs to be given a more central position in order to construct a more organic relationship between theory and reality. For
"the most extreme forms of the self-critical and anarchic models of
twentieth-century culture which modernism ushered can be seen
to depend on the existence of a post-colonial Other which provides
its condition of formation" (Ashcroft, Griffiths, and Tiffin, *The Empire Writes Back* 160). Euro-American culture, like its economy, is
built on the exploitation of non-Western peoples (see, for instance,
Rodney, *How Europe Underdeveloped Africa*),[18] while the Third
World itself cheers on, through the agency of a powerful comprador class, this civilizational deformity. The containment of Third
World peoples through a Westernized elite has always been a deliberate design of colonialism,[19] a policy that was most succinctly articulated in 1835 by Lord Thomas Babington Macaulay in what is
known as his "Minute on Education":

> We must at present do our best to form a class who may be
> interpreters between us and the millions whom we govern; a
> class of persons, Indian in blood and colour, but English in
> taste, in opinions, in morals, and in intellect. (qtd. in Ahmed,
> *Discovering Islam* 126)[20]

Thus the imperialists embarked on a campaign of cultural annihi-
lation, imposing new languages on their captives to disrupt the
necessary continuity between culture and language, causing a
massive identity crisis, including among the "interpreters" themselves (Soyinka's novel by the same title is an ironic illustration
of this confusion).[21] Hybridity and syncretism are then a state
of mind, the theory of most diasporic Third World intellectuals

(Ashcroft et al. 108; Brennan, "Rushdie, Islam, and Postcolonial Criticism" 271–76), intellectuals of the highest caliber suffering stoically, reaching out for a world that is no longer theirs, unable to feel at home in a world that has become theirs by default. Yes, homelessness-as-home, home-as-homelessness celebrated as cultural achievement by a Western academic apparatus eager to congratulate itself on the unmitigated pain of both Westernized intellectuals and indigenous peoples, an apparatus devoid of sentience and unable to break away from the imperatives of a narrow professionalism that insists on productivity avant tout, and rarely on genuine emancipation. This West has turned Rushdie's predicament into a cause célèbre, using his colonization to launch yet another wave of vicious attacks on an already traumatized people, transforming a native-born Indian from a Muslim family who has had to immigrate to England into a convenient hero, without ever pausing to remember the consequences of the other *fatwas* articulated, not by Iranian Ayatullahs, but by British Lords: Macaulay and Lytton in India, and Lugard in Nigeria. Instead of using this occasion for soul-searching and healing, the cultural apparatus rallied to reiterate that Western values are indeed universal, and that Islam and Islamists are yet to be civilized. On the thousandth day of the *fatwa*,[22] the *Times Literary Supplement* (8 November 1994) published the commentaries of prominent Western writers who used this occasion to depict Islam in the dark colors of the worst orientalism. Here are excerpts:

> Then came the holy war against *The Satanic Verses* in which the enemy was a single fiction, a single writer, and the whole might and money of the Islamic world was deployed in the *fatwa:* death to Salman Rushdie. (Nadine Gordimer)

> The lethal pitch of Islam is all the more understandable since Islam is among the youngest of the existing creeds; intolerance is the mark of its age as well as its means of transportation. (Joseph Brodsky)

> Clearly, fundamentalists are nowhere near accepting the vital Western principle of the rule of law, religious tolerance, and freedom of speech and enquiry—the underpinning of what V. S. Naipaul now identifies as "our universal civilization" . . .

> [Pressure must be increased] to secure the lifting of the
> *fatwa* . . . to persuade Islamic fundamentalism that it will re-
> main outcast until it comes to terms with Western standards of
> civility. (Ferdinand Mount)

How does a Muslim respond to this? Gordimer suggests that
such a publishing event is an innocent harmless act (although she
must have been aware of the death toll that resulted from it) and
transforms one leader's *fatwa* and a few million dollars into "the
whole might and money of the Islamic world." She implies that
writing in a global village dominated by former imperial languages
and powerful disseminating systems is a harmless activity, perhaps
just irritating; she thus fails to see, as does Ali Mazrui, how writing
itself can be a "lethal weapon" ("Satanic Verses" 132). In her view,
the whole Islamic world is complicit in the conspiracy to execute
Rushdie, while she never wonders whether the Islamic world, still
regularly bombed, harassed, and occupied, has any "might" at all.
The oil-producing Islamic countries drained their money reserves
to accommodate the U.S.-led imperialistic designs in the Gulf, an
event that only demonstrated how postcoloniality is an empty expression in the Arab world.[23]

Brodsky chose to attribute the "lethal pitch of Islam" and its
"intolerance" to the religion's youth (a rather intriguing argument
since Islam has been more tolerant than the Christian West, where
the oldest of monotheistic religions, Judaism, suffered relentless
persecutions that culminated in the Holocaust);[24] he is, however,
curiously silent about the newness of the "New World" itself, where
indigenous civilizations were gruesomely decapitated—to use
Marx's expression—and replaced by an imperial political and economic order that is still the nightmare of non-Western peoples.
Still, Muslims are condemned to remain uncivilized and barbaric,
as Ferdinand Mount clearly suggests, until they accept "the vital
Western principles of the rule of law, religious tolerance and freedom of speech and enquiry." Thus, a whole page in one of the
most prestigious book reviews in the West uncritically propagates
the supremacy of Western civility, carrying on the mission of orientalism, recently decried by a no less prestigious scholar, without
evoking the slightest sense of incongruity. The imperative of Western secularism, on which the whole edifice of Western scholarship

rests, remains the holiest of principles; its challenge may well mean an assault on the secular (Western) individual's being. If this can be understood, then one could begin to get a glimpse of what the ideology of Western secularism might mean to the Muslims' own sense of identity. Perhaps for this reason, Salman Rushdie "has been perceived by many Muslims as being guilty of cultural treason" (Mazrui, "Satanic Verses" 118).

Theoretically, Rushdie is a postcolonial writer who has been inserted in the postmodern moment by the Western cultural apparatus (Dirlik 348). Mark Edmundson, for instance, sanctified Rushdie as a "prophet" because *The Satanic Verses* "is infused with innovative power, with a capacity to prophesy, and maybe even to provoke change"; the novel, with its unprecedented creativity, is a "harbinger" for a "*positive* postmodernism" ("Prophet of a New Postmodernism" 62; author's emphasis). Not only is Rushdie's style "*post*-contemporary," but Rushdie himself is posthistorical, wanting "to be ahead of time, doing some of history's work for it" (62, 68). What is this exceptional talent that allows Rushdie to anticipate history? Rushdie's "rewriting of Muhammad . . . means speeding up the work of secularization by vaporizing—in good, negative postmodern fashion—the prophet's holy aura" (68). Partly for this reason, Muslim (or other Afroasian) intellectuals have found themselves drawn to the anti-Islamic camp to the point of absurdity. Qadri Ismail, for instance, claiming that Rushdie's novel speaks for the constituency of apostates in the Islamic world, sees Western liberalism (or neocolonialism) and Islamic fundamentalism as allies in the defense of purity, since both ideologies fear hybridity; *The Satanic Verses* becomes in this case a double-edged, simultaneous critique of both systems ("A Bit of This . . ." 123). But Aamir Mufti's more sober argument reiterates the same universal neo-orientalist statements Edmundson makes:

> By questioning the infallibility of the Revelation, by refusing to accept the required code of strict reverence in speaking of the Prophet and his close circle of relatives and companions, and, more generally, in secularizing (and hence profaning) the sacred "tropology" of Islam by insisting upon its appropriation for the purposes of fiction, [*The Satanic Verses*] throws into doubt the discursive edifice within which "Islam" has been produced in recent years. ("Reading the Rushdie Affair" 107)

Edmundson makes it clear that the desacralization of the Prophet Muhammed sacralizes Rushdie as an artist. Rushdie himself, being "a member of that generation of Indians who were sold the secular idea," ascribes powerful possibilities to art (*Imaginary Homelands* 16). For him, "redescribing the world is the first necessary step towards changing it," and good books should expand the horizons of possibility, even "when they endanger the artist by reason of what he has, or has not, *artistically* dared" (13–14, 15; author's emphasis).[25] The powers of art are unlimited: in its "secular definition of transcendence" it can replace religious dogma, while religious faith "must surely remain a private matter"; indeed, with the collapse of communism, literature is left alone to battle the sweeping march of capital by bringing certainties to a crisis ("Is Nothing Sacred?" 7, 9, 14).

That cultural practice could acquire revolutionary meaning seems to be a shared belief among certain postmodernists. Spivak, in a debate about postmodernity, argues that deglamorizing *grands récits* works against a capitalism that needs all the ammunition of unexamined certainties to carry on its mission of pillage (see *PC* 20–21). Perhaps it is this belief that has created an aura of radicalism around some cultural journals, where the main concern seems to be the dismantling of traditional convictions and the releasing of people into a liberating hybridity—the rapture of rupture, as Lyotard would have it. The revolutionary project having failed in France, the authoritarianism of grand narratives must now be denounced, and with it any visionary agenda of social reconstruction and a better world for humanity. The replacement of heroic idealism with theoretical playfulness, struggle with disenchantment, may just ominously signal the inability of Western oppositional forces to mount a credible resistance to the overwhelming power of transnational capital, partly because to the extent that they are an integral part of Western political culture, their alternatives are more likely to be coopted and reduced to variations on the single theme of secular democracy. This may explain why, even before Khomeini's *fatwa* was issued, Rushdie had been depicted as a besieged champion of freedom of speech in the West, from whose shores he dared the prime minister of an important Third World country to lift the ban on his book: "This is now," Rushdie wrote, addressing the late Rajiv Gandhi in the *New York Times*, "a matter between you and me."

While the political reasons that brought the *New York Times* (and other equally established papers) and Rushdie in alliance may be easy to surmise, the most disconcerting aspect of this gesture is to equate the ego of an ambitious writer—a writer who, as Ali Mazrui would say, "elevates the pleasures of art above the pain of society" ("Satanic Verses" 136)—with the awesome responsibilities of the head of a strife-ridden and religiously explosive state, a prime minister who would be assassinated precisely because he could not contain ethnic tension in his country. Ironies of history: it was Khomeini who replied a few months later, thus provoking massive indignation in the West and unveiling, once more, the incongruous face of orientalism. A furious debate erupted after the *fatwa* and reached every corner of the globe. *The Rushdie File* (edited by Appignanesi and Maitland, 1990) records its initial phases, which revolved around issues of censorship, responsibilities of writers, sources and markers of identity, and tolerance; but what really emerges from reading these various positions is that the project of the Enlightenment, with its premise of freedom of expression, is not—and has never been—as "universal" as the postcolonial writers so unequivocally state in their letter to the *New York Times* editor. For while freedom of expression is seen as a fundamental human right in Western democracies, Islam problematizes the very definition of the human, although an increasing number of Islamic scholars are also challenging the premises of Islamic law itself, eager to take the Islamic nation (*umma*) to a new plane of consciousness that is neither uncritically traditional nor blindly Western.

One of these reformers is Abdullahi Ahmed An-Na'im, the author of a study on civil liberties, human rights, and international law. An-Na'im, like practically all Islamists, reads the present Islamic resurgence as "the right to self-determination" (*Toward an Islamic Reformation* 10). But since concepts of historical Shari'a cannot be accommodated within the existing structure of the nation-state (whose viability An-Na'im doesn't question), the Shari'a, not being divine, must be revised to adapt to modern times; for despite the problematic applicability of Islamic law within secular global arrangements, "Islamic validity . . . is essential for the viability of the proposed reforms" (xv). An-Na'im, however, wants to identify a "common normative principle shared by all the major cultural traditions," and that is "the principle of reciprocity" (162–63). For him, "universal human rights are based on two primary forces that motivate all human behavior, the will to be live and the will to be free" (164). Still, An-Na'im doesn't define freedom, and so for an Islamic definition of freedom, we need to go back to his mentor, the late Sudanese scholar, Mahmoud Mohammed Taha.

In his controversial book *The Second Message of Islam*, Taha defines freedom as the overcoming of fear, since fear is the greatest obstacle to love and to a harmonious, balanced, and spiritual existence (67, 112, 129). Only Islam, which connects the individual with the community, is able to liberate people in this fashion, for Western civilization (not Christian), premised on a thoroughly materialistic view of life, has failed to create the conditions for a better world. And since Islam is a total way of life, freedom to develop means freedom from the various obstacles that hamper such development, including the freedom from political oppression and economic exploitation. Which is why Taha imagined a "superior state" that he called the "Good Society":

> The good society is one that is based on three equalities: economic equality, today known as socialism, or the sharing of wealth; political equality or democracy, or sharing in political decisions which affect daily life; and social equality which, to some extent, results from socialism and democracy, and is characterized by a lack of social classes and discrimination based on color, faith, race, or sex. In the good society, people are judged according to their intellectual and moral character, as reflected in their public and private lives and demonstrated in the spirit of public service at all times and through every means. Social equality aims at removing social classes and differences between urban and rural life by providing equal opportunity for cultural refinement. (153)

Such a society, furthermore, "enjoys tolerant public opinion, permitting different life-styles and manners, *as long as these are beneficial to society*" (153; my emphasis). This latter qualification needs to be highlighted for the crisis of contemporary Western society stems from its failure to produce a social imaginary that would give social existence a meaning that goes beyond the pursuit of elusive pleasures. It is precisely because capitalist modernity is experienced as a "loss,"[26] an anticultural process that fetishizes culture into marketable commodities, that Islam, drawing its inspiration from divine law, appears as a profoundly disturbing effect to the reigning global complacency. The Islamic social narrative is antimodern only to the extent that it refuses to treat free (bourgeois) expression as the finality of the social project; societies need to strike a balance between individual and communal needs, and Islam provides just one answer, which those who have despaired of the false promises (or premises) of capitalist modernity need to examine seriously, before they allow themselves to be ensnared by the myths which had nurtured them for so long. Secularism itself is originally a Western idea born out of specific historical circumstances,[27] and its rejection by many Muslims is part of the struggle for self-definition, which is an equally fundamental right. Most Arab intellectuals interviewed on the subject of human rights seem to agree that defining one's identity is an indispensable foundation for any discussion of human rights, which is one reason why the Westernized intellectuals' emphasis on liberty in the Arab world has only limited relevance. Indeed, according to one Moroccan graduate student, intellectuals have failed to account for the popular will, since Moroccans are mostly concerned about the erosion of their "human" and moral system (in the aftermath of colonialism), which is why Islamic groups are the "expression of the vital will of Moroccan society to maintain and perpetuate itself" (Dwyer, *Arab Voices* 139–40, 136, 138). "The liberation of our spirits from the hegemony of Western thought," wrote Salah Eddine Jourchi, an Islamist, "is an indispensable condition without which we will not free the land nor the economy and without which we will not manage to reunify our ranks," for to be alienated is to be underdeveloped, hence "the first step [in the process of liberation] is to destroy in ourselves the idol of the West" (Burgat 73). Unsurprisingly, Dwyer discovered that the Western notion of human rights is severely problematized, if not rejected out of hand, across the political spectrum, even in the most Westernized of Arab countries, such as Morocco, Tunisia, and Egypt. He then concludes that the Islamic resurgence is "a response to urgent contemporary problems," including "the desire to construct societies free from the ills of 'modern' Western society: its materialism, lack of social cohesion, lack of common purpose, absence of a sense of community" (215). Because the Islamist discourse, as Burgat observes, breaks away from the discourse of Western culture (121), it conforms, in concrete ways, to Fanon's prescription.

The preservation of community in Islam ultimately weighs more on the scale of justice than do the defying articulations of disenchanted individuals. Even the secular Article 19 of the International Covenant on Civil and Political Rights which protects freedom of opinion imposes restrictions for the "respect of the rights and reputations of others" and for "the protection of national security or of public order (*ordre public*), or of public health or morals" (*Rushdie File* 194). The idea of atomized individuals exercising their "rights" through participation in an electoral "democratic" process has no historical roots in the people's collective memory. When the West resorts to the moral argument of human rights, it precludes peoples' right to self-determination and totally downgrades the right to equal economic opportunity, since capitalism itself, the cornerstone of the West's—and especially, U.S.—ideology, is inherently a system of uneven development. Democratizing poverty and destabilizing threatening alternatives are what the carefully orchestrated human rights crusades amount to;[28] otherwise one would have to address freedom in capitalist democracies, such as the U.S., where the misinformed majority and the repressive apparatus of the state have managed to confine thought and privatize censorship:

> Every day of the week something is being censored in the U.S. media. Programs are denied funding for fear of offending advertisers, subscribers, mainstream religious zealots, powerful Jews, powerful Gentiles. Otherwise reputable publishers turn down manuscripts, edit out ideas, or surgically remove chapters likely to offend powerful groups in the nation. (Mazrui, "Satanic Verses" 126)[29]

So while freedom of speech remains a contentious and an unfinished project in the West—its meaning and extent defined by prevailing power relations—this right has been used to portray the widely diffused picture of an intolerant Islam, despite disclaimers by people who are more familiar with Islamic history. Though some leaders may have been perplexed by Khomeini's unilateral leadership in this matter, many Muslims read the freedom of speech principle as the latest tactic in the West's crusade against Islam,[30] a crusade that has managed to put Muslims on both sides of the divide—Rushdie (and other intellectuals) versus the protesting masses—in an extremely precarious situation that does nothing but exacerbate the pain of the colonized.[31] Although Rushdie wants to celebrate "hybridity, impurity, intermingling, the transformation that comes of new and unexpected combinations of human beings, cultures, ideas, politics, movies, songs" and "our mongrel selves" ("In Good Faith" 52); although he wants the "freedom to offend," "to satirize all orthodoxies, including religious orthodoxies" (53), *The Satanic Verses* is ultimately "the story of two painfully divided selves [Saladin Chamcha and Gibreel Farishta] and about "their quest for wholeness" (53).

To the extent that the novel struggles with questions of identity at home and in a racist imperial country, it is part of a larger Afroasian literary and cultural tradition, in which alienation bedevils ambitious and talented young people caught in the simultaneously promising and deadly web of Westernization. And if, as Mufti states, pastiche "becomes a means of appropriating and rewriting the colonial text" (111), this stylistic strategy—unpolished imitations of other writers' techniques—is, in fact, a nonstyle; it is, as Jameson argued, the hollowed artistic gesture of late capitalism (see "Postmodernism and Consumer Society"). So even the revolutionary potential ascribed to style cannot be taken seriously, for as with most cultural productions, it remains symptomatic of the larger and more concrete historical event of late or global capitalism. This is why I prefer the word "colonized" to "postcolonial": In what language does the Western academy—and the American one in particular—address Rushdie? If the dialogue is monolingual and conducted in Western terms, then only dazzling feats of self-deception, through the recourse to equally labyrinthine cultural theories, would manage to obfuscate the painful subjugation of the South to Western models of living. Cultural imperialism is real, and the presence of the Third World intellectual in the West—despite the proverbial exceptions and other conscious complicities—is a stark manifestation of this reality. Yet no leftist or radical Western scholar seems to measure accurately the degree of our alienation, to read the exotic presence of the Other in the Academy as a reminder of our vulnerabilities and organic uprootedness; for, even if Third World scholars prefer to be here—and we mostly do—we do it out of the paradoxical necessity to improve our lot by claiming our share in the dubious Western largesse.[32] It is yet to be proven that England is a more beautiful country than India, or that Western people are better than others; but what seems to be indisputably clear is the systematic exploitation of the non-Westerner in the last five hundred years or so, leading to a painful and maddening identity crisis whose symptoms have been unscrupulously interpreted to be the sign of a liberating order.

That the quest for (a lost) identity is the dominant theme in Rushdie's novel should make us look beyond the colorful posturing of theory and into the real meaning of pain and suffering that loss engenders. Whether Gibreel Farishta, the fallen movie star and satanic archangel, and Saladin Chamcha, the multi-vocal impersonator, are intertwined or not, their fall from the hijacked plane *Bostan* (garden of Eden?) is really a time of reckoning: at this stage, they have both, through different trajectories, reached an irreversible point of crisis. Their identities need to be urgently recovered if they want to avoid death ("*To be born again, first you have to die*"). Gibreel Farishta would eventually succumb, defeated by his ego, inflated on stages and broken by Allie. But Saladin seems to have embarked on a journey of healing and self-restoration (he recovers his real name, Salahuddin) in the end, finally coming to terms with a most traumatic past. Even the unbelieving skeptic Mizra Saeed Akhtar, who suffers from the postmodern affliction of emotional "detachment," of not being able "to connect" himself to "things, events, feelings" (490), and who is therefore unable to follow Ayesha's perilous crossing of the Arabian Sea, seems to yield to the mysteries of faith (507).

Let us also remember that it is Gibreel, troubled by doubt (92) and afflicted with schizophrenia (429), who dreams up (and distorts) the power of faith: Mahound, the intolerant prophet, with his "terrifying singularity" (102) within the religious multiplicity of Jahilia; Ayesha, in her carnivalesque, postmodernist journey amidst great social commotion in India (488); and the exiled Imam (whose resemblance to Khomeini is too striking to be a matter of coincidence) who condemns History as "the intoxicant, the creation and possession of the Devil, of the great Shaitan, the greatest of lies—progress, science, rights . . ." because "the sum of knowl-

edge was complete on the day Allah finished his revelation to Mahound" (210). Leaving all speculation about the author's inten-
tions aside, it is significant that both Mahound and the Imam, with
their firm (but satirized Islamic?) convictions, are the only successful revolutionaries in the novel; they are the creators of new social
orders, "inimical alternatives" to the ethos of (American) capitalism.[33] And while Khadija offers Mahound "the reassuring cer-
tainty" he needs, Gibreel is further weakened by the hybridized
Allie, "the bringer of tribulation, creatrix of strife, of soreness of
the heart" (321). Gibreel doesn't even have a Zeeny, the fatalist
intellectual of the homeland who interpellates Saladin back. He
finds no redemption, no inspiring source of hope; and so he is
"destroyed," as Rushdie puts it, "by the loss of faith" (*Imaginary*
431). Gibreel's blasphemous imaginings are "punishments and re-
tributions," while "the dream figures who torment him with their
assaults on religion are representatives of the process of ruination,
and *not* representative of the point of view of the author" (431;
Rushdie's emphasis).

The author is, on the contrary, and as I have tried to suggest,
another victim of Macaulay's scheme and its limitations. Like Salahuddin, he has been "Englished," as his alienation from his people
and culture increased (Ahmed, *Postmodernism* 121). He is the son
of Muslim elites who could not resist the temptation of the West.
As with most promising children of the early nationalist bourgeoi-
sie, he was sent to school in England, where he predictably lost
his faith:

> God, Satan, Paradise and Hell all vanished one day in my
> fifteenth year, when I quite abruptly lost my faith. I recall it
> vividly. I was at school in England by then. The moment of
> awakening happened, in fact, during a Latin lesson, and after-
> wards, to prove my new-found atheism, I bought myself a
> rather tasteless ham sandwich, and so partook for the first time
> of the forbidden flesh of the swine. No thunderbolt arrived to
> strike me down. I remember feeling that my survival con-
> firmed the correctness of my new position . . . (*Imaginary* 377)

There is no doubt that Rushdie's naive defiance of Islam is
merely the heartbreaking scream of another casualty of colonialism and the confused elite it created in its aftermath. One simply

cannot accept the rebellious gesture of an estranged 15-year-old as the legitimate and unchanging foundation of a new prophecy, a new theory; but one can recognize how such a boy, already a stolen resource, is transformed, through the ideological clutches of a particular form of secularism, into the reluctant accomplice of the West in its long and unmitigated genocidal war against difference, in general, and Islam, in particular. Only a cold scholarship with its myopic insistence on fact can fail to see the tragedy in this statement, the disorientation of a child exiled to England for no other reason but because that country had once occupied his. The same is true, in different degrees, of Third World intellectual giants such as Spivak and Said. The former, as I mentioned earlier, arrived in the U.S. at the age of 19 and has been a resident alien since 1966 (*PC* 75), while Said, always struggling with his exile, and now afflicted with a "chronically insidious disease," first visited the U.S. at the age of 16 ("Palestine Then and Now" 47). They—like most of us—all stayed in the West, speaking, writing, lobbying, while the indefatigable machinery of exploitation and barely disguised contempt for Muslims, and non-Westerners generally, perpetuates its historic mission of pillage, undaunted by a highly moral criticism whose dismissal could only mean the relinquishing of one's humanity.

The voice of the West's Other, spoken in indigenous idioms, must therefore be reasserted in order to force the complacent Western intellectuals who define themselves as progressive into a genuine, *multi-lingual* dialogue. Conviction is now growing that the monotheistic religion of Islam, premised on the notion of the sacred[34] and cultural authenticity, is the representative of much of the Third World in its struggle against what Ricardo Petrella has termed the "pax triadica"—i.e., the U.S.-Europe-Japan alliance against the South.[35] The challenge of Islam has become so pervasive that even magazines like the *Economist* are publishing dystopian fantasies about the rise of an Islamic empire, although—and this is one instance in which magazines display better judgment than erudite scholars and responsible politicians—they take their analysis beyond crude military calculations, or other equally hysterical warnings about the threat of Islam to cherished Western values—often expressions of a generalized false consciousness—such as "democracy," "freedom of speech," "human rights," etc.

The *Economist* simply subjects the whole project of the Enlightenment to critical scrutiny. That notion of "Reason," which Europeans congratulated themselves upon reaching in the 18th century,
led to a series of nightmarish revolutions and violent political
movements which devastated the whole world. In retrospect, however, the West is seen to have failed to realize that "it was time for
a readjustment":

> A new balance was needed between the analytic part of the
> human mind and the instinctive part, between rationality and
> feeling; only then could man address the world more steadily.
> And a new balance had to be struck between the claims of indi-
> vidual freedom and the claims of individual morality; only
> then could law and liberty swing evenly on the scales. Because
> they did not tackle these problems in time, the democracies
> marched straight from the climax of the 20th-century victory
> into anti-climax. They did not know what to do next. (153)[36]

Obviously, the *Economist* is warning the "democracies" that by
dispatching expeditionary forces and boycotting small countries
they will not reverse their decline and mend the fissures that are
growing within their ranks;[37] nothing short of a new way of seeing,
une autre manière de voir (the theme launched in recent years by *Le
Monde Diplomatique*), can change the course of the West's cultural
irrelevance to the majority of the people in the world. The
(Western-ized) intellectuals who continue to herald the virtues of
complex and puzzling theories of representation (such as homelessness and hybridity) from the pages of well-endowed journals
and the pulpits of prestigious universities, and who are fanatically
committed to secularism as the only "rational" way to deal with the
challenges of life, will then lose their credibility.[38] The time has
come to simply acknowledge that the Afroasian person (intellectual
or not) is in deep trouble today, persecuted by the tyranny of a
heartless capitalist régime which has cast its web across the globe,
and which rewards only those who—dazzled by the ephemeral
promise of the West—have unscrupulously abandoned the memory and wisdom of their ancestors. No amount of intellectual acro-
batics can erase this painful and dangerous reality. We must reclaim our resources, *ourselves,* our Rushdies and others like him.
Only self-sufficient and compassionate cultures in the South, moti-

vated by different ideals, can stem the massive flow of people and resources to the North,[39] and bring an end to the pain of displacement that Mark Edmundson wants to celebrate. The season of migration to the North must be replaced by other, more pleasant and enriching seasons; seasons of stability and confidence; seasons of migrations not impelled by necessity and dependence. When that happens—and it will—the disturbing discourses of orientalism and racism will turn into the distant echoes of a culture that has condemned itself into regression. The West will then evoke pity, not horror.

Notes

1. The fear of Islam is being played out in dramatic ways on the European stage, for instance. Turkey is being kept out of the European market partly because of its dominant religion, Islam. And Bosnia is being annihilated out of existence for very much the same reasons. Public political discourse in the U.S. doesn't, of course, state this, but occasionally there are hints that one reason why Bosnians are being abandoned to their deadly fate is the West's unstated fear of Islam. On September 3, 1992, the Republican Task Force on Terrorism and Unconventional Warfare issued an executive summary that warned against the rise of Islamic militancy in Europe, with the expanding Muslim population, estimated, according to this summary, to constitute 25% of Western Europe's population by the year 2000. This memo resorted to some of the most abject forms of distortions, such as Muslims' practice of "blood vengeance" and "the killing of females." These unfounded concerns, expressed at the highest level of the U.S. government, were never mentioned in public. Susan Sontag did, however, allude to the West's anti-Islamic predisposition as a cause for resigning to the genocide of a people. The reason why very few artists—and for that matter, intellectuals—are concerned with Bosnia, she suggested, is because the term Muslim is a "turnoff." Half a year later, the *New York Times* made the same suggestion. On the exclusion of Turkey from the European Community, see Scott L. Malcomson, "Heart of Whiteness," 10–14. The Republican memo was published in *The Link* 26 (1993): 3; Susan Sontag's interview appeared in the *MacNeil/Lehrer Newshour* (3 Aug. 1993). Finally, see Roger Cohen, "West's Fears In Bosnia: 1) Chaos, 2) Islam," E3.

2. Walter Benjamin would argue that modern art, for instance, is characterized by the stripping away of the aura that emanates from the organically rooted artistic production, and is an inextricable part of a culture's collective self-expression. Art is now for exhibition, a reified practice transformed into a commodity devoid of any historical content. See his "The Work of Art in the Age of Mechanical Reproduction," 217–51.

3. By "theoretical" Islam, I simply mean the general Qur'anic rules that characterize Islam and Muslims. While the interpretations of these rules have been mostly historical events, to question certain foundational rules (such as prayer, fasting, a certain diet, etc.) is principally to reject Islam itself. The heterogeneities

of Islam, while affirmed, should not obliterate the equally important universal dimensions of the religion. Moroccan Islam may take on different characteristics from, say, Indonesian Islam; but both Indonesian and Moroccan Muslims are connected by their adherence to the same faith, and to the belief, for instance, that gambling is not permitted by the Islamic religion.

4. One must continue to stress the gross violations of basic human rights (complex as this concept may be) in much of the Third World, and the Arab and Islamic worlds in particular. This pervasive condition has crippled intellectual inquiry and coopted many scholars; but although they must be held accountable, these pathological Third World tyrannies should be situated within larger global configurations, in which the dominant logic at the end of this century is the extraterritoriality of capital and the reduction of most governments into guardians of (foreign) investments. Third World nations in the postcolonial era have mostly been police states, but with the acceleration of capitalist globalization, they are in competition to sell themselves as "stable" havens with cheap and semi-skilled labor. Even regions in the First World have begun to act like Third World countries, offering big incentives and "parks" for industries willing to relocate.

5. Christopher Miller struggles at length with the "paradox" of using the mediation of the Western methodological device of anthropology to study African literature. He finally chooses the dialogic gesture to reduce the impact of ethnicity (Anglo-Eurocentrism) and relativize his beliefs; and he rightly notes that "unless the Western critic attempts to suspend—to hold at least in temporary abeyance— the systematic criteria and judgments that emanate from Western culture, ethnocentrism will persist forever" (*Theories of Africans* 65; also see chapters 1 and 2). Miller is well aware that leaving Africans alone might put him "out of business altogether," as Weber states (28), but, like Spivak, he nevertheless goes on to defend his undertaking as best as he can. Linda Alcoff also struggled with this issue in the pages of this journal, although she offers a somewhat modified approach to this dilemma. Alcoff calls on speakers to (1) exercise restraint (since speech is mastery); (2) "interrogate the bearing of our location and context . . ."; (3) be accountable for their utterances; and (4) treat discourse as an "*event*" which includes speaker, words, hearers, location, language, and so on." The difference here is accountability ("The Problem of Speaking for Others" 5–32). But to define the context of our speech risks becoming an infinitely (and unnecessarily) regressive matter if we don't begin from the simple assumption that we are speaking from within an academic and intellectual apparatus that is thoroughly informed by a capitalist ethic that, among other things, refuses to acknowledge that the most humane social agendas may also fulfill and be tainted by the requirements of specific institutional structures.

6. What the black historian may have intuitively objected to in Said's presentation has been documented and clarified by Aijaz Ahmad. In a recent essay, Ahmad shows us how Said has been thoroughly subjected to the very Orientalist tradition he has denounced in *Orientalism*. According to Ahmad, the "high humanism" of this tradition is what prompts Said's beliefs in the liberal virtues he often evokes and calls for. Said seems "transfixed by the power of the very voice" he criticizes. Ahmad argues that the categories of "orientalism" and "third world female subaltern" are perfectly suitable for privileged Third World intellectuals who nevertheless need "documentary proof that they have always been oppressed" ("Orientalism and After" 98–116). Moreover, Said's inarticulated political position (in fact, his tacit condoning of U.S. hegemony in *Orientalism* itself) has been noted by Sadik Jalal al-'Azm in "Orientalism and Orientalism in Reverse," 5–26, especially 16–18.

7. Albert Hourani, the late eminent historian of the Arabs, saw the resurgence

of Islam as the inevitable "third wave" of Arab nationalism. See Judith Miller, "The Islamic Wave," 24. In his magnum opus, *A History of the Arab Peoples* (1991), he had shown that Islam is what facilitated the expansion of Arabic (and therefore of Arabism), legitimated and toppled governments, that the concept of the *umma* (community of believers) bonded Arabs like no other system could, and that the call for a properly applied Islam has always been the rallying cry of the "proletariat" in its resistance to the despotic "alliance of interests" (137). Although Hourani seemed to recognize that the dominant ideology of nationalism may be coming to an end through the pressures of Islam, and although he acknowledged elsewhere that to understand Islam one needs to have a living relationship with it (see *Islam in European Thought*, 4), he was unable to transcend the "guild orthodoxies" of his secular profession by predicting at the end of his *History* an unlikely secular arrangement for the Arab peoples, vaguely informed by a few Islamic principles (458).

8. The same has been true of dominant multicultural theories in the U.S. George Yúdice has shown how American multiculturalism, based on identity politics, universalizes its project, and obliterates postcolonialist struggles against [U.S.] imperialism. Seen in this light, U.S. multiculturalism ends up, wittingly or not, serving transnational capital's interests (coopting indigenous resistance through the dissemination, via powerful and well endowed media, of one particular version of identity). See George Yúdice, "We are *Not* the World," 202–16. The Coca-Cola Company, whose major income is outside the U.S., has already "banished" words such as "domestic" and "foreign" from its vocabulary, and is therefore ahead of many cultural and educational institutions. See Roger Cohen, "For Coke, World Is Its Oyster," D1, 5.

9. Fanon writes scathingly about Westernized intellectuals who "take up a fundamentally 'universal standpoint'" (*The Wretched of the Earth* 218–19). Moreover, the Westernized intellectual often fails to "measure the real situation which the men and the women of his country know" (223). Fanon's denunciation of this type of intellectuals also echoes the black woman historian's reservations about Said's cosmopolitanism. Fanon himself, we should remember, had taken a universalist position in *Black Skin, White Masks;* his transformation may indicate his closer identification with the wretched.

10. Academicians tend to be a dogmatic lot. In the U.S., once the secular model displaced the religious foundations of the university in the 19th century, the spiritual dimensions of life were virtually excluded from the curriculum. "Academic fundamentalism is the issue," wrote Page Smith in a recent book on higher education in America, "the stubborn refusal of the academy to acknowledge any truth that does not conform to professorial dogmas." In this world, "certain ideas are simply excluded, and woe to those who espouse them. Such individuals are terminated, lest their corruption spread to others" (*Killing the Spirit* 5).

11. The specter of Islamic fundamentalism permeates the American cultural apparatus at every level. The May 1994 issue of the *World Press Review* is entitled "Fear of Islam," and asks whether it is "a real world menace, or just the latest 'evil empire.'" Sections on Islamic and Middle Eastern or Arab Studies are expanding in good bookstores, while, according to a colleague who took a Foreign Service exam, the assumption that Islam may be the next "evil empire" can be easily surmised from the test.

12. Awareness of situational constraints would, as noted earlier, take us back to the rather schizophrenic gesture of perpetually qualifying assertions. Since, as Linda Alcoff suggests, writers are to be accountable, then such a principle seems to have been masterfully eluded in the case of Rushdie. If speech is an "event,"

then why do these critics object to Khomeini's response, which is, strictly speaking, another form of speech, the articulation of a *fatwa*? My goal here is not just to show why the theory of discourse as praxis inevitably falls into difficult contradictions; but I also want to emphasize that while Islam-as-alternative is gaining wider legitimacy among larger segments of the masses in the Islamic world, secular scholars continue to imperil the legitimacy of their own profession by making such claims.

13. For a good account of the paganism of U.S. (and Western) capitalist culture, see Erich Fromm, *To Have or To Be?*

14. A similar argument has been presented by 'Alija 'Ali Izetbegovic, the President of Bosnia at the time of this writing. Progress is a materialist process that is carried out in a civilization, while spirituality is a feeling that gives life to culture. Science cannot account for the act of creation, without which there would be no civilization to start with; only art (poetry, painting, music, etc.) that has its genesis in inspiration can. See his *Islam Between East and West* (1984). The notion of "progress" (together with that of nationalism) is furthermore losing its intellectual force in the West. For the failure of this project, see Christopher Lasch, *The True and Only Heaven* (1991) and Serge Latouche, *L'Occidentalisation du Monde* (1989). By the end of 1992 (the quincentennial of an ominous year for indigenous peoples), newspapers and articles were prophesying the decline of the concept—and the total ideology of the Enlightenment. See John Lukacs, "History, Wild History," A 25. A further and more poignant example of how mainstream periodicals are questioning the hegemonic principles of the Enlightenment will be provided at the end of this essay.

15. For Lyotard, the text is also an "*event*" (81), but it is an "event" that is blissfully unrepresentable (since this assumption prevents the oppressiveness of totalities and activates differences). No wonder, then, Fredric Jameson reads a certain despair in Lyotard's theory, perhaps prompted by the failure of the Left in France. See Jameson's foreword to Jean-François Lyotard's *The Postmodern Condition*.

16. This should be a concern for Westerners too, especially those who are struggling to expand freedom of speech in Third World countries. The "corporate takeover of public expression" is the subtitle of Herbert Schiller's book on the vanishing spaces of public expression and the rise of corporate discourse in the West. The ramifications of the corporate monopoly over speech in the U.S. are yet, in my view, to take their rightful place in cultural and literary studies. See Herbert Schiller, *Culture Inc.* (New York: Oxford University Press, 1989) and Edward Herman and Noam Chomsky, *Manufacturing Consent* (New York: Pantheon, 1988). The corporate control of the media and cultural enterprises continues unabated. See Geraldine Fabrikant, "Viacom is Winner Over QVC in Fight to Get Paramount," 1+; Clyde Farnsworth, "Canadian Media Giants to Merge," D1. Time Warner Inc. already is the "world's largest media and entertainment company" and "the world's #1 copyright owner, creator, and distributor." See *Hoover's Handbook of American Business 1994*, 1036–37. In such conditions, the bourgeois preoccupation with freedom of speech risks becoming a vacuous expression that, among other things, reflects the false consciousness of intellectuals living under the iron laws of capitalism. We go back to Fanon's injunction: liberation first!

17. Another example of how the theme of alienation is veiled in theory is Saree S. Makdisi's reading of Tayeb Saleh's *Season of Migration to the North* in the same *Critical Inquiry* issue that invited Bilgrami to define Muslim identity. In this reading, Saleh's novel reflects the transitional phase between traditionalism and mod-

ernism; that the unstable and "multilayered" (808) text, with its "different regis-
ters of textuality, narrative, form chronology, and history" (808) prevents closure,
and points toward the direction of synthesis, of hybridity where the future of a
postimperial Arab nation lies. Said, on the other hand, sees the novel as a "rewriting of Conrad's *Heart of Darkness*" ("Criticism" 43), although it enlarges the scope
of consciousness "which has heretofore always been an exclusively European observer of consciousness." Why both critics cannot bring themselves to read the
novel as the record of tragic suffering by a very intelligent but profoundly hurt
and alienated man (Mustafa Sa'eed), who is "no longer at ease" despite his attempt to reimmerse himself back in the traditions of his culture and who most
probably chooses death in the end, instead of the torments afflicting him, can
only be explained by the inability of dominant Western theories to explain the
predicament of Muslims at the present. If one is to find an analogy with Conrad's
novel, the most obvious one is not a vaguely defined "consciousness," but the
concrete and deadly legacy of a cold imperialism that drives perceptive humans
insane in the end.

18. For a most recent assessment of the African condition, see *Dissent* (Summer
1992); for an illustration of how Western financial organizations continue to drain
the Third World generally of its resources, see *Race and Class* (July–Sept. 1992).

19. The creation of missionary schools and Western universities in the Middle
East is part of this pattern. The American University of Beirut (AUB), for example, consciously aims at producing a Westernized Arab leadership. See Robert
D. Kaplan, "Tales from the Bazaar," 46. La Francophonie is a continuation of
imperialism through language, despite claims by the non-French that they are
advantaged by the fact that they speak more than one language. French in the
Maghreb, for example, continues to be the symbol of privilege, although it is
being gradually (and I think unsuccessfully) supplanted by English. The opening
of a private, American-style university in Ifran, Morocco, complete with a board
of trustees and high tuitions, is a dramatic illustration of this departure from
French tutelage. As far as I know, this would be the first time in the history of
Moroccan higher education that the primary language of instruction would be
English. For a brief description of the opening ceremony (January 1995) and how
the university was built, see the international Arabic newspaper *Al-Quds Al-Arabi*
(16 Jan. 1995), 12.

20. The mélange that postmodern and postcolonial theories sometimes celebrate may suggest that global intermixing is a process that has grown out of a
natural process of globalization, and not a deliberate strategy of colonialism carefully orchestrated by the imperialists in the 19th century. On March 14, 1878,
Lord Lytton, viceroy of India (1876–80), spoke before his Legislative Council and
outlined his strategy of Westernizing India and other peoples, saying: "It is a fact
which there is no disguising . . . and also one which cannot be too constantly or
too anxiously recognized that . . . we have placed, and must permanently maintain ourselves at the head of *a gradual but gigantic revolution—the greatest and most
momentous social, moral, and religious, as well as political revolution which, perhaps, the
world has ever witnessed*" (qtd. in Theodore H. Van Laue, *The World Revolution of
Westernization* 15; original emphasis).

21. Ngugi Wa Thiong'o has worked tirelessly to emphasize the primacy of language in reconstructing a cultural imaginary. In his latest book, *Moving the Center*
(1993), which builds on many of the arguments in *Decolonizing the Mind* (1986),
he shows that the African elites have been designed to perpetuate neocolonial
structures, while the peasants and the masses, through their marginalization, pre-

served native customs and languages. The cultural control of the Third World (dissemination of certain ideas, inventing a mutilated consciousness, false self-perceptions, etc.) are an integral part of the imperialist project, because this generalized cultural confusion weakens resistance (51, 54). The writer in the neocolonial state must therefore align her/himself with the people (74) and make an attempt to restore African languages, despite the loud cynical cries of the Europhones (21).

22. The drums of violence are always beating for Arabs and Muslims. CNN had a countdown before the bombing of Baghdad; now the *fatwa* seems to have launched another chronology, another calendar, though its purpose (besides the pious statements of solidarity with Rushdie) is not exactly clear.

23. See, for instance, Youssef Ibrahim, "The Arabs Find a World in Which They Count Less," E3. The gradual impoverishment of oil-producing Arab countries has been widely reported in recent years. Saudi Arabia, Kuwait, Iraq, Libya, and Algeria have all suffered from some aspect of Western imperialism, including the fixing of oil prices. For an examination of how the West gained from the sale of petroleum and the Arabs lost, see Sarkis, "L'inquiétante baisse des revenus du pétrole," 6. For the depletion of Saudi money, see two articles in the *New York Times* (22–23 Aug. 1993) and an editorial significantly titled "Saudis Without Dollars" (25 Aug. 1993, A14). The Gulf War cost an estimated $676 billion in 1990–91. See Ibrahim, "War Is Said to Cost the Persian Gulf $676 Billion in 1990–'91," 14. Yet, despite this massive economic bloodletting, Saudi Arabia continues to infuse its money in the American economy, allowing it to survive in the near future. See Friedman, "Saudi to Buy $6 Billion in Jets Built in the U.S.," 1+; Andrews, "AT&T Wins $4 Billion Saudi Project," D1+. Meanwhile, the mismanagement of Kuwaiti investments overseas has led to billions of dollars in losses. See particularly the case of Kuwaiti investments in Spain in Cohen, "Big Wallets and Little Supervision," D1, 20.

24. Jews fared better under Islamic rule. See Bernard Lewis, *The Jews of Islam* (1984).

25. The prophetic dimensions of this sentence (written in 1982) have been tested by history. As I am writing this, Rushdie remains in hiding, presumably under the protection of Scotland Yard, the reputable security agency of the country that had been a direct cause for the trauma of his people. I find it a bit ironic—albeit thoroughly understandable—that imperialist powers seem to be the ones most concerned about his safety!

26. See Tomlinson's analysis of Cornelius Castoriadis' critique of modernity in *Cultural Imperialism* 164; also see Latouche, *L'Occidentalisation du Monde.*

27. Professor Bernard Lewis, before the eruption of the Gulf War on January 17, 1991, explained to a Jewish audience in Israel that "secularism in its modern political connotation, the idea that religion and authority, church and state are distinct and different and therefore ultimately separable, is in a profound sense Christian." The long history of schism and heresy in Christendom has no parallels in Jewish and Islamic histories. "There is nothing," says Lewis, "in Islamic history remotely comparable with such epoch-making Christian events as the Christological controversies, the schism of Photius, which split the Greek and Latin churches, the Reformation, the holy office of the Inquisition and the bloody religious wars of the 16th and 17th centuries which in effect compelled Christians to secularize their states and societies in order to escape from the vicious circle of persecution and conflict. Muslims encountered no such problem and therefore required no such solution." See Bernard Lewis, "Secularism in the Middle East."

28. While this policy succeeded in breaking up the Soviet Union, China's lead-

ership is proving to be more formidable and resilient. That the human rights campaign against China is an attempt to open up the system can hardly be disputed. In 1988, a Reagan-appointed U.S. panel predicted that China would be the second largest economy in 2008; in 1989, the human-rights campaign was launched. A similar procedure is being applied to indebted Arab countries through the U.S. Agency for International Development (AID), whereby the process of democratization would exonerate the comprador class from its responsibility, democratize poverty, and, at the same time, counter the rise of Islam as an alternative ideology. See Zaidi, "American Human Rights for China!," 15–16; Miskin, "AID's 'Free Market' Democracy," 33–34. Secular forces in the Arab world are now introducing the notion of "civil society" to secure the democratic process. In Egypt, the Ibn Khaldun Center has been created for this purpose, but its founder, and the leading proponent of this movement, Saad Eddin Ibrahim, seems to have suspect credentials. See Zubaida, "Islam, the State and Democracy," 2–10, and Beinin, "Aspects of Egyptian Civil Resistance," 38–39. The "democracy industry," according to William I. Robinson, has "replaced anticommunism as the ideological justification for what is in fact the self-interest of a rapacious elite. It also assumes the same combination of self-righteousness, semi-religious fervor, and cynicism as fueled anticommunism." Termed "low intensity democracy," "its primary goal is to assure political stability in an integrated global economy dominated by the North" ("Low Intensity Democracy," 45, 40).

29. The control of thought by an anti-intellectual disposition of the "majority" in the U.S. did not escape Alexis de Tocqueville's observations. He noted that there is no refuge for the dissenter in the American democracy, for the power of the majority is more overreaching than that of the monarch: it not only controls actions, but also influences desires, shapes will, and prescribes behavior. "In America," de Tocqueville adds, "the majority has enclosed thought within a formidable fence. A writer is free inside that area, but woe to the man who goes beyond it." See *Democracy in America*, 223–35. The criminalizing of the "alien" is a well-established pattern in the U.S., including "alien" ideas such as "communism." For an excellent account of this tradition, see David Bennett, *The Party of Fear* (1989); for how the repressive measures taken against "communism" during the McCarthy era affected thought and the lives of intellectuals even within the relatively sheltered universities, see Ellen Schrecker, *No Ivory Tower* (1986).

30. For a brief account of several reactions in the Arab world, see *al-'Alam* (international magazine) 22 Oct. 1988 and 10 April 1989. The film and television industries in Egypt are now being used to demonize Islamic militants, proving, once again, that art, often dependent on patronage, is almost always political. See Hedges, "Battling the Religious Right: The Celluloid Front," A4.

31. A great number of Arab and Muslim writers and intellectuals have written in favor of Rushdie, and their statements were published in book form, initially in France. They wrote in support of his freedom to speak, although not everyone listed seems to have read Rushdie's novel, *The Satanic Verses*. Some even used this occasion to launch attacks on the patriarchy or to advance their own agendas for a project of secularization in the Islamic world. In my view, only two writers stand out for the depth and historical perspectives of their analyses. Mohammed Arkoun, a prominent Islamic scholar in France, while insisting on Rushdie's right to freedom, placed the controversy in the larger context of the West's repudiation of the spiritual, a West which, "under the cover of a defense of 'freedom of expression,' in fact seeks to debase Islam and prove that all the old talk about the civilizing mission of the European colonial powers is and has always been fundamentally valid. . . . Thus, merely to protest against the intolerance of Muslims

alone means covering over with a veil of silence some things that represent a decisive aspect of the whole battle that has involved Rushdie" (47). Amin Maalouf, the famous author of *The Crusades Through Arab Eyes*, reminds the reader that "a billion Muslims have the impression of living in a foreign, hostile, indecipherable universe," that such conditions engender grave dilemmas which, unless resolved, will probably lead to even greater dramas (217). See *For Rushdie.*

32. The Moroccan feminist Fatima Mernissi remarks on the general "malaise" that affects both the highly educated and the most impoverished members of the Third World with a sense of "self-depreciation," leading them to immigrate to "the very paradoxical West" ("un Occident très paradoxal"). See Mernissi, *La peur-modernité*, 78.

33. In one of his books, Henry Munson, Jr., after announcing that he has "no sympathy for anyone who seeks to force society to conform to sacred scripture" (ix–x), seems to argue that uncompromising secular tyrannies, untroubled by human rights considerations, is one of the viable strategies to contain Islamic revolutions (ix). For Munson, Jr., Marxism and Islamism are "inimical alternatives" to American interests (137). That his book, *Islam and Revolution in the Middle East*, was published by Yale (1988) illustrates the extent to which Orientalist scholarship persists even in the most respected academic circles.

34. "Where nothing is sacred, every belief becomes revisable," notes Ahmed in *Postmodernism and Islam* (13). The persistence of the "sacred" in even the most revolutionary régimes, such as the Sandinista one in Nicaragua, is testimony that no utopian project of society can easily dispense with it. Rigoberto López Pérez, the Nicaraguan poet who sacrificed himself to rid his country of dictatorship, is now endowed with a shrine. "The creative or spiritual, and its product the sacred, needs to receive scientific recognition as a valid expression of human life . . ." (Bretlinger, "Socialism and the Sacred" 27–43). Terry Eagleton also argues that "deeply persistent beliefs" must be taken seriously, for they are the real expression of the people whom many of us seek to emancipate (*Ideology* 12–13). But Bosnian President Izetbegovic would argue that it is precisely because secular interpretations cannot penetrate to the structure of faith that they are simply condemned to failure.

35. For an explanation of how Islam is now the leading voice of the indigenous South, see Mazrui, *Cultural Forces in World Politics*, especially the chapter, "Changing the Guards from Hindus to Muslims," 208–26. Petrella's definition of "pax triadica" is in his article by the same title.

36. See "Looking Back from 2992."

37. For a reassessment of U.S. military strategies in relation to the Islamic threat, see interview with Alain Joxe in *Le Monde* (22 Dec. 1992): 2; and Alain Joxe, "Humanitarisme et empires," 1, 6–7. For the U.S. flexible military strategy in the post-Cold War era, especially in relation to the Third World, see Schirmer, "Access: Imperialist Expansion in the Post Cold-War Era," 38–51.

38. Edward Said continues to make a compelling argument for intellectual secularism as the best defense against strong political or religious commitments because, as some former Communists would testify, "gods" fail in the end. Understandable as this proposition may be, we must remember that there is no neutral secular space in which we can ultimately find refuge from the temptations of this world. Universities and journals are implicated in a larger system which, in the U.S., is inescapably informed by the capitalist—and hence, indirectly, by the imperialist—ethic. Many scholars, in an attempt to assuage their consciences and eradicate nagging contradictions, see the American university as captive of its

own bourgeois contradictions, allowing freedom of speech, and thus, in a way, being condemned to tolerate radical views. But a quick glance at the hierarchical structure and budgetary operations of a university would soon reveal that the spaces it opens for critique are, in large measure, dependent on capital, investments, joint ventures, and state economies. Furthermore, many prestigious universities, citadels of "serious" scholarship, were established by tycoons and robber barons, and are still supported to this day by corporate contributions. In short, there is no reason to believe that the liberal arts are not beholden to capital as the sciences are. For a recent article by Edward Said on the virtues of secularism, see "Gods That Always Fail." For a brief history of higher education in the U.S., see Page Smith, *Killing the Spirit.* For the relationship between capital and science, see Mandel, *Late Capitalism,* 249; Fisher, "Profits and Ethics Clash in Research on Genetic Coding," 1+; Browne, "End of Cold War Clouds Research as Openings in Science Dwindle," 1+. For corporate contributions to universities ($600 million in 1986 for research and development), see Calvin Sims, "Business-Campus Ventures Grow," *New York Times* (14 Dec. 1987); qtd. in Schiller, 86.

39. According to Bernard Valcourt, Employment and Immigration Minister of Canada, around 80 million people, worldwide, were actively looking for a home in the early 1990s. See Clyde H. Farnsworth, "Canada Tightens Immigration Law," *New York Times* (22 Dec. 1992) : A11.

Works Cited

Ahmad, Aijaz. "Orientalism and After: Ambivalence and Cosmopolitan Location in the Work of Edward Said." *Economic and Political Weekly* 25 July 1992: 98–116.

Ahmed, Akbar S. *Discovering Islam: Making Sense of Muslim History and Society.* London: Routledge, 1988.

———. *Postmodernism and Islam: Predicament and Promise.* London: Routledge, 1992.

Al-'Azm, Sadik Jalal. "Orientalism and Orientalism in Reverse." *Khamsin* 8 (1981): 5–26.

Alcoff, Linda. "The Problem of Speaking for Others." *Cultural Critique* 20 (Winter 1991–92): 5–32.

Andrews, Edmund. "AT&T Wins $4 Billion Saudi Project." *New York Times* 10 May 1994: D1+.

An-Na'im, Abdullahi Ahmed. *Toward an Islamic Reformation: Civil Liberties, Human Rights, and International Law.* Syracuse: Syracuse UP, 1987.

Appiah, Kwame Anthony. *In My Father's House: Africa in the Philosophy of Culture.* New York: Oxford UP, 1992.

Ashcroft, Bill, Gareth Griffiths, and Helen Tiffin. *The Empire Writes Back: Theory and Practice in Post-Colonial Literatures.* London: Routledge, 1989.

Beinin, Joel. "Aspects of Egyptian Civil Resistance." *Middle East Report* 179 (Nov.–Dec. 1992): 38–39.

Benjamin, Walter. *Illuminations.* New York: Schocken, 1969.

Bennett, David. *The Party of Fear: From Nativist Movements to the New Right in American History.* Chapel Hill: U of North Carolina P, 1989.

Bilgrami, Akeel. "What Is a Muslim? Fundamental Commitment and Cultural Identity." *Critical Inquiry* 18 (Summer 1992): 821–42.

Brennan, Tim. "Rushdie, Islam, and Postcolonial Criticism." *Social Text* 31/32 (1992): 258–76.

Bretlinger, John. "Socialism and the Sacred." *Monthly Review* 44 (Oct. 1992): 27–43.

Browne, Malcolm. "End of Cold War Clouds Research as Openings in Science Dwindle." *New York Times* 20 Feb. 1994: 1+.

Burgat, François. *The Islamic Movement In North Africa.* Austin: Center for Middle Eastern Studies, U of Texas, 1993.

Cohen, Roger. "Big Wallets and Little Supervision." *New York Times* 28 Sept. 1993: D1+.

———. "For Coke, World Is Its Oyster." *New York Times* 21 Nov. 1991: D1+.

———. "West's Fears in Bosnia: 1) Chaos, 2) Islam." *New York Times* 13 March 1994: E3.

Dirlik, Arif. "The Postcolonial Aura: Third World Criticism in the Age of Global Capitalism." *Critical Inquiry* 20 (Winter 1994): 328–56.

Dwyer, Kevin. *Arab Voices: The Human Rights Debate in the Middle East.* Berkeley: U of California P, 1991.

Eagleton, Terry. *Ideology.* London: Verso, 1991.

Edmundson, Mark. "Prophet of a New Postmodernism." *Harper's* Dec. 1989: 62–71.

Esposito, John L. *The Islamic Threat: Myth or Reality?* New York: Oxford UP, 1992.

Fabrikant, Geraldine. "Viacom is Winner Over QVC in Fight to Get Paramount." *New York Times* 16 Feb. 1994 (nat'l. ed.): 1+.

Fanon, Frantz. *The Wretched of the Earth.* Trans. Constance Farrington. New York: Grove Weidenfeld, 1968.

Farnsworth, Clyde. "Canadian Media Giants to Merge." *New York Times* 9 March 1994: D1.

Fisher, Lawrence. "Profits and Ethics Clash in Research on Genetic Coding." *New York Times* 30 Jan. 1994: 1+.

For Rushdie. New York: Brazillier, 1994.

Friedman, Thomas. "Saudi to Buy $6 Billion in Jets Built in the U.S." *New York Times* 17 Feb. 1994 (nat'l. ed.): D1+.

Fromm, Erich. *To Have or To Be?* 1976. New York: Bantam, 1981.

Harvey, David. *The Condition of Postmodernity.* Oxford: Blackwell, 1989.

Hedges, Chris. "Battling the Religious Right: The Celluloid Front." *New York Times* 18 April 1994: A4.

Herman, Edward, and Noam Chomsky. *Manufacturing Consent: The Political Economy of the Mass Media.* New York: Pantheon, 1988.

Hourani, Albert. *A History of the Arab Peoples.* Cambridge: Belknap/Harvard, 1991.

———. *Islam in European Thought.* Cambridge: Cambridge UP, 1991.

Huntington, Samuel P. "The Clash of Civilizations?" *Foreign Affairs* 72 (Summer 1993): 22–49.

Ibrahim, Youssef. "The Arabs Find a World in Which They Count Less." *New York Times* 5 April 1992: E3.

———. "War Is Said to Cost the Persian Gulf $676 Billion in 1990–'91." *New York Times* 4 April 1993: 14.

Ismail, Qadri. "A Bit of This and a Bit of That: Rushdie's Newness." *Social Text* 29 (1991): 117–24.

Izetbegovic, 'Alija 'Ali. *Islam Between East and West.* Indianapolis: American Trust Publications, 1984.

Jameson, Fredric. *The Political Unconscious: Narrative as a Socially Symbolic Act.* Ithaca: Cornell UP, 1981.

———. "Postmodernism and Consumer Society." *Postmodernism and Its Discontents.* Ed. E. Ann Kaplan. London: Verso, 1988. 13–29.

JanMohamed, Abdul. "Wordliness-without-World, Homelessness-as-Home: Toward a Definition of the Specular Border Intellectual." *Edward Said: A Critical Reader.* Ed. Michael Sprinker. Oxford: Basil Blackwell, 1992. 96–120.

Joxe, Alain. "Humanitarisme et empires." *Le Monde Diplomatique* Jan. 1993: 1+.

Kaplan, Robert D. "Tales from the Bazaar." *Atlantic* Aug. 1992: 37–61.

Lasch, Christopher. *The True and Only Heaven: Progress and Its Critics.* New York: Norton, 1991.

Latouche, Serge. *L'Occidentalisation du Monde.* Paris: La Découverte, 1989.

Lewis, Bernard. *The Jews of Islam.* Princeton: Princeton UP, 1984.

———. "Secularism in the Middle East." Rehovat: Weizmann Institute of Science, 1991. 3–36.

"Looking Back from 2992." *Economist* 26 Dec. 1992–8 Jan. 1993: 17–19.

Lukacs, John. "History, Wild History." *New York Times* 8 Jan. 1993: A25.

Lyotard, Jean-François. *The Postmodern Condition: A Report on Knowledge.* Trans. Geoff Bennington and Brian Massumi. Minneapolis: U of Minnesota P, 1984.

Makdisi, Saree S. "The Empire Renarrated: *Season of Migration to the North* and the Reinvention of the Present." *Critical Inquiry* 18 (Summer 1992): 804–20.

Malcomson, Scott L. "Heart of Whiteness." *Voice Literary Supplement* March 1991: 10–14.

Mandel, Ernest. *Late Capitalism.* London: Verso, 1978.

Mazrui, Ali. *Cultural Forces in World Politics.* Portsmouth: Heinemann, 1990.

———. "Satanic Verses or a Satanic Novel?" *Third World Quarterly* 12 (Jan. 1990): 116–39.

McClintock, Anne. "The Angel of Progress: Pitfalls of the Term 'Post-Colonialism.'" *Social Text* 31/32 (1992): 84–98.

Mernissi, Fatima. *La peur-modernité.* Paris: Albin Michel, 1992.

Miller, Christopher L. *Theories of Africans: Francophone Literature and Anthropology in Africa.* Chicago: U of Chicago P, 1990.

Miller, Judith. "The Islamic Wave." *New York Times Magazine* 31 May 1992: 24.

Miskin, Al. "AID's 'Free Market' Democracy." *Middle East Report* 179 (Nov.–Dec. 1992): 2–10.

Mufti, Aamir. "Reading the Rushdie Affair: An Essay on Islam and Politics." *Social Text* 29 (1991): 95–116.

Munson, Henry, Jr. *Islam and Revolution in the Middle East.* New Haven: Yale UP, 1988.

Petrella, Ricardo. "Pax triadica." *Le Monde Diplomatique* Nov. 1992: 32.

(The Holy) *Qur' an.* Trans. Abdullah Yusuf Ali. Various publishers.

Robinson, William I. "Low Intensity Democracy: The New Face of Global Domination." *CovertAction* Fall 1994: 40–47.

Rodney, Walter. *How Europe Underdeveloped Africa.* 1972. Rev. ed. Washington: Howard UP, 1981.

Rushdie, Salman. "In Good Faith." *Newsweek* 12 Feb. 1990: 52–57.

———. *Imaginary Homelands.* London: Granta, 1991.

———. "Is Nothing Sacred?" *Granta.* 1990. ("The Herbert Read Memorial Lecture." 6 Feb. 1990)

———. *The Satanic Verses.* New York: Viking, 1989.

The Rushdie File. Ed. Lisa Appignanesi and Sara Maitland. Syracuse: Syracuse, 1990.

Said, Edward. *Covering Islam.* New York: Pantheon, 1981.

———. "Criticism/Self-Criticism." *Lingua Franca* Feb.–March 1992: 37–43.

———. *Culture and Imperialism*. New York: Knopf, 1993.
———. "Gods That Always Fail." *Raritan* XIII (Spring 1994): 1–14.
———. *Orientalism*. New York: Vintage, 1979.
———. "Palestine, Then and Now." *Harper's* Dec. 1992: 47–55.
Said, Edward, Gayatri Spivak, Akeel Bilgrami, Ibrahim Abu-Lughod, Eqbal Ahmad, and Agha Shahid Ali. "Antithetical to Islam." Letter to the Editor. *New York Times* 17 Feb. 1989: A38.
Sarkis, Nicolas. "L'inquiétante baisse des revenus du pétrole." *Le Monde Diplomatique* Feb. 1993: 6.
Schiller, Herbert. *Culture, Inc.: The Corporate Takeover of Public Expression*. New York: Oxford UP, 1989.
Schirmer, Daniel. "Access: Imperialist Expansion in the Post Cold-War Era." *Monthly Review* 45 (Sept. 1993): 38–51.
Schrecker, Ellen. *No Ivory Tower: McCarthyism and the Universities*. New York: Oxford UP, 1986.
Shohat, Ella. "Notes on the 'Post-Colonial.'" *Social Text* 31/32 (1992): 99–113.
Smith, Page. *Killing The Spirit*. New York: Penguin, 1990.
Soyinka, Wole. *The Interpreters*. 1965. Portsmouth: Heinemann, 1970.
Spivak, Chakravorty Gayatri. "Can the Subaltern Speak?" *Marxism and the Interpretation of Culture*. Ed. Cary Nelson and Lawrence Grossberg. Urbana: U of Illinois P, 1988. 271–313.
———. *The Post-Colonial Critic: Interviews, Strategies, Dialogues*. Ed. Sarah Harasym. New York: Routledge, 1990.
Taha, Mahmoud Mohammed. *The Second Message of Islam*. Trans. Abdullahi Ahmed An-Na'im. Syracuse: Syracuse UP, 1987.
Tocqueville, Alexis de. *Democracy in America*. 1835–40. Ed. J. P. Mayer and Max Lerner. Trans. George Lawrence. New York: Harper, 1966.
Tomlinson, John. *Cultural Imperialism*. Baltimore: Johns Hopkins UP, 1991.
Van Laue, Theodore. *The World Revolution of Westernization: The Twentieth Century in Global Perspective*. New York: Oxford UP, 1987.
Wa Thiong'o, Ngugi. *Decolonising the Mind: The Politics of Language in African Literature*. Portsmouth: Heinemann, 1986.
———. *Moving the Centre: The Struggle for Cultural Freedoms*. Portsmouth: Heinemann, 1993.
"Who Needs the Great Works?" *Harper's* Sept. 1989: 43–52.
Yúdice, George. "We are *Not* the World." *Social Text* 31/32 (1992): 202–16.
Zaidi, Nayyar. "American Human Rights for China!" *Impact* 22 (11 Dec. 1992–7 Jan. 1993): 15–16.
Zubaida, Sami. "Islam, the State and Democracy." *Middle East Report* 179 (Nov.–Dec. 1992): 2–10.

Despotism from Under the Veil: Masculine and Feminine Readings of the Despot and the Harem

Inge E. Boer

D espotism figures as a persistently dominant concept in West-ern representations of the Orient.[1] Because of concepts com-monly related to despotism, such as polygamy, the harem, and the presumed oppressed position of women under despotism, repre-sentations of Oriental women have been affected in particular.

Montesquieu's *De l'esprit des lois,* published in 1748, has been instrumental in establishing despotism as a basically *political* sys-tem.[2] Simultaneously, through the Greek *despotes,* meaning "mas-ter over slaves in a domestic space," despotism maintains a link with the domestic. This linkage between despotism and the domes-tic is present in various forms in *De l'esprit des lois.* Given the ex-traordinary influence of Montesquieu's work, the specific position despotism occupies in his analysis of different forms of govern-ment, and the reproduction of his ideas in representations of the Orient, the study of representations of Oriental women necessi-tates an analysis of Montesquieu's ideas on despotism. Montes-quieu's seemingly inevitable logic of oppression operates on the

© 1996 by *Cultural Critique.* Winter 1995–96. 0882-4371/96/$5.00.

Western representation of Oriental women, and thus they too become defined, through his definition of despotism.

The first part of this article, therefore, focuses on three different relations between despotism and domestic space in *De l'esprit des lois* in order to uncover the implicit inequalities of power in Montesquieu's system of ordering and to explore the way in which gender intersects with those relations. The three relations indicated are, first, that between the monarchy and the republic, on the one hand, and despotism, on the other; second, that between the despot and his subjects generally speaking; and third, that between the master and his slaves.

Pierre Bourdieu argues that Montesquieu is not by accident led to pose explicitly the question of the link between domestic rule and the political in *De l'esprit des lois,* because

> it is there in fact that, in addition to sexuality and politics, the threads of conscious reasons become knotted—where it is a matter of "domestic servitude" in the sense of "control over women"—with the hidden chain of unconscious socially organized phantasms—where it is a matter of control *exercised by* women (with the theme of *ruse,* the power of the weak) and of despotism as the only means left to men to escape from the control of women. (Bourdieu 235; original emphases)[3]

I want to take the domestic in a somewhat broader sense than Bourdieu so as to bring all the connotations of the domestic into play. The domestic, according to the *Oxford English Dictionary,* signifies that which pertains to the house(hold), that which pertains to a particular or to one's own country, and that which pertains to what is domesticated.

The second part of my analysis foregrounds the domestic space, the term mostly silenced in Montesquieu's investigations. My examination of *Lettres persanes* and of a recent analysis of the seraglio by Alain Grosrichard, *La structure du sérail,* is meant to show how the political and the domestic converge in the representations of the harem. Both texts hinge on a system of surveillance, which reproduces a dominant and dominating masculine perspective and whose forces work toward control of the women in the harem. The fear of a revolt by the women is countered by the regulation of their visibility. To render an account of but one aspect of the complex interaction in the harem—that is, by emphasizing the despot's point of view—maintains women as the object of surveillance.

Therefore, in the third section, I will juxtapose these two texts with the so-called *Turkish Embassy Letters* by Lady Mary Montagu. Her letters, although partaking in a dominant mode of representing Oriental women, provide critical instances that arrive at a partial difference in scopic regimes. From a perspective "within" the harem, achieved through the narratological conception of a first-person embedded discourse, the letters by Lady Montagu show how surveillance also provides possibilities for resistance. My reading of the *Turkish Embassy Letters* proposes alternative perspectives that draw attention to a system of communication among women that goes unnoticed and that also point out the potentially threatening character of women in the harem, where they confront the despot as a group. I aim at an analysis in which the monolithical and unidirectional character of relations among despotism, the domestic, and ensuing scopic regimes are subverted. A deconstructive and feminist critique of the hierarchical ranking inherently present in Western representations of the Orient, and of women in the Orient in particular, provides possibilities for women's empowerment and pleasure that have received very little attention until now.

1. Despotism as Boundary Marker

In *De l'esprit des lois*, despotism evolves from a comparison— is meant to discriminate in order to establish the identities of the republic, the monarchy, and despotism, respectively, and thereafter to show the inevitability of an order.[4] Montesquieu starts with the "essence" or nature of these three government types, which he defines in terms of power and how power is exercised:

> the republican government is that in which the body or only a part of the people is possessed of the supreme power; monarchy that in which a single person governs but by fixt and established laws; a despotic government, that in which a single person directs everything, without rule or law, by his own will and caprice. (II: 1; translation modified)

The nature of the types of government functions as the point of departure, enabling subsequent deductions. The nature of each type is directly related to its laws because "[l]aws in their most general signification, are the necessary relation derived from the nature of things. In this sense all beings have their laws . . ." (I: 1). By ordering the different forms of government, a principle of ranking is established.

Considering the way a government is related to its laws, it is clear that despotism shortcircuits every intended comparison by the nonexistence of laws. For if everything has its laws, then what place does despotism occupy? In Louis Althusser's words, despotism constitutes "the limit government, and already the limit of government" (75). Despotism becomes the boundary marker, while simultaneously occupying a place that cannot be theorized, outside the perception of what constitutes a government. Ernesto Laclau and Chantal Mouffe use the term antagonism to define this condition:

> Antagonism, as a witness of the impossibility of a final suture, is the "experience" of the limit of the social. Strictly speaking, antagonisms are not *internal* but *external* to society; or rather, they constitute the limits of society, the latter's impossibility of fully constituting itself. (125)[5]

Having established the nature of monarchy, republic, and despotism, Montesquieu infers the principle of the three government types that "are from thence most naturally derived" (III: 2). Whereas virtue is the principle of the republic, honor is that of the monarchy and fear constitutes the principle of despotism (III). One of Montesquieu's major concerns, however, lies with the potential corruption of the republic, and especially the monarchy, through their principle, by which they would fall prey to despotism: "The principle of monarchy is corrupted, when the first dignities are marks of the first servitude, when the great men are stripped of popular respect, and rendered the low tools of arbitrary power" (VIII: 7).

From these remarks about the nature and principle of the various government types, some notions concerning Montesquieu's way of ordering can be derived. The nature and principle

of government constitute the framework on which the whole system of differentiation is built. Despotism works within this framework as the representation for what is "other" to the West, and
more specifically to France. Montesquieu establishes this relation
through the opposition of France as domestic space, on the one
hand, and non-European regimes, in particular regimes in the
Orient such as the Ottoman Empire and Persia, on the other.
France functions as domestic space from which notions of "self"
spark off differences, differences all converging in the repetition
of despotism as the most alien conceivable. Despotism functions as
the *degré zéro* in Montesquieu's system of ordering.[6]

Montesquieu constructs a hierarchy where despotism functions as an opposite to the pair republic/monarchy. But, simultaneously, this pair is continually in danger of falling prey to despotism
through the corruption of the principle of republic/monarchy. It
implies that despotism is always lurking in the background as a
presence within the "self" (Althusser 65–67; Grosrichard 61). The
clear boundaries that Montesquieu drew between despotism, on
the one hand, and the republic and the monarchy, on the other,
thereby tend to become blurred, thus severely testing Montesquieu's construction of differences.[7]

The Despot and His Subjects: A Reign of Fear
Montesquieu's fear of the monarchy's slide into despotism already hints at a second relation between despotism and domestic
space, that is, the relation between the despot and his subjects. The
despot reigns through fear, but, as Montesquieu indicates, "a
timid, ignorant and faint-spirited people have no need for a great
number of laws" (V: 14). Despotism appears to be trapped in a
vicious circle constructed by Montesquieu. Fear rules over people,
who are unworthy, it seems, of laws, and thus a despot has a free
hand imposing his will. The assumption that timidity and igno-
rance belong almost as natural characteristics to people in a despotic state contrasts sharply with virtue and honor, belonging respectively to the republic and the monarchy. It raises the question
how a system functions without laws or order, where absolute servitude of the subjects determines their relationship to the despot, a
system, in short, where "man is a creature that submits to a creature that demands" (III: 10; translation modified).

Montesquieu's well-known theory of climate provides the un-
derpinnings for this relationship of the despot and his subjects—
of the political and the domestic. Climate, in Montesquieu's view,
influences the temperament of (wo)man; there are physiological
differences between those living in cold climates and those living
in hot climates. He argues that climate, as an inescapable fate, determines one's behavior and thus creates a fundamental difference
between people from the North and those from the South.[8] So
physiological differences lead to naturalized character traits.
People from the North have "a greater boldness, that is, more
courage; a greater sense of superiority, that is, less desire of revenge; a greater opinion of security, that is, more frankness, less
suspicion, policy and cunning" (XIV: 2). What this statement implies is that people from the South are less confident or coura-
geous, have more desire for revenge, are suspicious and shrewd,
and abound with rumors. Montesquieu illustrates this opposition
with, among other examples, Asia, where cold climate zones border immediately warm climates. "From hence it comes, that in Asia
the strong nations are opposed to the weak; the warlike, brave,
and active people touch immediately on those who are indolent,
effeminate, and timorous; the one must therefore conquer, and the
other be conquered" (XVII: 3). The relations between people from
the North and those from the South are embedded in inequalities
of power and indicate a colonialist impulse on the part of the
North. The possession of power by people from the North is directly linked to activity, courage, and a liking for war, implying that
masculine traits belong to a discourse of authority and domination.
What is implicit in the first half of the comparison is overtly stated
in the second: those dispossessed of means of power, due to the
warm climate, are fearful and effeminate. Montesquieu's logical
conclusion is that the powerful conquer the weak or, in his implied
terms of gender, that the masculine conquers the feminine. We
might then conclude that the whole discourse on despotism,
through its nature and principle informed by and founded on the
climate theory, is embedded in gendered relations and inequalities
of power.[9]
    The despot becomes a paradoxical figure in Montesquieu's
representation in that his subjects blindly obey him, but, as the
climate theory implies, both the despot and the subjects are gov-

erned by their senses. Moreover, as Montesquieu states, the despot is hidden from his subjects: "one does not know in which state he is. Luckily, man is such in this country that they only need a name to govern them" (V: 14; my translation). Fear as the principle of despotism seems to be the true master, creating a system where a name is enough to keep the subjects in line. The domestic space does not need a visible ruler in the form of a master. The ultimate transparency of power is established by absence. According to Montesquieu, the despot's power is represented through delegation: "It is therefore more natural for him to resign it to a vizir and to invest him with the same power as himself. The creation of the vizir is a fundamental law of this government" (II: 5) and "[i]n a despotic government power passes completely onto the hands of the person to which one entrusts it. The vizir is the despot himself; and every particular officer is the vizir" (V: 16; my translation).

Each House Is a Separate Empire
So far I have analyzed two different relations between despotism and the domestic. The first was that of France as a domestic space from which despotism differed as the most alien form of government. The second relation derives from despotism in that the relationship between the despot and his subjects is specified. In fact, Montesquieu's systematization of despotism works as a set of Russian dolls. The delegation of power points at yet another level of relation between despotism and domestic space as it stretches from the highest level—with the delegation of power from the despot onto the vizir—to the lowest, that is, with the passage of power from the despot to the master of a household. Therefore, following Montesquieu's logic, the relationship between the master and his slaves/women can be seen as the third main relationship between despotism and domestic space. It is this transference of one meaning of domestic to another through the despot that makes for the gendering of the Orient. Indeed, that which determines the despot with regard to his subjects is doubled in the individual relationship between the sexes. As Montesquieu states, "[i]n despotic states each house is a separate empire" (IV: 3; translation modified).

Two notions are particularly important in connection with the relationship of the master to his women: polygamy and the harem. In eighteenth-century accounts, the seraglio of the despot is mostly taken as the exemplary space wherein the master (the despot) is portrayed in relation to women (his women in the harem). Both the harem and polygamy were intensely scrutinized phenomena as well as sources for speculation and fantasy in the West.[10] Montesquieu believed that in Asia and Africa more women than men were born, which contributed, just like the climate, to the feminine characteristics of those regions (XVI). Moreover, according to Montesquieu, women in despotic states were themselves an object of luxury, kept under surveillance in the harem to ascertain their availability for the master (VII: 9).

The harem seems to be the knot that ties notions about the "other" together. Women form the lowest level in the whole chain of being in the despotic state evoked by Montesquieu. The guarding of women is not only naturalized through a system of relations where domination is located in the first term, in despot(ism) or the master, but also hinges on the perceived potential of "escape" for women from surveillance, traditionally represented in the form of lesbianism. The suppression of women takes on a form where force and violence become justified methods to maintain the structure of power relations. I think a double fascination sets in motion a fantasy that is perpetuated not only because the locus of this fantasy was unavailable and impenetrable for Western men, but also because it integrated fantasies of identification with the position of the despot and fantasies about female sexuality as "naturally" predicated upon relations of domination.

I perceive Montesquieu's system of despotism as a model in which the first term is privileged and endowed with power, whereas the second term represents the oppressed. One relation implied but never spelled out in Montesquieu's representation of despotism is that of the West as the absent despot with regard to the Orient as the oppressed. If we see the West as the place from which representations emanate and as that which defines the terms of the relationship, we might see how the position of the West as the despot was naturalized and made transparent through the very projection of despotism on the Orient.

From this point of view, it is possible to rework the relations previously understood as hierarchical and to show that no term is merely an element of domination or repression. Montesquieu set up a system where the Orient functioned as "other," defined from within a domestic space, that of France as a national state. If, in contrast, we see the Orient as domestic space, as that space which the West wishes to domesticate, the West/France becomes the space from which both fear and representation emanate. Western representation endows the Oriental despot with masculine traits: for example, through his absolute political power in relation to his subjects and his absolute sexual power in relation to women. As we have already seen, the Orient was perceived as a feminine space influenced by climate and easily subjected to passions. Despite the endowed masculinity, the Oriental despot functions himself as a domesticated space. How then do we perceive the despot? And how do we interpret the role of women as they seem to end up again at the receiving end of the power chain?

2. Reading from the Despot's Point of View

Reading along the lines of Montesquieu's logic of ordering showed the tensions present in his systematization. As Bourdieu indicated, despotism seemed the only means left to men to escape from the control of women. The harem will thus be the focal point in the following analyses as we turn our attention to the domestic space. Rendering the harem a central position does not necessarily lead to a divergence from the despot's point of view, as interpretations of *Lettres persanes* and *La structure du sérail* indicate. Next, in part three, I will suggest a reading against the grain, reading the gendered relations converging in representations of the harem differently, that is, from "within" the harem.

In order to emphasize the oblique status of such a reading, I will first elaborate further on a masculine reading of the despot and his relation to the harem. Alain Grosrichard centers his study, *La structure du sérail,* on the position of the despot. In addition to Montesquieu's theory of despotism, he bases his argument mainly on travel journals and descriptions of the Ottoman Empire from the seventeenth and eighteenth centuries. Grosrichard regards Montesquieu's representation of despotism as a phantasm, but I contend that he builds his analysis on a similar phantasm. At times it is very difficult to decide whether Grosrichard uses the travel journals and other contemporary sources as representations or as a "reality." The travel journals were repetitive in their compulsive desire to "penetrate" the world of the harem and the despot. The phantasm unveiling this space, stereotypically represented in highly sexualized imagery, is once more repeated by Grosrichard, who, while analyzing the despot's role, becomes enveloped in the same discourse used in the travel journals.

Grosrichard's account of representations of harems in eighteenth-century texts takes the form of what might be called a guided tour. After an elaboration on the despotic state, Grosrichard considers the harem. The narrative of the seclusion of the seraglio—a seclusion that becomes more closely guarded as one advances toward the center, the actual harem—leads us through this hothouse of violence and jealousy, sexuality and surveillance. With descriptions entitled "Anatomy of the Seraglio" and "Curtain Raiser," the harem becomes a theatrical performance with the readers as spectators/voyeurs and Grosrichard as director.

I consider Grosrichard a good example of what Bourdieu describes thus: "And nothing then prohibits the rationalizing intention, which defines the 'scientific' mythology, to re-cover the mythic narrative with a 'rational' account which *doubles* and *represses* it at the same time" (Bourdieu 235; original emphasis). Hence, Grosrichard's account, while analyzing those travel journals, is the next in the chain of representations of a phantasm. To make things worse, the discourse silences parts of these representations at the same time.[11]

This problem is particularly clear in his analysis of the despot in the seraglio:

> But what strikes the travellers as much perhaps as that exacerbated femininity, avid for the phallus in all its states and forms—in short, simply hysterical—is that this femininity gives itself as an uncountable multiplicity of practically interchangeable specimen. . . . Everything takes place as if the primary object of the despot's jouissance was not so much woman as all *women*. Certainly, in the seraglio the despot is the only one able to enjoy the other sex. But it is less the *other* sex that he enjoys than its multiplicity that, in contrast to his own unity, characterizes the inferior. (Grosrichard 177, 178; original emphasis).

Grosrichard seems more concerned with the system of surveillance and the preservation of the despot's power (representing, and generalizing into, the phallus) than with the position of those placed under surveillance. The unity of the despot is duplicated in his gazing over a multiplicity of women, who all lose their individuality. It resembles a Foucauldian panopticon, where the controlling eye of surveillance establishes and maintains power relations. Grosrichard casts representations of the harem in terms of surveillance, which does not only preserve the despot's power and point of view, but also ascertains his own privileged position. The unsettling consequences of giving up a reproduction of the despot's point of view would disrupt the reassuring gesture that women are under control, as my analysis of the braiding of hair will show.[12]

Grosrichard's use of the Foucauldian panopticism and especially a Lacanian interpretation of the (preservation of the) phallus therein centers on the figure of the despot around whom the whole system of control and surveillance evolves:

> But rumor has it that a captivated lewdness burns in the inaccessible core of the seraglio and that the piercing gaze of the old [guardian] women, watchful for every trace of jouissance stolen from the master, risks at any moment to be deceived, despite all the precautions. (177)

The system is directed toward one point, the pleasure of the despot, and above all, his sexual pleasure. It starts with his scopic privilege over the other inhabitants of the seraglio, who are related to him in a greater or lesser degree of servitude. Moreover, Grosrichard argues that all harem inhabitants reinforce the despot's position by identification through a lack. Deaf-mutes, eunuchs, and women affirm that the despot has the power of speech, of communication in general, and of the phallus in particular. Ultimately, all the systems of mutual control work in one direction: "Everything converges toward this blind spot, this imaginary hearth of jouissance, that is the harem . . ." (158). Grosrichard's account is largely written from the despot's point of view; that is, his scopic privilege is reproduced. Moreover, to call the harem a blind spot means that it is never possible to theorize *from* that space because it is bound to remain unknown. Later in this article, I will attempt to do exactly that, to read from "within" that spot, which seems to be a blind spot in a male perspective and imagination.

The harem is prominent in Montesquieu's *Lettres persanes* as well, but the representation of the harem as the space fully dominated by the despot's desire and the response of the women to this desire is played out to its tragic end. It shows the havoc caused by a system of control gone haywire, with the women again victims of the forced imposition of the despot's point of view.

A Persian nobleman, Usbek, travels to Paris with his companion Rica. Usbek's correspondence can be divided into two parts: the letters he writes from Paris to friends about French culture, and his letters to the women he leaves behind in his harem. In their responses, the women testify about their loneliness in Usbek's absence and of their desire for him. The eunuchs who were supposed to control the harem have more and more difficulty in maintaining order with the prolonged absence of Usbek. Finally the system of control collapses, strained to its limits, as the increasingly anxious sequence of letters from several eunuchs shows. The principal eunuch writes Usbek in despair:

> Things here have arrived at a state that can no longer be tolerated. Your wives have supposed that your departure gave them complete impunity and dreadful things have happened. I tremble myself at the horrible account I am about to give you. (Letter CXLVII)[13]

Usbek responds in kind and delegates his full power to the eunuch:

> Receive by this letter unlimited power over all the seraglio. Command with authority equal to mine. Let fear and terror run with you; . . . Let all be in consternation and in tears before you. Interrogate the whole seraglio. (Letter CXLVIII)

When these measures prove to be insufficient, Usbek orders his eunuchs to kill all the women guilty of disobedience. Roxane, who apparently was Usbek's most trusted and beloved wife, writes him a shocking farewell:

Yes, I deceived you; I corrupted your eunuchs, made sport of your jealousy, and *learned how to make your frightful seraglio into a place of delight and pleasure*. . . . I have lived in slavery, but I have always been free; I reformed your laws by those of nature, and my spirit has always held to its independence. (Letter CXXI; my emphasis)

Usbek has been deceived by the appearance of submission, but ultimately he must learn that nobody can be controlled completely.

Julia Douthwaite argues that the battle that erupts in the harem is a battle between mutually opposing codes: women see the harem as prison, whereas Usbek (although influenced by French ideas about the Orient) maintains that it is a "sweet retreat." Roxane is the one who reveals best the hypocrisy of the harem and changes it into a place of female delight and pleasure, a women's place. She redefines the concepts of Usbek's vocabulary and thus redefines female existence against his restrictive norms. The novel, however, closes with a conventional conclusion: Roxane's death. Douthwaite does not interpret Roxane's suicide as a gesture of final freedom nor as a universal condemnation of all sexual tyranny, but rather as "the logical climax of Usbek's moral and affective 'mauvaise foi,' the ultimate clash between his abstract political philosophizing and the concrete reality of his domestic despotism" (64–78). This "solution," however, is fully in line with a recourse to male domination and control, where insubordination by women is punished so that patriarchal order can reestablish itself.

3. Reading from "Within" the Harem

Montesquieu's *Lettres persanes* form a stark contrast with the letters from Constantinople by Lady Mary Wortley Montagu,[14] written during the years 1717–1718. The *Turkish Embassy Letters*, as they were called, were published for the first time in 1763, a year after her death. They immediately won high acclaim. In his complete edition of Lady Montagu's letters, Robert Halsband concludes that the *Turkish Embassy Letters* are not actual letters, but that "in the main Lady Mary compiled her Embassy letters from actual letters which she 'edited' by transposing sections and otherwise manipulating them to achieve a more artistic collection" (I: xvi).

Therefore, I will analyze Lady Montagu's letters as representations and focus mainly on her attention for and description of the position of women in the Ottoman Empire.[15]

It is striking to see how Lady Montagu divides the subjects of her writing among her addressees. In the letters to Alexander Pope and the Abbé Conti, for example, she addresses questions related to the organization of the Ottoman Empire and Islam, and refutes the faulty representations given by earlier travellers. Her letters to women, especially those to her sister, Lady Mar, deal extensively with the position of women and her visits to women's quarters. The comparison of the position of English and Turkish women turns out favorably for the latter.

Contrary to travel accounts by previous writers, which kept repeating the by then familiar stereotypical tale of women's oppression in the Ottoman Empire, Lady Montagu emphasizes the liberty of Turkish women:

> Now that I am a little acquainted with their ways, I cannot forbear admiring either the exemplary discretion or extreme stupidity of all the writers that have given accounts of 'em [Turkish women, IB]. Tis very easy to see they have more liberty than we have, no Woman of what rank so ever being permitted to go in the street without 2 muslins. . . . You may guess how effectually this disguises them, that there is no distinguishing the great lady from her Slave, and 'tis impossible for the most jealous Husband to know his Wife when he meets her, and no Man dare either touch or follow a Woman in the street. (Letter to Lady Mar, I: 328)

The liberty of Turkish women finds expression, ironically, in their dress. The very dress meant to keep the women from being looked at provides possibilities for masquerade and free movement. This point of view emphasized by Lady Montagu contrasts sharply with the current interpretation of women's dress as oppressive only. Another source for a certain freedom of action, Lady Montagu states, is the disposal Turkish women have over their dowries. "Neither have they much to apprehend from the resentment of their Husbands, those ladys that are rich having all their money in their own hands, which they take with 'em upon a divorce with an addition which he is oblig'd to give 'em" (I: 328). Taking the financial position of English women, or even worse, that of French women, into account, it must have impressed Lady Montagu that Turkish women enjoyed certain financial privileges.[16]

Lady Montagu is equally impressed by the availability of exclusively female spaces like baths, where women have the chance to meet. She perceives the baths as a women's coffee house, where the latest news and gossips are exchanged. Rank or standing are effaced: "all being in the state of nature, that is, in plain English, stark naked, without any Beauty or defect conceal'd, yet there was not the least wanton smile or immodest Gesture amongst 'em" (Letter to Lady Mar I: 313). Lady Montagu cannot, however, escape from the fact that she herself proved to be an incursion in this egalitarian female domain. As she watches the women, she is fully dressed in a riding dress that she doesn't want to take off despite the encouragement of the women present in the bath. Reluctantly, and only after repeated requests, she shows the women her stays, "which satisfy'd 'em very well, for I saw they believ'd I was so lock'd up in that Machine that it was not in my own power to open it, which contrivance they attributed to my husband" (I: 314).[17]

Although Lady Montagu takes great pains to show and subvert the presuppositions of her male predecessors, she nevertheless does not escape from common fantasies about Oriental women. No immodest gestures, she informs her addressee, were perceived by her. The fact that Lady Montagu explicitly mentions the absence of wanton smiles or immodest gestures implies that she did expect their occurrence. The fantasy that women, waiting in frustration for the attention of their master, would start sexual relations among themselves, was commonly referred to in seventeenth-century travel journals, and, as this detail suggests, it informs Lady Montagu's discourse as well.

On some occasions she has difficulty in warding off her attraction for the women she meets or the scenes unfolding before her eyes, as Lowe (*Critical Terrains* 47) also argues. Writing to her sister, who always receives the most intimate details of Lady Montagu's adventures, she relates her visit to the beautiful Fatima. She is dumbfounded with so much beauty:

I was struck with admiration that I could not for sometime speak to her, *being wholly taken up in gazing.* That surprising Harmony of features! that charming result of the whole! that exact proportion of Body! that lovely bloom of her Smile! But her Eyes! large and black with all the soft languishment of the bleu! After my first surprize was over, I endeavor'd by nicely examining her face to find out some imperfection, without any fruit of my search but being clearly convinc'd of the Error of that vulgar notion, that a face perfectly regular would be agreable . . ." (Letter to Lady Mar I: 350; my emphasis)

Lady Montagu excuses herself for speaking about beauty in terms of such enchantment, and phrases her appreciation in the form of a defense of divine creation versus human creation. She compares her description of Fatima with the way writers speak about statues or paintings.

I think I have read somewhere that Women always speak in rapture when they speak of Beauty, but I can't imagine why they should not be allow'd to do so. I rather think it Virtue to be able to admire without any Mixture of desire or Envy. The Gravest Writers have spoke with great warmth of some cele-brated Pictures or Statues. The Workmanship of Heaven cer-tainly excells all our Weak Imitations, and I think has a much better claim to our Praise. (I: 351)

Lady Montagu's claim that human beauty exceeds artistic produc-tion is substantiated and reinforced by attributing to it a divine origin. The aesthetic value of pictures and sculptures is no more than a weak imitation and is therefore less to be admired. The admiration Lady Montagu projects onto Fatima is virtuous, be-cause not tainted, as she claims, by desire or envy.

Yet Lady Montagu has to exert herself to show distance or disinterested praise while she is captured by the obvious appeal of Fatima. The rapture about Fatima is augmented by the dance her slaves perform.

This Dance was very different from what I had seen before. Nothing could be more artfull or more proper to raise *certain Ideas,* the Tunes so soft, the motions so languishing, accompa-ny'd with pauses and dying Eyes, halfe falling back and then

recovering themselves in so artfull a Manner that *I am very positive the coldest and most rigid Prude upon Earth could not have look'd
upon them without thinking of something not to be spoke of.* (I: 351;
my emphases)

Lady Montagu's emphasis on the artful manner in which the
dance was executed strives to include her audience, her sister, in
the effects the dance has on Lady Montagu herself. The double-
talk, alluding both to sexual desire and a tender melancholy,
speaks of lack of control. The control that Lady Montagu was more
or less able to sustain in her description of Fatima—a virtuous admiration without desire or envy—breaks down under the forceful
impression that would have led any woman, even the coldest and
most rigid prude, let alone herself, to sexually charged fantasies.
But at the same time the male discourse she uses does not give her
the means to talk of what she experiences. Lowe (*Critical Terrains*
47) phrases Lady Montagu's rapture in terms of homoeroticism
and makes explicit what in my opinion is exactly what cannot be
expressed.

Clearly, Lady Montagu perceives the places where she meets
women as "women's own spaces." To argue that the harems or
baths, for that matter, are utterly controlled spaces is to forget that
they can also be seen as relatively "safe" spaces where women can
be among themselves. Baths and harems, without doing away completely with the fact that women were kept under surveillance,
serve equally as places for exchange of information and learning
by and through women. The dominant masculine representation
of women waiting in agony for the master, separated from each
other by their desire for him, sustains the effort to divide and rule
over women and leaves out this crucial understanding of a feminine space.

Therefore, I want to take up an argument made by Lowe and
carry it further. Lowe (*Critical Terrains*) argues that

the harem is not merely an orientalist voyeur's fantasy of imagined female sexuality; it is also a possibility of an erotic universe in which there are no men, a site of social and sexual
practices that are not organized around the phallus or a central male authority. (48)

The practices Lowe refers to can take place in the absence of men, but that is not a necessary condition. The bonding between women might lie beyond or outside male perceptions and fantasies and might express itself in terms of female sexuality—sexuality understood in a broad sense—which is pleasurable and "autonomous."

Braiding Hair: Countering the Despot's Gaze

Through an analysis of a repetitive element in Lady Montagu's letters, I will elaborate how social and sexual practices of women in a feminine space lead to a partial difference in scopic regimes and means of expression. The first is related to the social environment in which women operate and communicate; the second goes back to the fact that the despot's privileged gaze is focused on female sexuality.

Lady Montagu's letters revealed a repetitive element, the braiding of hair or braided hair, that could be taken as a metaphorical representation of the harem: a female representation of learning, communication, and production in sharp contrast with male representations. In her letters to women in England, and again specifically in those to her sister, Lady Montagu relates her encounters with Turkish women by giving descriptions not only of the magnificence of their dress, but also of their elaborately braided hair. In the baths of Adrianople, Lady Montagu comments, for example,

> to see so many fine women naked in different postures, some in conversation, some working, others drinking Coffee or sherbet, and many negligently lying on their Cushions while their slaves (generally pritty Girls of 17 or 18) were employ'd in braiding their hair in several pritty manners. In short, tis the Women's Coffee house, where all the news of the Town is told, scandal invented, etc. (Letter to Lady Mar I: 314)

The mention of braided hair and its braiding can be discarded as merely a detail, but changing the perspective of analysis into that in which the detail takes prominence leads to a different and differing story. As Naomi Schor has argued,

> [t]o focus on the detail and more particularly on the *detail as negativity* is to become aware . . . of its participation in a larger semantic network, bounded on the one side by the *ornamental*,

with its traditional connotations of effeminacy, and on the other, by the *everyday*, whose "prosiness" is rooted in the domestic sphere of social life presided over by women. (4; original emphases)

The insistence of the detail, gendered as feminine as Schor asserts, in its repetitive occurrence allows it to gather significance. Braiding hair is one of those activities that combines the ornamental, embellishing women, and the everyday in its casual ordinariness.

The braiding of hair can be analyzed as a means of communication, as something that women perform on each other in their own spaces. Lady Montagu's repeated representation of braided hair signifies that hair is the chain that links one narrative of female production to another. By that I mean that Lady Montagu notices the braided hair or the braiding of hair and writes about it to female addressees. Ultimately, it is my interpretation and reading back along the chain that forms the provisionally last station in this process of the production of meaning. To be sure, I am not interpreting Lady Montagu's representation of braided hair in relation to women's spaces in order to establish or arrive at any kind of truth about "reality" in the harem. Nor do I attempt, using the expression "from 'within' the harem" in this analysis, to speak for women in the harem. In the first place, the harem is largely a fictional notion, and one can hardly take any real space represented as a harem to be described by that notion. In the second place, the women in this fictional harem do not speak, which constitutes a silence that urges further investigation. Not to be attentive and responsive to the silences would reproduce the oppression present in the representations of those women. Instead, I explore the alternative ways in which the inhabitants of the harem do "speak." As I have suggested, they express themselves to each other in alternative ways, and the braiding of hair is one such means of communication. The women's response to the presence of Lady Montagu is another. I take the semiosis thus conceived as an expression of a "first person" that is just like first person narrators whose discourse is embedded in a "third person" narration of the Western traveller.

According to narratology, each text is uttered by a speaker— a function rather than an individual—who may embed another speaker's discourse in his or her own. In that way, multiple and fractured voices can be braided together. The plurality of such structures recalls Bakhtin's notion of polyphony; yet within this narratological conception, plurality is also accounted for in terms of relative subordination. Thus, viewing the braiding of hair as an embedded first person narrative accounts for both these women's access to a culturally specific form of expression and their relative confinement within it.[18]

Hair is not something that has been theorized about as such, but I think the significance lies in the braiding. We can argue that braiding hair is a form of weaving. The warp and woof of weaving resembles the braiding of hair into tresses, adding ribbons and pearls, as the women in the harem do, to achieve intricate patterns. The detail of braiding hair, through the gendering of the detail itself and because it is an activity performed by women, begs the issue of femininity, that is, femininity considered in the context of social and sexual practices. In his article "Femininity," Freud links up the two practices, although his focus is very much directed toward the sexual aspects of weaving.

Freud (*New Introductory Lectures*) examines weaving—the one meager share, a detail one could say, that he grants women in the discoveries and inventions in the history of civilization—in connection with shame and women's concealment of genital deficiency.

> Shame, which is considered to be a feminine characteristic *par excellence* but is far more a matter of convention than might be supposed, has as its purpose, we believe, concealment of genital deficiency. We are not forgetting that at later times shame takes on other functions. It seems that women have made few contributions to the discoveries and inventions in the history of civilization; there is, however, one technique which they may have invented—that of plaiting and weaving. If that is so, we should be tempted to guess the unconscious motive for the achievement. Nature herself would seem to have given the model which this achievement imitates by causing the growth at maturity of the pubic hair that conceals the genitals. The step that remained to be taken lay in making the threads adhere to one another, while on the body they stick into the skin and are only matted together. (117; original emphasis)

Freud mixes two voices in his statement that shame has concealment of genital deficiency as its purpose. At first Freud attributes the claim that shame is a feminine characteristic par excellence to the voice of common knowledge. The second voice—that is, Freud's claim to "know" the *real* purpose—distances and mixes in with this common knowledge, only to reascertain that shame *is* a feminine characteristic. This short section on shame takes a position within an argument about penis-envy, a female trait, as Freud asserts. Weaving in this context seems to fall from the skies unless we assume that the shame motive works here as well. And that is exactly what Freud is aiming for. He is able to guess the unconscious motive for weaving and relegates the female invention to female sexuality. Women merely imitate nature by weaving, that is, weaving their pubic hair, and their only accomplishment is that they make the threads adhere to each other. By weaving, women, out of shame, try to block the gaze of men. As Sarah Kofman (48–49) has argued, by imitating nature, women keep men from the horror of looking at the gaping wound of genital deficiency, reminding men of their own fear of castration.

Freud's interpretation of weaving is very much written from a male perspective, where weaving has no other function but to conceal genital deficiency from male eyes. I will return to this aspect of visuality later in this article. Instead of interpreting weaving as a screen to block the female genitals from male sight, let us assume possibilities where weaving/braiding takes on other functions, both as a social and sexual practice. What if weaving is considered a woman's business, performed by women for women? What if weaving/braiding involves a lot of pleasure? What if braiding brings out unsuspected aspects in the relation between the despot and the women in the harem? I will consider braiding as such practices in order to argue for alternative perspectives, which pay close attention to potentialities of pleasure and empowerment for women.

Nancy Miller (79) argues that to focus only on the texture of the weaving, or on the braided hair as such, is to lose sight of the producer of the texture. It would dissolve the subject, the one who does the weaving/braiding, into the production process, which makes the subject into someone suspended in a continual moment of fabrication. I want to read the braided hair both as texture and as a product produced by women.

If we go back to Lady Montagu's description of women in the

baths of Adrianople, we, as readers, are participants in her representation of activities going on in the bathhouse. Women are talking, working, drinking coffee, and braiding, and are being braided
upon. The braiding of hair is embedded in activities of exchange,
among women. The analogy with coffee houses is evoked, which
were mainly male domains for discussion, information exchange,
and male bonding. In this respect, I would argue that the braiding
of hair takes place in an environment defined as a women's space
as a part of a process of production of knowledge, information,
and pleasure. I read the braided hair as a sign, inscribed by a process of production by women. Lady Montagu "reads" braided hair
too, describing the headdress of women in general in Adrianople.
She observes that on one side of their head women wear a cap
embroidered with jewels. "The Hair hangs at its full length behind,
divided into tresses braided with pearl or riband, which is always
in great Quantity. I never saw in my life so many fine heads of hair.
I have counted 110 of these tresses of one ladys, all natural . . ."
(Letter to Lady Mar I: 327). It is hard to believe that Lady Montagu actually counted all those tresses, but it is more a representation of Lady Montagu's claim for exactitude in her observation.
Moreover, it is an indication for the special attention paid to the
braided hair of women, adorned with pearls and ribbon. Counting
them involves touching, which implies a bodily participation in the
community of women.

Observation and visibility play an important role in Lady
Montagu's representation of Turkish women in a double sense: as
a claim for exactitude and for the knowledge of the spectator. The
following fragment, recounting her entrance into Fatima's house
and the previous examples given, may serve as an illustration for
my point:

> I was met at the door by 2 black Eunuchs who lead me
> through a long Gallery between 2 ranks of beautiful young
> Girls with their hair finely plaited almost hanging to their Feet,
> all dress'd in fine light damasks brocaded with silver. *I was sorry
> that Decency did not permit me to stop to consider them nearer* . . . (Let-
> ter to Lady Mar I: 349; my emphasis)

On the one hand Lady Montagu operates within an "ethnographic"
and "epistemological" framework, where description and observa-

tion are aids for the representation of women as cultural "others."
On the other hand, her encounters with women both question and
partly reaffirm fantasies about Oriental women. The observation
of braiding/braided hair works in this respect on several levels,
namely as a source of an anxiety and fear and as a source to assume
power, as another of Freud's texts will demonstrate.

In Freud's text "Medusa's Head" (212–14),[19] visuality in combination with hair is foregrounded. Luce Irigaray (11–133) has argued that visuality is a main ground for Freud's establishment of
sexual difference. With regard to Medusa's head, the visual in relation to sexual difference takes on a special significance: "To decapi-
tate = to castrate. The terror of Medusa is thus a terror of castration that is linked to the sight of something" (212). Like the little
boy discovering the "castration" of woman at first sight, the apper-
ception of Medusa's decapitated head evokes the fear of castration.

Freud then moves away from decapitation to the hair on Medusa's head, frequently represented in the form of snakes in works
of art:

> It is a remarkable fact that, however frightening they may be
> in themselves, they nevertheless serve actually as a mitigation
> of the horror, for they replace the penis, the absence of which
> is the cause of the horror. This is a confirmation of the techni-
> cal rule according to which a multiplication of penis symbols
> signifies castration. (212)

The hair/snakes on Medusa's head therefore signifies two things:
it replaces the penis so as to mitigate for men the horror of its
absence, and because of the multiplicity (of penis symbols) it signifies castration. Therefore, the multiplicity of penis symbols shows
that woman is castrated and provokes at the same time a castration
anxiety in men.[20]

Relating Freud's analysis of Medusa's head to Lady Montagu's representation of women's braided hair, I propose to read the
multiple tresses of the women as figurations of Medusa's head. If
we go back to the situation in the harem, the despot in traditional
representations exercised a reign of fear. The whole harem economy was organized around the despot's scopic privilege and the
preservation of his phallus. But let us assume another scenario in
which the despot is confronted with a multiplicity of women wear-

ing their hair in multiple braids intertwined with pearls and ribbons. The sight of the braided hair multiplied by the number of
women would in Freud's analysis evoke a castration anxiety on the
part of the despot (an anxiety which had already become reality
for the many eunuchs in the seraglio). It is an anxiety that only the
master can "enjoy," as he was supposedly the only one allowed to
see the women in his harem. Instead of a reign of terror exercised
by the master, women remind him time and again of the possibility
of losing his penis. Who exercises power in this space? Hélène Cixous's assertion (279–98) that Medusa is beautiful and laughing
does not alleviate the fears of man, because women's laughter will
only reinforce his anxiety. They are (temporarily) out of his control, and he might be the butt of the joke.[21]

In this respect, it is revealing to see how the hairdo of harem
women was represented in Western imagery (Fig. 1). Elaborately
decorated with ribbons and pearls, the headdress reminds us of
familiar representations of Medusa's head topped with snakes. Interestingly enough, an engraving of Lady Montagu (Fig. 2) depicts
her with the same elaborate hairstyle as worn by the harem women
in the previous image.[22] It is possible to read these representations
in several ways: as close resemblances of representations of Medusa's head causing anxiety and fear among men, while securing
women's castration, or as a representation of braiding as a female
production. The fact that Lady Montagu is represented with the
same hairstyle as the harem women in Fig. 1 can be seen as Lady
Montagu "gone native"; that is, she has been braided upon. But
I think that we cannot interpret either of these representations
"outside" the confines of a dominant male discourse. The fact that
I indicated ways in which braiding hair or braided hair can be read
differently was meant to acknowledge that signs can be read in
different ways. I also have suggested that a process of renegotia-
tion by women for male-defined words, which cannot be acknowledged by dominant discourse, is possible. The braiding of hair,
therefore, can also, but not only, be read as a process of rewriting.

Hélène Cixous states in "The Laugh of the Medusa" that:

> writing is precisely the *very possibility of change*, the space that
> can serve as a springboard for subversive thought, the precur-
> sory movement of a transformation of social and cultural struc-

Fig. 1. Corneille de Bruyn, *Voyage au Levant*. [Amsterdam] 1714, Dept. of Rare Books, University of Amsterdam, Fig. 35, UBA: 1151 B 12.

Fig. 2. Engraving of Lady Mary Wortley Montagu as "The Female Traveller." Dept. of Rare Books, Princeton University Libraries, Ex 3862. 7. 64.

tures. . . . It is by writing, from and toward women, and by taking up the challenge of speech, which has been governed by the phallus, *that women will confirm women in a place other than that which is reserved in and by the symbolic, that is, in a place other than silence.* Women should break out of the snare of silence. *They shouldn't be conned into accepting a domain which is the margin or the harem.* (283; last emphasis mine)

In opposition to Cixous, I would argue that even women in the harem break the silence in building on their bodies by writing, that is, braiding onto each other. In this case, writing represents a change in the harem, since the master cannot master women by instilling them with fear but instead is reminded of his fear of castration by a multiplicity of women with braided hair. The braiding performed on them by other women in their own spaces offers possibilities for women's empowerment and pleasure that strikes at the heart of the relation between master and women as perceived in traditional male Western representations.

Notes

I have benefited greatly from discussions with Mieke Bal, Thomas DiPiero, Ali Behdad, and Bonnie Smith.

1. The Orient has had different meanings in the course of time and could in its most extended form signify a region including the Middle East, the Indian subcontinent, and the Far East. My use of the term is limited to the Islamic/Arab world as it existed in the period 1750–1850.

2. The quotes in the text are taken from the English translation *The Spirit of Laws*. Book numbers (in Roman numbers) and chapter numbers (in Arabic numbers) will be given in the text. At times parts remained untranslated in this edition, in which cases I used for my own translation Charles-Louis de Secondat, Baron de Montesquieu, *De l'esprit des lois* (Paris: Librairie Garnier Frères, 1927).

3. All translations are mine unless otherwise indicated.

4. Montesquieu's project of "naming" despotism can be understood in the Foucauldian analysis of the episteme of the Classical Age, which is based on identity and difference. In contrast with the sixteenth-century episteme, which considered resemblance as a potentially endless process of proliferation, "[f]rom now on, every resemblance must be subjected to proof by comparison, that is, it will not be accepted until its identity and the series of its differences have been discovered by means of measurement with a common unit, or, more radically, by its position in an order" (Foucault 55).

5. For a further elaboration of the notion of antagonism in connection with Lacanian concepts of subjectivity and ideology, see Slavoj Žižek.

6. Tzvetan Todorov in *Nous et les Autres* (403–21) interprets *De l'esprit des lois* as a plea for the moderation of power. Therefore, according to Todorov, Montesquieu depicts despotism in its bleakest terms. Todorov, however, reads Montesquieu in the terms that the latter sets up for his ordering, but Todorov does not interpret the consequences of Montesquieu's ordering.

7. The threat of despotism served at least partially as an argument for a class-related struggle fought in France. Montesquieu's fear of the monarchy falling prey to despotism was a barely veiled criticism of the way in which the French nobility was deprived of its particular liberties by the French crown. By urging the monarchy, that is, post–Louis XIV France, to value the nobility, who keeps honor and service to the king in high esteem, Montesquieu makes himself a spokesperson for the disenfranchised nobility. This backdrop to *L'esprit des lois* has been recognized by many, as it has been recognized in similar fashion in *Lettres persanes* (for example, see Althusser 61–85; Behdad 109–26; Lowe, "Rereadings in Orientalism" 115–43). In *Critical Terrains* (55–62, 73–74) Lowe modifies her stance somewhat with respect to despotism. She argues that in *Lettres persanes*, Montesquieu both allegorizes anxieties and tensions in eighteenth-century France and presents a French image of its cultural other. I will consider Montesquieu's personal diatribes as contextual to a broader framework of constructing despotism as a necessary attribute of the Orient.

8. Montesquieu is not always consistent in his use of geographical indications, and certain slippages occur. Starting out with a distinction between cold and hot climates out of which ensues a North-South division (XIV: 1–3), Montesquieu proposes as examples England as a Northern state and Spain, Italy, and India as Southern states. Shifting then from a North-South division to a West-East distinction (in which the first term remains implicit), South and East become almost interchangeable (XIV: 4). In a discussion of the relation between the laws of domestic slavery and the nature of the climate (XVI), the same shift from South to East occurs (XVI: 2, 10). Within the logic of these shifts, similar slippages between North and West are implied.

9. Lisa Lowe ("The Orient as Woman" 44–58) argues that the relations between the West and the Orient can be defined as spatial in the eighteenth century, whereas during the nineteenth century these relations became gendered. See in contrast Pierre Bourdieu (227–41), who locates the gendered relations between the West and the Orient already in the eighteenth century.

10. The concern with polygamy and the harem had in part to do with the demographic question whether polygamy stimulated or hampered population increase and with a debate about natural law. See, for further discussions, Bourdieu (227–41) and Grosrichard (145–48). For contemporary accounts and comments, see the *Journal Etranger* of November 1756 and November 1757. For a thorough account of the imperial harem institution and woman's important role in power structures of the Ottoman Empire of the sixteenth and seventeenth centuries, see Leslie Pierce.

11. For a thorough analysis of the perils and possibilities surrounding the interpretation of visual and textual representations of women in a colonial context, see Mieke Bal ("The Politics of Citation").

12. Grosrichard cites in passing some revealing passages about women in Persia who participate in a private council "which ordinarily preponderates over all and which gives the law to all. It is held between the mother of the King, the Grand Eunuchs and the most clever and favored mistresses" (207). The Sultane Validé,

the mother of the despot, plays an important role not only by participation in a legislative council, but also as the guardian of the Sultan's seal, hidden in the depths of the seraglio. If we take the Sultan's seal as representing the full powers of the despot, then it is noteworthy that a woman guarded these powers, and thus by extension his identity. The name of the despot was the only thing needed, as Montesquieu argued, to govern the people in a despotic regime, rendering extraordinary powers to the guardian of the name/the seal. See also Fatima Mernissi and Leslie Pierce, who emphasizes the political role of the Sultane Validé, which is not often recognized in Western sources.

13. All references to Montesquieu's *Lettres persanes* in the text will be by the number of the letter.

14. Lady Montagu's husband was sent to Constantinople as the English ambassador to the Ottoman Empire. He was credited with securing the English interests during negotiations taking place between Russia and the Ottoman Empire. The couple arrived in Constantinople in April 1717. In September of the same year, he was recalled from his duties by the king, and he and Lady Montagu left Constantinople in July 1718.

15. See also Billie Melman (77–98) for an analysis of Lady Montagu's letters.

16. A full account of Lady Montagu's own problems with her father about her dowry in relation to her suitor, Wortley, is given in the introduction by Dervla Murphy in *Embassy to Constantinople: The Travels of Lady Mary Wortley Montagu* (10–24). See also Robert Halsband (13–17) and Billie Melman (88).

17. For a reading of Lady Montagu's letters about her visits to Turkish bathhouses and the influence of those letters on Ingres' paintings, see Wendy Leeks (29–38). For an analysis of Lady Montagu's conception of liberty, see Melman (85–98).

18. I thank Mieke Bal for suggestions toward these notions. See Bakhtin for his concept of polyphony. For a further discussion of embedded first person narratives, see Mieke Bal (*Narratology* 119–27).

19. Further page references are made in the text.

20. See also Sarah Kofman's analysis (82–85) of Freud's text on Medusa's head.

21. See also Neil Hertz (27–55), who consistently associates Medusa's head with a horrifying physiognomy.

22. For the phenomenon of cultural cross-dressing, see my article "This Is Not the Orient" (211–20).

Works Cited

Althusser, Louis. *Politics and History: Montesquieu, Rousseau, Hegel and Marx*. Trans. Ben Brewster. London: NLB, 1972.

Bakhtin, Mikhail. *Problems of Dostoevsky's Poetics*. Ed. and trans. Caryl Emerson. Minneapolis: U of Minnesota P, 1984.

Bal, Mieke. *Narratology: Introduction to the Theory of Narrative*. Trans. Christine van Boheemen. Toronto: Toronto UP, 1985.

———. "The Politics of Citation." *Diacritics* 21.1 (1991): 25–45.

Behdad, Ali. "The Eroticized Orient: Images of the Harem in Montesquieu and His Precursors." *Stanford French Review* 13 (1989): 109–26.

Boer, Inge E. "This Is Not the Orient: Theory and Postcolonial Practice." *The*

Point of Theory: Practices of Cultural Analysis. Ed. Mieke Bal and Inge E. Boer. New York: Continuum; Amsterdam: Amsterdam UP, 1994.

Bourdieu, Pierre. "La rhétorique de la scientificité: contribution à une analyse de l'effet Montesquieu." *Ce que parler veut dire: l'économie des échanges linguistiques.* Paris: Fayard, 1982.

Cixous, Hélène. "The Laugh of the Medusa." Trans. Keith Cohen and Paula Cohen. *The Signs Reader: Women, Gender and Scholarship.* Ed. Elisabeth Abel and Emily K. Abel. Chicago: U of Chicago P, 1983.

Douthwaite, Julia. "Female Voices and Critical Strategies: Montesquieu, Mme de Graffigny, and Mme de Charrière." *French Literature Series* 16 (1989): 64–78.

Foucault, Michel. *The Order of Things: An Archaeology of the Human Sciences.* New York: Vintage, 1973.

Freud, Sigmund. "Femininity." *New Introductory Lectures on Psychoanalysis.* Trans. and ed. James Strachey. New York: Norton, 1965.

———. "Medusa's Head." *Sexuality and the Psychology of Love.* Ed. Philip Rieff. New York: Macmillan, 1963.

Grosrichard, Alain. *La structure du sérail: la fiction du despotisme asiatique dans l'Occident classique.* Paris: Seuil, 1979.

Halsband, Robert, ed. *The Complete Letters of Lady Mary Wortley Montagu.* 3 vols. Oxford: Clarendon P, 1965.

———. *The Life of Lady Mary Wortley Montagu.* London: Oxford UP, 1960.

Hertz, Neil. "Medusa's Head: Male Hysteria under Political Pressure." *Representations* 4 (1983): 27–55.

Irigaray, Luce. "The Blind Spot of an Old Dream of Symmetry." *Speculum of the Other Woman.* Trans. Gillian C. Gill. Ithaca: Cornell UP, 1985.

Kofman, Sarah. *The Enigma of Woman: Woman in Freud's Writings.* Trans. Catherine Porter. Ithaca: Cornell UP, 1985.

Laclau, Ernesto, and Chantal Mouffe. *Hegemony and Socialist Strategy: Toward a Radical Democratic Politics.* Trans. Winston Moore and Paul Commack. London: Verso, 1985.

Leeks, Wendy. "Ingres Other-Wise." *The Oxford Art Journal* 9.1 (1989): 29–38.

Lowe, Lisa. *Critical Terrains: French and British Orientalisms.* Ithaca: Cornell UP, 1991.

———. "The Orient as Woman in Flaubert's *Salammbô* and *Voyage en Orient.*" *Comparative Literature Studies* 23.1 (1986): 44–58.

———. "Rereadings in Orientalism: Oriental Inventions and Inventions of the Orient in Montesquieu's *Lettres Persanes.*" *Cultural Critique* 15 (1990): 115–43.

Melman, Billie. *Women's Orients. English Women and the Middle East, 1718–1918: Sexuality, Religion and Work.* London: Macmillan, 1992.

Mernissi, Fatima. *Sultanes oubliées: femmes chefs d'Etat en Islam.* Paris: Albin Michel, 1990.

Miller, Nancy. "Arachnologies: The Woman, the Text, and the Critic." *Subject to Change: Reading Feminist Writing.* New York: Columbia UP, 1988.

Montesquieu, Charles de Secondat, Baron de. *De l'esprit des lois.* 1748. Paris: Garnier-Flammarion, 1979.

———. *Lettres persanes.* 1721. Paris: Garnier-Flammarion, 1964.

———. *Persian Letters.* Trans. George R. Healy. Indianapolis: Bobbs-Merrill, 1964.

———. *The Spirit of Laws.* 1721. A Compendium of the First English Edition. Ed. David Wallace Carrithers. Berkeley: U of California P, 1977.

Pick, Christopher, ed. *Embassy to Constantinople: The Travels of Lady Mary Wortley Montagu.* London: Century, 1988.

Pierce, Leslie P. *The Imperial Harem: Women and Sovereignty in the Ottoman Empire*. Oxford: Oxford UP, 1993.
Schor, Naomi. *Reading in Detail: Aesthetics and the Feminine*. London: Methuen, 1987.
Todorov, Tzvetan. *Nous et les autres: la réflexion française sur la diversité humaine*. Paris: Seuil, 1989.
Žižek, Slavoj. *The Sublime Object of Ideology*. New York: Verso, 1989.

Black and White World: Race, Ideology, and Utopia in *Triton* and *Star Trek*

David Golumbia

[In *Triton*], a certain masculine psychology, treated as a social object, is analyzed down into its conflicting elements until it can no longer be radically distinguished from a certain 'femininity' that men begin by defining and distinguishing as wholly apart from and supplementary to the masculine.
　　　　　　　　　　　　　　　—Delany, "Interview" 42

One of the key questions on the contemporary agenda concerns the cultural construction of whiteness. One of the signs of the times is that we really don't know what "white" is.
　　　　　　　　　　　　　　—Mercer, "Skin Head Sex Thing" 205

This is an essay about utopian representations of race. More generally, it examines the project of imagining a future in which contemporary racial problems—specifically the conflicts between blacks and whites in the U.S.—have been, to whatever degree this may be possible, resolved. This project interests me for what might be called negative and positive hermeneutic reasons. The negative reasons have to do with the common representation in utopian fictions and science fiction of futures in which "racial problems" have been erased; that sort of fiction demands a critique on specifically ideological grounds. The positive motivation for this project is to work toward opening at least some critical space to discuss the possibility of resolving some of our contemporary problems about race, to ask what the spaces for such solutions might look like.[1]

Methodologically, this paper is part of a larger project that will apply ideological criticism to social issues, such as race, gender, and sexuality, especially in terms of the utopia/ideology dialectic that is so visible in science fiction. In applying ideological analysis to these social issues, one main benefit is the opportunity to deconstruct those less-than-visible, neutralizing, and neutering terms that occupy central positions in social ideologies: to penetrate these blinding, perhaps because white, places, where no one has gone before. In order to look at blackness in *Star Trek* we need also to look at what *Star Trek* says about whiteness, at the way whiteness maintains its ideological grip. This deconstructive analysis is similar to the one Samuel R. Delany enacts in *Triton:* to deconstruct utopian aspirations—which means precisely not to discount them altogether—in part by critically dismantling juridical norms of whiteness, masculinity, and "straight" sexuality.

Triton, written in 1973 and 1974 and published in 1976, offers its reader the subtitle "An Ambiguous Heterotopia," which science fiction readers will recognize as a commentary on, and reaction to, Ursula K. LeGuin's 1974 novel *The Dispossessed,* subtitled "An Ambiguous Utopia." I want to focus here on the shift in Delany's novel from "utopia" to "heterotopia," and to use briefly *The Dispossessed,* itself a sophisticated and highly critical version of utopia, as a foil for *Triton* to try to get at that deconstructive operation. I will also discuss the way Delany shifts from the classically heroic utopian center of consciousness to a villainous one. The specific characteristics of Bron Helstrom, *Triton*'s protagonist, provide some suggestive hints toward the complex operation of the contemporary Science Fiction Utopian Imaginary, pointing, in a sociological sense, toward, and even representing, a particular, hopeful future, intending to "defamiliarize and restructure our experience of our own present" in Fredric Jameson's words ("Can We Imagine the

Future?" 151), but at the same time functioning as the Imaginary *of* our present.

Delany's use of the term "heterotopia" comes from Foucault's *The Order of Things*, itself published in English just before composition started on Delany's novel. The relevant passage is found in the Preface to that work and is quoted as the epigraph to Appendix B of *Triton:*

> there is a worse kind of disorder than that of the *incongruous,*
> the linking together of things that are inappropriate; I mean
> the disorder in which fragments of a large number of possible
> orders glitter separately in the dimension, without law or ge-
> ometry, of the *heteroclite;* and that word should be taken in its
> most literal, etymological sense: in such a state, things are
> "laid," "placed," "arranged" in sites so very different from one
> another that it is impossible to find a place of residence for
> them, to define a *common locus* beneath them all. *Utopias* afford
> consolation: although they have no real locality there is never-
> theless a fantastic, untroubled region in which they are able to
> unfold; they open up cities with vast avenues, superbly planted
> gardens, countries where life is easy, even though the road to
> them is chimerical. *Heterotopias* are disturbing, probably be-
> cause they secretly undermine language, because they make it
> impossible to name this *and* that, because they shatter or tangle
> common names, because they destroy 'syntax' in advance, and
> not only the syntax which causes words and things (next to
> and also opposite one another) to "hold together." (Foucault
> xvii–xviii; Delany 345)[2]

Delany invokes Foucault in part to oppose LeGuin's usage of "uto-pia" in *The Dispossessed,* although he clearly admires that book. And of course *The Dispossessed* is itself not a conventional utopian work, which is why LeGuin calls it an "ambiguous utopia." In fact, as Jameson and others have pointed out, LeGuin's novel is in many ways determinedly dialectical, and therefore determinedly and di-alectically opposed to uncritical notions of utopia. But what Delany seems to take from *The Order of Things* is that very Foucauldian notion of "the heteroclite," that sense of a pervasive but uncategor-izable irregularity in any given order, of an unavoidable resistance to a clearly established regime of Truth.

Delany points toward the heteroclite utopia, though in an unexpected way, when he says in a recent interview that

> "[h]eterotopia" is, after all, a real English word. It's got several
> meanings. You can find it in the *OED*. If you do, you'll find it
> has some meanings that, I'd hope, apply quite directly to the
> book. ("On *Triton* and Other Matters" 318)

This is a more cunning claim than it may seem, because, although
"heterotopia" does occur in the *OED*, it is offered only as an alternate term for "heterotopy," a term from physiology, which has two
principal definitions: the general physiological notion of "displacement in position, misplacement," and the specific meaning in pa-
thology of "the occurrence of a tumour in a part where the elements of which it is composed do not normally exist." No usage
of "heterotopia" itself is provided. In that same interview Delany
himself asserts that "a major definition of 'heterotopia' is its medical meaning. It's the removal of one part or organ from the body
and affixing it at another place in or on the body. That's called a
heterotopia. A skin graft is a heterotopia. But so is a sex-change"
(319).

Although these meanings do not precisely conform to the dictionary definitions of heterotopy, they resonate with the concerns
of *Triton*, whose main character, Bron Helstrom, Delany wants his
readers to dislike strongly.[3] One of Bron's main problems has to
do with his sexual relationships—Bron is absolutely unable to understand or empathize with his partners, especially a woman he
seems actually to love, called "The Spike." So it comes as a pretty
large surprise when, in the last quarter of the novel, Bron decides
without warning to change his sex, which Delany portrays as a
simple and common operation on Triton.

As Jameson has noted, "in utopian discourse it is the narrative
itself which tends to be effaced by and assimilated to sheer description, as anyone knows who has ever nodded over the more garru-
lous explanatory passages in the classical utopias" ("Of Islands and
Trenches" 16). But what Delany, in this sense partly like LeGuin
before him, injects into the utopian narrative is character: the
reader is granted descriptions of Triton's utopian society only
through the eyes of a character who the reader is supposed to rec-

ognize not only as "unreliable" but as morally compromised, seriously unable to comprehend the world in which he lives. This puts him at odds with the utopian aspirations of the narrative description, and it sets him apart from Shevak, narrator of *The Dispossessed*, who for all that book's admitted ambiguity toward utopia per se nevertheless functions as a relatively stable and sympathetic center of consciousness.[4]

In denying the reader this center, Delany lodges one of his principal critiques of the utopian genre and of utopian thinking in general. Not only does he refuse the reader the ability to imagine herself in "the utopian place," but he puts in that place a figure whose function is exactly to force a critique of the overriding and mainstream ideology upon which the very idea of utopia itself rests. In other words, by injecting into the very center of his utopia an ideologically compromised and therefore representative figure of white, "straight," masculinity, Delany paradoxically injects into his utopia a heteroclite element, an element that refuses his utopia the closure or order his (uncritical) readers may desire. In that sense, he specifically and deliberately makes his utopia a "place of difference," an ideal world that by definition cannot be fully described or apprehended.

Bron, who transcends traditional boundaries of gender in an ultimately conservative and traditional manner, presents an odd locus of identification for the present-day reader. He willingly undergoes a transformation that an individual in our time, living according to Bron's beliefs and the ruling ideology, would refuse even to consider. This crucial displacement of ideology and utopia, including their displacement onto an organic as well as a characterological site, helps to fix the general displacement that *Triton* seeks to enact. It is in this respect that the notion of utopia—not as a projection of future social hopes but rather as a doubled reflection of our own society and the forms of its ideology—emerges. As Delany says in the same interview from which I have already quoted, "SF is not about the future. SF is in dialogue with the present. It works by setting up a dialogue with the here-and-now, a dialogue as intricate and rich as the writer can make it" ("On *Triton* and Other Matters" 320). That is Jameson's perspective on SF as well, but what I am suggesting is that the combination of SF and utopia produces a form that exists in a kind of unique tension, that serves at once to project *and* to mask the present-day ideology in which it is constructed *and also* to project deformations and corrections of the social hopes lodged within that ideology.

This heady mix of ideological, Imaginary, and social functions is well summed up by the social structure of Triton, in which every sort of imaginable (and several unimaginable) genders and sexualities coexist peacefully, and also by Bron himself, a man whose notion of masculinity reflects directly on our own most central and (until recently) least-examined notions of sexuality. The racial makeup of Triton, too, is remarkably fluid, and it is no accident that one of Bron's primary goals after his (or her) sex change operation is to have a relationship with Sam, a prominent diplomat, and significantly a "good-looking, friendly, intelligent" black man with an "amazing mind" and a "magnificent body" (30–31), who previous to the narrative proper undergoes an FTM (female-to-male) sex change operation himself.

I lack the space here to go deeply enough into the specific ways in which the novel lodges its critique of hegemonic masculinity—and, indeed, hegemonic whiteness—against and through Bron. Instead, I have tried only to point out the ways in which the novel's struggle against utopia in and of itself produces a "heterotopia," which I will read as a displacement of utopian and ideological forces into itself, a self-conscious rereading of the form of utopia that allows a multi-valenced presentation of the central and in some important sense unexaminable grounds on which any dominant ideology rests itself. It is not hard to infer that Delany is aware of what Jameson calls the disjunctive process out of which utopias must always be produced.[5] In Jameson's view, that process, minus a critical understanding, leads to a "desperate formalism"; without a critical understanding of the disjunctive nature of utopia, its function can too easily be to deconstruct itself within its own ideological contradictions.

This brings me to *Star Trek,* which I hope to have now situated in the contexts of both SF and utopia.[6] In many crucial ways, *Star Trek* embraces uncritically the utopian forms that LeGuin and Delany, in diverse ways, take as their objects of critical scrutiny. The episode of *Star Trek* I would like to deal with is the one called "Let That Be Your Last Battlefield" (episode number 70, which first aired on 10 January 1969), which stars Frank Gorshin as Bele, a representative of the government of the remote planet Cheron. Bele has been chasing a fugitive named Lokai across the galaxy for "more than 50,000 of your terrestrial years," because Lokai is guilty of inciting revolution and treason, which have resulted in the deaths of thousands of his fellow Cheronites. For my discussion here, the salient fact, which readers familiar with the series will no doubt remember, is the skin coloring of Bele and Lokai: like all members of the ruling class of Cheron, Bele is stark black on the right side and stark white on the left, while Lokai, like all members of the oppressed class, has just the opposite pigmentation. Interestingly, the show wants us to believe that this skin coloring corresponds to regular human skin tones for blacks and whites, even though the colorings as they appear on Bele and Lokai are charcoal black and chalk white—diametric opposites, but also costumer's colors. To be sure, the general liberal-humanist point the show is making is laid right on the surface by this arrangement: the accidents of the history of racial division are arbitrary, as offensive as Bele's insistence that the viewer of the show and the observer on the *Enterprise* should be able to directly *see* that Lokai is of an "inferior breed" because he is "black on the right side." Of course, the viewer sees no such thing. Like the crew of the *Enterprise,* the show's viewer sees Lokai and Bele as fundamentally of the same species, fundamentally "human" (in whatever sense "aliens" are human), fundamentally equal; their quarrel at base is pointless, like racial conflict on our own Earth; we should all act like members of one glorious Federation, "containing" multitudes.

Now this in part unobjectionable liberalism is surely part of the texture of *Star Trek* in general and this episode in particular, and I do not imagine that it can be entirely gainsaid. Nevertheless, the particular context of this show is fascinating, as Spock might say, as is the context in which the show's liberal message about race is delivered. This context is interesting in at least four specific ways, and in these ways it helps to expose the inner workings of what might be called the "logic of race in *Star Trek,*" which is much more polished, distracting, and reified in other episodes and in *The Next Generation* and *Deep Space Nine,* and depends as much on a logic of whiteness as of blackness.[7]

The first point has to do with the reduction of racial conflict in human history to pure pigment, which erases cultural and political

difference in favor of a formal matter that is realized only morpho-
logically—much like the costumer's coloring that displaces real human skin tones. The equivalence of color implied by the somatic
representation of black and white on Lokai's and Bele's bodies
(really, in the episode, faces) radically rewrites human racial conflict: in fact, it is what allows the condescending and conservatively
utopian recountings of human history in the episode. In one of
the episode's most strangely reflective scenes, for example, Lokai
sits in the crew lounge and tries to radicalize Sulu, Chekov, and
several other crew members and convert them to his cause, which
is clearly meant to reflect on African-American history: his people
were enslaved for thousands of years by people in Bele's class; they
were freed thousands of years ago, but the freedom they achieved
was greatly restricted, completely conditioned by the oppressive
ideology of the ruling class, and so forth. Indeed, it is clear that
the words Lokai utters are the words of civil rights activists at the
very time the show was being produced and aired. Lokai explains
the difficulty in transmitting the urgency of his story by saying that
"[t]here is no persecution on your planet." Sulu concurs: "There
is no such persecution today." The scene is doubly reflective, since
on one reading what Lokai is trying to do is to make white people
understand the plight of blacks in America—this is the very discourse out of which his words arise. But in terms of its Imaginary
function, the scene represents our present-day world as having rid
itself of the very conflict on which the show hinges. Curiously, and
in a suggestively supplementary way, Spock stands outside the
crew lounge during this scene, just listening; no mention is made
further on in the episode of his overhearing it; he utters no judgment on it in particular.

   This brings me to the second, even more plainly ideological,
part of the show's contextualization of the race issue. Because in
the midst of the civil rights era, this supposedly liberal program,
while explicitly aligning Lokai's cause with the cause of African-
Americans, and providing plenty of evidence for the justness of
that cause, explicitly and determinately refuses to endorse him in
any way. This is attributed to Lokai's somewhat open predilection
to violence (already hardly an ideologically innocent representation), but it extends further, so that only the barest hint is ever
given of anyone on board the *Enterprise* saying directly that Lokai

and Bele are in every sense equal, and specifically that they are morally equal with the crew members themselves.

Rather, "equality" is troped in the episode in terms of disruptive emotion, namely "hatred." (I should mention here that "emotion" plays a crucial role in the construction of normative ideologies of the "human" in Star Trek, but I will have to address that elsewhere.) Whenever Lokai and Bele are portrayed as equals, it is directly related to their mutual hatred and to their own "race's" hatred of the other's "race," and it is this hatred that is portrayed as specifically equivalent: no gesture is ever made at implying that Lokai might in any sense be *justified* in hating the representative of a race who has overtly and covertly enslaved him and his people for thousands of years.[8]

The ending of the episode is no less telling. After an interminable amount of wrangling over the control of the ship—I will return to this in a moment because it is also highly suggestive—at the end of the show the Enterprise arrives at Cheron, only to discover that the planet has been destroyed utterly: no Cheronite is left alive but for Lokai and Bele themselves. The planet's destruction is conveyed to the viewer in another remarkable way, because the scenes of burning buildings and fire-choked streets must have been eerily familiar to any contemporary viewer of the episode: they look just like the riots, especially the Watts riots, which occurred during the several summers prior to the production and airing of this episode in early 1969. Certainly this helps to explain some of the antirevolutionary bias of the show, but I also think it reflects something far deeper. It is fascinating, for example, that no one on the Enterprise guesses that Bele and Lokai will beam down to the planet surface to continue their fight (Kirk even asks, "Where can they run?"). It is as if the awful energy they contain—which burns visibly red-hot and threatens literally to tear the Enterprise apart when Bele and Lokai fight—must be put back where it belongs, in what is in some sense "our" world.

This helps provide a context for the astonishing exchange which ends the show, during which nearly every regular cast member is present on the bridge:

Uhura: It doesn't make any sense [that is, Bele and Lokai returning to Cheron to continue their fight].

> **Spock:** To expect sense from two mentalities of such extreme viewpoints is not logical.
> **Sulu:** But their planet's dead; does it matter now which one's right?
> **Spock:** Not to Lokai and Bele. All that matters to them is their hate.
> **Uhura:** Do you suppose that's all they ever had, Sir?
> **Kirk:** No. But that's all they have left. Warp factor 2, Mr. Sulu. Set course for Starbase 4.

That the producers and writers of the show put these words in Uhura's mouth is really remarkable. It is difficult to watch Nichelle Nichols saying that she does not understand why Lokai would hate Bele or why Lokai would want a revolution, considering what her role represents on *Star Trek* (for example, as half of the famous first-ever "interracial kiss" on broadcast U.S. television), and, in this respect alone, what her personal feelings about the civil unrest of the sixties might be. I am not implying that the sort of violent and anarchic demonstrations of the Watts riots might have been actively endorsed by a mainstream TV show. However, it is astounding that Uhura is not only made to say that she cannot understand the *basis* for the conflict but that she is also actively, grammatically chastised by Spock, the representative of white rationality, for not being "logical," which can be read as something far worse.

It is not hard to understand why the TV executives and producers might be interested in containing the violent energy represented by the Watts riots and other racial and civil unrest of the 1960s. And they do a good job of it, too: I think that is how we should read the remarkable fact that the *Enterprise* happens to arrive at Cheron at just the precise moment when the planet is still in flames, yet every one of its inhabitants has been killed: it is a moment of profound suspense, when the very elimination of the human from the field of ideology allows the inverse pull of utopia to take a final and terrifying hold. But it is clear that a further kind of containment is enacted in this episode, in no small part by having Uhura, and Sulu as well, pose the questions they do at the show's end, and by having Spock and Kirk be the authority figures who provide interpretive readings of Bele's and Lokai's fight.

And this brings me back to the two further contextualizations of racial conflict within the episode. The first has to do with the bizarre dramatic theme of the show, namely, that Bele is able somehow to assert mental control over the ship and thus to direct it wherever he wants. Of course, the show never explains how it is that Bele has this ability while Lokai does not. But the terror this causes within the crew is emphasized over and over, so that almost immediately on the discovery of the fact Kirk threatens to destroy the entire ship, which is depicted in the rather famous self-destruct sequence. Rather than just dropping Lokai and Bele off on their home planet and allowing them to continue their conflict by themselves, Kirk chooses to destroy the *Enterprise*. (Here, at least, the show implies that this is because Kirk wants to protect Lokai from persecution, though that is never overtly stated.) Well, what is Kirk afraid of? The answer is, of course, the destruction, or maybe better the deconstruction, of the entire rational-logical structure of the Federation, that control over ideology maintained by utopian representation and figured here by both Kirk and Spock and several times referred to in the show as the ultimate, unquestionable repository of authority. Insofar as that rational-logical structure, the Federation, represents the white power structure in place in the U.S. (and the neutralizing and blinding ideology upon which it rests), the show offers us the spectacle of that power structure and of what we might call hegemonic whiteness watching the Watts riots in horror, while relying on its utopian displacements to make those conflicts strange, alien, not part of "us" and significantly not our fault. This is what antiutopian critical theorists point to as the sustaining features of utopia, features that contrast strongly with the critical heterotopian strategies developed by Delany in *Triton*.

In fact, though, this reading has a resistant underside, in part because the presence of both black and white on both Bele and Lokai's bodies is meant to implicate, again in a liberal-humanist fashion, white people particularly in the irrationality of race hatred and oppression. But this admission, always lurking at the edges of the show, threatens as well literally to tear the *Enterprise* apart, even to inspire the adherents of the *Enterprise* to destroy themselves rather than choose sides in the conflict they supposedly can rationally mediate. The Federation's utopia has no tools with which to intervene, to understand, such conflict; after all, it is not "logical," apparently, to attempt to extricate oneself from a millenniums-old oppression. I think this accounts for one of the oddest moments in all of *Star Trek:* after Bele relinquishes mental control of the *Enterprise* for the second time, Kirk asks Sulu whether control has returned to the helm. Sulu, beaming, as if under the influence of drugs or in some other state of beatitude, looks up at the camera and at Kirk and declares, "It's beautiful, Captain." What has been returned so sublimely, of course—in a moment of not just intellectual but fetishized and even sexualized joy—is not command of the ship so much as the assurance that the Federation's rational ideology will not be torn asunder from within, the assurance that *Star Trek* will still be able successfully to displace present-day conflict onto utopianized, science-fictional futures. That project, and also the very project of the white majority to maintain rational distance from and control over the energies loosed by U.S. racial conflict, is radically endangered in the ideological Imaginary, and it is that endangerment which is enacted and displayed in "Let That Be Your Last Battlefield."

The show provides one final contextualizing device that illustrates this conflict, or perhaps lack of conflict, through its frame narrative. At the beginning of the episode the *Enterprise* is en route to Ariannus, a planet on the "commercial lanes" which is "under attack by bacterial contamination." In between Lokai's two attempts to take control of the ship, the *Enterprise* completes this frame mission with a startling lack of drama. Eventually, the ship releases tanks of bactericide from high above Ariannus; during this scene there is strictly speaking no dramatic conflict pending between Lokai and Bele or in the frame story so that Scotty just sits in the Captain's chair and says things like "[f]inal run completed, Captain." The lack of dramatic energy here, I think, functions as a supplement, foregrounding the unrealizable utopian effort of the show: to decontaminate itself of the racial conflict, of the call to take sides, and of the Federation's (that is, U.S. racial ideology's) complicity in the very conflict which Bele and Lokai are meant to displace. This dispassionate decontamination is precisely what the ideological work of the episode is meant to enact, and precisely what it, like any straightforward representations of utopia, cannot accomplish.

The logic of race in *Star Trek* operates more smoothly and is more fully reified in *The Next Generation* and *Deep Space Nine* than in the original show. I want to end this discussion by speculating briefly on what goes on in these shows. I will concentrate on *The Next Generation* because *DS9*, whatever else can be said about it, seems very much in its nascent stages at the time this essay is being written.

It seems useful to me to begin with a very provocative statement by the *Village Voice* writer Jeff Salamon, who recently wrote there that

> the Federation-Klingon alliance reads like a straightforward colonialist narrative: we get to see Worf grow progressively more human, but neither Riker nor Picard seems even remotely influenced by Klingon culture. ("Race Men and Space Men" 47)

This seems just right to me. One of the neutralizing functions of the white ideology of *Star Trek* is to portray the Federation as normative in every respect, so that the basic categorical term "the Federation" admits of no actual qualities but only positive valuations. Being an officer, but specifically a human officer of the Federation (or a member of one of the races that is marked as basically human, as is Ensign Ro, though her case itself is telling), means that one is granted the full range of human emotion and, significantly, human potential. Being a member of any "other" race—especially Klingon or Ferengi, or a villainous race like the Romulans or the Cardassians—means that one's character and characteristics are largely determined by one's membership in that race. A human is not anything in particular, and a Federation officer who is human, whatever else he or she may be, is only presumed to be a "good person" unless shown otherwise. A Klingon is presumed to be warlike and overly concerned with "honor," interested in animalistic sex, and a good fighter; a Ferengi is assumed to be unintellectual and greedy, sneaky, and pathetically desirous of sex with people who are too good for him or her; Cardassians are treacherous, cunning, and cruel; and so on.

In its most basic form, this very opposition underlies that logic or economy of race that exists in more overt form in "Let That Be

Your Last Battlefield." In the utopia of the Federation, difference is played down, supposedly because differences make no *negative* difference, but as a reflection of our own present that representation exists precisely to highlight and objectify difference and to reinscribe the notion that "others" have "difference," while "we"— "core" humans who populate the Federation—manifest only "goodness" and heterogeneity. Every time you hear Worf talk about "honor," you can be sure that racism is not dead, that it is written at the deepest levels into the most intimate hopes and projections of even those creative people who believe, earnestly I would guess, that they have the betterment of humankind at heart.

Think, though, about the racial makeup as it has been set up on the *Enterprise.* You basically have three races represented there, although it may appear to be four. The first is white humans, among which we must count most of the personnel who display flexibility in terms of being able to apply their skills other than at their central command station (for example, even though Worf was originally head of engineering, for some reason this expertise is no longer mentioned): these include Picard, Riker, Dr. Crusher, O'Brien, even at times Wesley Crusher and Tasha Yar. Even in this mixed group, it is the women who cannot translate those skills as fluidly as the men can—Dr. Crusher is only the doctor; Tasha Yar is only the security chief; Troi, an alien who is marked by the "sensitivity" and "empathy" associated with being empathic, has been shown to be terrified by the command chair to which she is entitled as an officer with rank (and the actresses who portray these characters have each complained about the producers refusal to give them important and flexible roles). An exception might be Ensign Ro, who has shown a certain amount of cross-disciplinary ability in some shows; notably, though, she is marked by her unacceptably aggressive sexuality, normally coded as a male emotion on *Star Trek,* and which itself may have to do with her being marked as fundamentally "alien," though generically human (in certain ways, an equation much like the one that rules Spock's behavior).

Let us say, these are the "white" people on the *Enterprise:* the more centrally white you are, the greater your abilities and the more your personality is supposed to be able to handle difference and to account for it. As I have shown, at least a tentative gender-oriented dividing line can be drawn that makes ability in this regard highly dependent on maleness. Notice that Picard is in this sense marked especially as a central and neutral exponent of Federation ideology: he is visibly and traditionally English, but his name encompasses French people in general (the ancestral enemies of the English) and a specific French person (so as to mark out that coding especially strongly), Jean-Luc Godard, a notably subversive, creative member of the French body politic. Thus, Picard can at once signal the great heterogeneity reserved only for humans in *Star Trek*'s utopia.

Now before turning to the explicitly "not-human" members of the crew, let me turn to the important transitional case, Data. Like Spock, Data might be seen as the ultimate distillation of the Federation's utopian representation of rational-logical control over nature, over ideology. Like Spock, Data can at times serve as a representative of Otherness and at times as the purest and most commodified representation of the self-as-desired-object; he is the essence of the Federation in both its conscious utopian aspirations and in its Imaginary, unconscious underside. And in both cases his overriding need and desire is the same: to be human, not to be Klingon, "alive," Ferengi, even Terrestrial, but to be "human," which means to feel emotion. I will return to this highly provocative point in a second. But think of that desire to be human because it resonates in at least two ways: one is the implicit denial in the very heart of Federation ideology that eliminates vast and important fields of experience and difference so that the representation it makes to itself is significantly homogenized. It also resonates in that what Data most wants, to be human, stands in for what all non-Federation and Federation nonhumans want in the supposedly postcolonial utopia of *Star Trek:* not only to join the Federation (why? answers are rarely provided, and thinking about this produces highly provocative and suggestive speculations), but to "become" the Federation, to lose difference, to become neutral, human, but really white, to exist really outside of ideology.

This leaves us with the blacks on board the *Enterprise,* and here we have to include Worf because he is played by Michael Dorn, who is African-American, and I do not think it possible to argue that this is merely a serendipitous fact. Worf, Geordie, and Guinan are the three blacks onboard the *Enterprise,* and they form a fascinating trio. Worf, as I have already expressed, stands in as *TNG*'s chief representative of otherness qua otherness: through those familiar and ugly tropes of "honor" and "warrior," to say nothing of the hideous and in some ways demeaning makeup that he wears, Worf is consistently marked as alien and other and is continually put under pressure to explicate or defend his otherness or to capitulate to Federation ways. In a well-known episode where all the crew and the ship's computer have their memories wiped away by a manipulative alien named MacDuff (!), significantly it is only Worf who guesses incorrectly as to his place in the crew hierarchy, and of course he guesses that he is the Captain because he is a "warrior." In a moment of true *TNG* condescension, no one wants to argue about whether Picard or Worf is really Captain, but the viewer is consistently aware of Worf's hubris, and Picard "forgives" Worf fully when their memories return, but the viewer cannot shake the feeling that it is precisely Worf's race that has inspired him to think too much of himself, and wrongly to perceive himself central in a world where his very difference precludes him from being so.

Significantly, Geordie, who also has some of that "skill-transfer" ability I've identified as a mark of the white, neutral ideology of *Star Trek*, has an always-marked disability. Not surprisingly, although his lack of "natural vision" is supposed to be more than made up for with the visor that allows him to see well beyond the normal spectrum, in an episode where his deepest desires are revealed, they turn out to be the sexually fetishized desire to "see normally."

This leaves us with Guinan. My understanding is that Whoopi Goldberg petitioned the producers of *Star Trek* for a long time to have a character like Guinan introduced on the show, and it is not surprising that in this character, marked as she is in various negative ways, we see at least some hint of a complex response to utopian projections of the "race problem." The negative markers for her include not being a real member of the ship's crew, being a bartender, and being consulted mainly when there is some matter of "cultural or historical sensitivity" with which to deal. But the positive markers are significant: she has a deep and long-standing relationship with the Captain, and we are made to know that he relies on her opinions, in at least some matters, quite strongly; her history and the history of her planet are mentioned often; she has a different take on the Federation's business than most of the other

members of the crew. Guinan's character does not escape the problematic racist Imaginary of *Star Trek* (and neither does Benjamin
Sisko, the commander of *Deep Space Nine*), but at least she points
toward a more complex and critical engagement with the deep
divisions in the controlling ideologies of our time.

Both *Triton* and *Star Trek* demonstrate how the ideological and
the utopian are inextricably intertwined. There can be no projection of our own present without a supplement, the Imaginary of
that present, and similarly no projection of the future without the
Imaginary of that future (that is, in Althusserian terms, the ideological Real of our present).[9] *Triton* gestures toward the critical
imagining of real futures, ideals that may help to destabilize our
own reified ideologies through the heteroclite disruption of the
naturalizing and neutralizing processes of ideological construction. In contrast, "Let That Be Your Last Battlefield" and the character arrangement of *Star Trek: The Next Generation* show how easy
and dangerous it is to repeat our own ideological, racist Imaginary
when we project our futures uncritically.

Notes

    An earlier version of this paper was presented at the Center for the Study of
Black Literature and Culture at the University of Pennsylvania, March 1993. I
thank Houston Baker and Stephen Best for providing me with the opportunity
to speak in that heady environment. In addition to them and the congenial audience at the talk, I want to thank Rebecca Bach, Herman Beavers, Anne Cubilie,
Suzanne Daly, Judy Filc, and an anonymous reader for *Cultural Critique* for their
helpful comments and suggestions on this essay.
    1. The notion of positive and negative hermeneutics is due to Jameson, *The
Political Unconscious*. This analysis relies specifically on the understanding of the
dialectical interplay between ideology and utopia that Fredric Jameson describes
in *The Political Unconscious* and elsewhere, and which has precedents in the work
of Ernst Bloch and other critical theorists; at the same time, it proceeds from my
own interest in science fiction as a genre, which Jameson and Tom Moylan especially have identified as a site for significantly revealing ideological constructions.
For overviews of the ideology and utopia controversy, see Jameson, *Marxism and
Form, The Political Unconscious,* and "Of Islands and Trenches"; Bloch, *The Utopian
Function of Art and Literature;* Mannheim, *Ideology and Utopia;* and Moylan, "The
Locus of Hope" and *Demand the Impossible*. The following provide overviews of the
relationship between science fiction and utopian writing and discourse, all from
Marxist-critical perspectives: Jameson, "Of Islands and Trenches" and "Progress
Versus Utopia"; Moylan, "Beyond Negation" and *Demand the Impossible;* Williams,

"Utopia and Science Fiction"; Easthope, "The Personal and the Political"; and Somay, "Towards an Open-Ended Utopia."

My analysis takes race for its site of investigation and theories about the scenic and screening functions of ideology as its mechanisms, but it proceeds as well from the following: the work of Stuart Hall; Jane Gaines's seminal essay "White Privilege and Looking Relations" and Manthia Diawara's related work in "Englishness and Blackness"; the critical and fictional work of Samuel R. Delany and critical works on him and on the African-American woman SF writer Octavia Butler; recent writings in black cultural theory like those collected in *Screen*, "Last Special Issue on Race," edited by Isaac Julien and Kobena Mercer, and the *Black Popular Culture* anthology assembled by Michele Wallace and Gina Dent. But, as my epigraphs from Delany and Mercer indicate, my specific goal here is to isolate and analyze structures of ideological normalization, especially racial normalization, and to examine how these instantiate themselves in utopian discourse—meaning, especially, how the structures of whiteness are defined and constructed. This follows from Delany's work, but more so from Mercer's essay and from Richard Dyer's important essay, from that same issue of *Screen*, called "White," where Dyer writes that "the property of whiteness" to be everything and nothing, is the source of its representational power" ("White" 45). For Hall, see "The Whites of Their Eyes" and "Black Popular Culture." Relevant works by Delany include "The Semiology of Silence," "Afterword," "Street Talk/Straight Talk," "Interview," and the articles in *The Jewel-Hinged Jaw* (in particular, see "To Read *The Dispossessed*" 218–83 in that volume); for articles on him, in addition to the articles on utopian SF already cited, most of which contain substantive sections on *Triton*, see Govan, "The Insistent Presence of Black Folk." On Octavia Butler, see Zaki, "Utopia, Dystopia, and Ideology," and Foster, "Octavia Butler's Black Female Future Fiction." Also see the Delany and Mercer articles cited in the epigraphs to this essay. For an overview of representations of African-Americans in U.S. SF, see James, "Yellow, Black, Metal and Tentacled."

For discussions of utopia in relation to feminism—a subject too complex to be addressed in the main body of this essay, but which functions with a dynamic similar to the one described here—see Pearson, "Where No Man Has Gone Before"; Barr, ed., *Future Females;* Barr and Smith, eds., *Women and Utopia;* Bartowski, *Feminist Utopias;* Gubar, "Feminism and Utopia"; and Pfaelzer, "The Changing of the Avant Garde: Feminist Utopia."

2. All emphases are Foucault's. I have altered the quoted selection slightly to bring Foucault's writing about the "heteroclite" into focus.

3. On the role of character, and Bron in particular, in *Triton*, see Massé, "Individual Expectations in *Triton*"; Somay, "Towards an Open-Ended Utopia"; Moylan, "Beyond Negation" and *Demand the Impossible.*

4. Both Moylan and Jameson, among others, make this point about *The Dispossessed.*

5. Cf. Jameson:

> The utopian narrative might be described as one which, having come into being by a radical act of disjunction, must then summon up all of its energies into a 'motivation' of that initial disjunction into an elaborate, endless, impossible demonstration that such unimaginable separation from the inextricable totality of Being of that "real" world in which history and indeed the reader himself exist was in fact 'imaginable' in the first place. The ultimate subject-matter of utopian discourse would then turn out to be its own conditions of possibility as

discourse. Yet such desperate formalism, and the spectacle of a genre lifting itself up into being by its own bootstraps, is perhaps only the obverse and the corollary of its most genuine chance for authenticity: for it would follow, in that case, that utopia's deepest subject, and the source of all that is most vibrantly political about it, is precisely our inability to conceive it, our incapacity to produce it as a vision, our failure to project the other of what is, a failure that, as with fireworks dissolving back into the night sky, must once again leave us alone with *this* history. ("Of Islands and Trenches" 21; emphasis in original)

6. For more on mass culture and ideology, and specifically on the place of television in ideological critique, see White, "Ideological Analysis and Television." For a discussion of television theory and race ideology, see Hall, "The Whites of Their Eyes." For a theoretically sophisticated discussion of television and ideology, see Ronell, "Video/Television/Rodney King." For discussions of utopia and ideology in relation to mass culture, see Jameson, "Reification and Utopia in Mass Culture" and Heath, "*Jaws*, Ideology and Film Theory."

7. For discussions of race in *Star Trek: The Next Generation* and *Deep Space Nine* that bear importantly on this discussion, see Davis, "Space Is the Place," Minkowitz, "Deeper and Deeper," and Salamon, "Race Men and Space Men." For a suggestive comparison of *Star Trek* and *Star Trek: The Next Generation*, see Wilcox, "Where Others Have Gone Before." *Star Trek: The Next Generation* is discussed more fully in the final part of this essay.

8. Indeed, the trope of "hatred" is among the most common means for discussing racial difference in *Star Trek*, particularly with regard to the Klingons, which unsurprisingly places the cause of hatred in the Klingons—meaning in this sense blacks—themselves. On this logic see Hall, "The Whites of Their Eyes." Conveniently, Klingons, like other races in the world of the Federation, can serve as representations of Mongols as well as African-Americans, just as Spock can represent both Japanese and white Americans. On some of these issues, see Salamon, "Race Men and Space Men."

9. For more definitions and discussions of the Real and the Imaginary, in both ideological and psychoanalytic terms, see Žižek, *Sublime Object of Ideology*, and Althusser, *Lenin and Philosophy* and *For Marx;* for the Lacanian origin of the terms see, for example, his *Écrits* and *Four Fundamental Concepts of Psychoanalysis*. The reading here has been greatly influenced by feminist rereadings of these materials, such as the one found in Rose, *Sexuality in the Field of Vision*.

Works Cited

Althusser, Louis. *Lenin and Philosophy and Other Essays*. Trans. Ben Brewster. New York: Monthly Review P, 1971.

———. *For Marx*. London: Verso/New Left Books, 1977.

Barr, Marleen, ed. *Future Females: A Critical Anthology*. Bowling Green: Bowling Green UP, 1981.

Barr, Marleen, and Nicholas D. Smith, eds. *Women and Utopia: Critical Interpretations*. Lanham: UP of America, 1983.

Bartowski, Frances. *Feminist Utopias*. Lincoln: U of Nebraska P, 1989.

Bloch, Ernst. *The Utopian Function of Art and Literature: Selected Essays*. 1974. Trans. Jack Zipes and Frank Mecklenburg. Cambridge: MIT Press, 1988.

Davies, Philip John, ed. *Science Fiction, Social Conflict and War.* Manchester: Manchester UP, 1990.

Davis, Erik. "Space Is the Place." *Village Voice* 38.8 (23 Feb. 1993): 46–47.

Delany, Samuel R. Afterword. *Stars in My Pocket Like Grains of Sand.* 1984. New York: Bantam, 1990. 376–85.

———. Interview. *Diacritics* 16.3 (Fall 1986): 27–45.

———. *The Jewel-Hinged Jaw: Notes on the Language of Science Fiction.* New York: Berkley, 1977.

———. "The Semiology of Silence." *Science-Fiction Studies* 14, Part 2.42 (July 1987): 134–64.

———. "Street Talk/Straight Talk." *Differences: A Journal of Feminist Cultural Studies* 3.2 (1991): 21–38.

———. *Triton.* New York: Bantam, 1976.

———. "On *Triton* and Other Matters: An Interview with Samuel R. Delany." *Science-Fiction Studies* 17, Part 3.52 (Nov. 1990): 295–324.

Dent, Gina, ed. *Black Popular Culture: A Project by Michele Wallace.* Seattle: Bay Press, 1992.

Diawara, Manthia. "Englishness and Blackness: Cricket as Discourse on Colonialism." *Callaloo* 13.4 (Fall 1990): 830–44.

Easthope, Anthony. "The Personal and the Political in Utopian Science Fiction." Davies 50–67.

Foster, Frances Smith. "Octavia Butler's Black Female Future Fiction." *Extrapolation* 23.1 (Spring 1982): 37–49.

Foucault, Michel. *The Order of Things: An Archaeology of the Human Sciences.* New York: Vintage, 1971.

Gaines, Jane. "White Privilege and Looking Relations: Race and Gender in Feminist Film Theory." *Cultural Critique* 4 (Fall 1986): 59–79.

Govan, Sandra Y. "The Insistent Presence of Black Folk in the Novels of Samuel R. Delany." *Black American Literature Forum* 18.2 (Summer 1984): 43–48.

Gubar, Susan. "Feminism and Utopia." *Science-Fiction Studies* 13, Part 1.38 (March 1986): 79–83.

Hall, Stuart. "What Is This 'Black' in Black Popular Culture?" Dent 20–33.

———. "The Whites of Their Eyes: Racist Ideologies and the Media." *Silver Linings: Some Strategies for the Eighties, Contributions to the Communist University of London.* Ed. George Bridges and Rosalind Brunt. London: Lawrence and Wishart, 1981. 28–52.

Heath, Stephen. "*Jaws*, Ideology and Film Theory." *Popular Television and Film.* Ed. Tony Bennett, Susan Boyd-Bowman, Colin Mercer, and Janet Woollacott. London: BFI/Open UP, 1981. 200–05.

James, Edward. "Yellow, Black, Metal and Tentacled: The Race Question in American Science Fiction." Davies 26–49.

Jameson, Fredric. "Of Islands and Trenches: Neutralization and the Production of Utopian Discourse." *Diacritics* 7.2 (Summer 1977): 2–21.

———. *Marxism and Form: Twentieth-Century Dialectical Theories of Literature.* Princeton: Princeton UP, 1971.

———. *The Political Unconscious: Narrative as a Socially Symbolic Act.* Ithaca: Cornell UP, 1981.

———. "Progress Versus Utopia; or, Can We Imagine the Future?" *Science-Fiction Studies* 9, Part 2.27 (July 1982): 147–58.

———. "Reification and Utopia in Mass Culture." *Social Text* 1.1 (Winter 1979): 130–48.

Julien, Isaac, and Kobena Mercer, eds. *The Last Special Issue on Race. Screen* 29.4 (Autumn 1988).

Lacan, Jacques. *Écrits: A Selection.* 1966. Trans. Alan Sheridan. New York: Norton, 1977.

———. *The Four Fundamental Concepts of Psychoanalysis.* 1973. Trans. Alan Sheridan. New York: Norton, 1981.

LeGuin, Ursula K. *The Dispossessed: An Ambiguous Utopia.* 1974. New York: Avon, 1975.

Mannheim, Karl. *Ideology and Utopia: An Introduction to the Sociology of Knowledge.* Trans. Louis Wirth and Edward Shils. New York: Harcourt, 1936.

Massé, Michelle. "'All You Have to Do Is Know What You Want': Individual Expectations in *Triton.*" *Coordinates: Placing Science Fiction and Fantasy.* Ed. George E. Slusser, Eric S. Rabkin, and Robert Scholes. Carbondale: Southern Illinois UP, 1983. 49–64.

Mercer, Kobena. "Skin Head Sex Thing: Racial Difference and the Homoerotic Imaginary." *How Do I Look? Queer Film and Video.* Ed. Bad Object-Choices. Seattle: Bay Press, 1991. 169–210.

Minkowitz, Donna. "Deeper and Deeper." *Village Voice* 38.8 (23 February 1993): 46.

Moylan, Tom. "Beyond Negation: The Critical Utopias of Ursula K. LeGuin and Samuel R. Delany." *Extrapolation* 21.3 (Fall 1980): 236–53.

———. *Demand the Impossible: Science Fiction and the Utopian Imagination.* New York: Methuen, 1986.

———. "The Locus of Hope: Utopia Versus Ideology." *Science-Fiction Studies* 29, Part 2.27 (July 1982): 159–66.

Pearson, Jacqueline. "Where No Man Has Gone Before: Sexual Politics and Women's Science Fiction." Davies 8–25.

Pfaelzer, Jean. "The Changing of the Avant Garde: The Feminist Utopia." *Science-Fiction Studies* 15, Part 3.46 (Nov. 1988): 282–94.

Ronell, Avital. "Video/Television/Rodney King: Twelve Steps Beyond *The Pleasure Principle.*" *Differences: A Journal of Feminist Cultural Studies* 4.2 (1992): 1–15.

Rose, Jacqueline. *Sexuality in the Field of Vision.* New York: Verso, 1986.

Salamon, Jeff. "Race Men and Space Men." *Village Voice* 38.8 (23 Feb. 1993): 46–47.

Somay, Bülent. "Towards an Open-Ended Utopia." *Science-Fiction Studies* 11, Part 1.32 (March 1984): 25–38.

White, Mimi. "Ideological Analysis and Television." *Channels of Discourse, Reassembled: Television and Contemporary Criticism, Second Edition.* Ed. Robert C. Allen. Chapel Hill: U of North Carolina P, 1992. 161–202.

Wilcox, Clyde. "To Boldly Return Where Others Have Gone Before: Cultural Change and the Old and New *Star Trek*s." *Extrapolation* 33.1 (Spring 1992): 88–100.

Williams, Raymond. "Utopia and Science Fiction." *Science Fiction: A Critical Guide.* Ed. Patrick Parrinder. New York: Longman, 1979. 52–66.

Zaki, Hoda M. "Utopia, Dystopia, and Ideology in the Science Fiction of Octavia Butler." *Science-Fiction Studies* 17, Part 2.51 (July 1990): 239–51.

Žižek, Slavoj. *The Sublime Object of Ideology.* New York: Verso, 1989.

"Let Freedom Ring!": Free Jazz and African-American Politics

Charles Hersch

On August 28, 1963, Martin Luther King stood before 250,000 black and white Americans and proclaimed, "Let freedom ring!" urging citizens to "transform the jangling discords of our nation into a beautiful symphony of brotherhood" (*Words* 97). In his writings, King called for the creation of a "redemptive community" in which "mutual regard" and equality would replace racial hierarchy and distrust. In this community, argued King, cohesiveness would not hamper, but instead would enhance, individuality.

Three years earlier such a community had been represented in aesthetic form by eight musicians in a recording studio. If the result was not a "symphony" per se, these musicians nevertheless pioneered a style of music called "free jazz" that musically expressed some of the ideas about freedom that were becoming prominent in the struggles of African-Americans for justice. This essay argues that "free jazz" represented political freedom in two ways: negatively, by rejecting musical rules and conventions that restricted individual expression and discarding traditional hierarchical roles within the small group; and positively, by musically cre-

© 1996 by *Cultural Critique*. Winter 1995–96. 0882-4371/96/$5.00.

ating a group of equals that, in accord with King's idea of the redemptive community, maximized individual expression while maintaining great cohesiveness. The musical principle underlying this reconciliation of individual and group was polyphony, the simultaneous presence of independent melodies.

The essay begins by chronicling the representation of political themes in jazz from its beginnings to the "free jazz" of the Sixties. I then examine the conception of freedom contained in the idea of the "redemptive community" and show how it had been anticipated, in incomplete form, by pre-Sixties jazz. The main part of the essay shows how the Sixties jazz of Charles Mingus and Ornette Coleman brought to fruition the musical representation of the redemptive community. Finally, I argue that "free jazz" turned away from the musical embodiment of freedom in the face of America's resistance to its realization in society.

I

As an assertion of individual and group identity in the midst of a society that has sought to ignore or destroy it, jazz improvisation has from the beginning had political overtones for African-Americans.[1] The actual representation of political themes in jazz developed gradually. The pre-jazz spirituals sung by slaves represented a yearning for freedom as the songs spoke of the "Israelites" in bondage to the Egyptians. As jazz developed, some composers took up racial themes. Duke Ellington in the 1930s and 1940s saw his music as a celebration of black culture, in pieces like "Harlem Air Shaft," "Take the 'A' Train," and "Black and Tan Fantasy."[2] In his words,

[m]y men and my race are the inspiration of my work. I try to catch the character and mood and feeling of my people. The music of my race is something more than the American idiom. It is the result of our transplantation to the American soil, and it was our reaction to plantation days, to the life we lived. What we could not say openly we expressed in music. The characteristic, melancholic music of my race has been forged from the very white heat of our sorrow and from our gropings. (Lambert 22)

However, despite Ellington's claim that "social protest and pride in the Negro have been the most significant themes we've done" and that "in that music we have been talking for a long time about what it is to be a Negro in this country" (Hentoff, *Jazz Is* 30–31), jazz pieces were rarely explicitly political. Jazz's status as "entertainment," particularly in the popular white "swing" bands, hampered the development of political aspects of the music. Billie Holiday's 1939 recording of "Strange Fruit," a poem about lynching, represented an important exception.

In the Forties, however, many jazz musicians reacted against the cooptation of their music by mainstream white society by creating new styles that could not be so easily assimilated. The first such style became known as "bebop" (or "bop"). On the one hand the beboppers' rebellion was musical. They created jazz that was so difficult that whites could not easily copy it and so intense that one was unlikely to dance to it or even listen casually.[3] But the beboppers rebelled through their lifestyle as well. The bebop musician was nonconformist in several ways—in his unconventional dress and mannerisms (goatee, horn-rimmed glasses, beret), in his use of drugs (especially heroin), and in his language. Words like "crazy" as a term of approbation called into question mainstream norms and standards of rationality, while a term like "dig" proclaimed the value of looking underneath the surface of society (Walton 97; Sidran 109).

Bebop was not the only culturally assertive style of jazz to come out of the postwar period, however. The Forties saw a style called "rhythm and blues" that more explicitly expressed black cultural pride in both its lyrics and its "funky," "bluesy," and "soulful" music.[4] Coinciding with a new phase of black political activism, in the Fifties jazz itself joined this trend with a style known as "hard bop," featuring musicians like Horace Silver and Art Blakey. In addition to the gospel and "rhythm and blues" influence, this music's cultural assertiveness is apparent in song titles of the time, from the use of black argot ("Cookin'," "Dis Hyeah") to references to Southern Black Church experiences ("Wednesday Night Prayer Meeting," "The Sermon," "The Preacher") to evocations of Africa ("Africa," "Bantu," "African Violets") (Kofsky 41–49).

The Sixties brought the political potential of earlier jazz to fruition. Most jazz musicians were not political activists; however, they did express political ideas and sentiments through their music. Sometimes the politics was overt, through lyrics, or song and album titles. Max Roach's *Freedom Now Suite* chronicled through music and lyrics the struggles of blacks to be free, from slavery to the present. In 1963 John Coltrane wrote a song entitled "Alabama," based on the cadences of a Martin Luther King speech, memorializing four black children killed in the bombing of a church (Cole 150).[5]

Most of the time, however, the political meaning was communicated more subtly, through purely instrumental music. Such music was not linked to a particular platform or party but instead reflected, and reflected upon, the experience of African-Americans in the Sixties. As Coltrane put it, when asked whether "political issues and social issues that Malcolm talked about" were important,

> [o]h, they're definitely important; and as I said, the issues are a part of what *is* at this time. So naturally, as musicians we express whatever is. (Kofsky 227)

Yet the music did more than represent what existed; it contained an alternative vision as well. Coltrane said that "in music I make or I have tried to make a conscious attempt to change what I've found" and that "music is an instrument [that] can change the initial thought patterns that can change the thinking of the people." He also called music an expression of "higher ideals" (Kofsky 227).

The most important such ideal for activists and musicians in the early Sixties was "freedom." Jazz musicians self-consciously linked political freedom for blacks—emancipation from racist restrictions—with musical freedom, the liberation from accepted musical rules. Album and song titles of the time make this connection explicit: "Suite Freedom," *The Freedom Rider, Free for All,* and "The Freedom Suite." "Let Freedom Ring!" was both an exhortation in Martin Luther King's "I Have a Dream" speech and the title of a jazz album in the early Sixties. Not all these albums were "free jazz," as the avant-garde style came to be known, but the connection between musical and political freedom remained. As Coltrane put it in 1962, "we all know that this word which so many seem to fear today, 'Freedom' has a hell of a lot to do with this music" (Simpkins 160).[6]

II

The meaning of freedom for Coltrane and other musicians can only be understood in the context of the growing African-American civil rights movement of the late Fifties and Sixties. For those in the forefront of the movement in the early Sixties—Martin Luther King and SNCC organizers—the immediate goal was the dismantling of the system of racial inequality in America.[7] They called for liberal or negative freedom, liberation from constraints. Yet such a liberation, while a necessary first step, was not enough; the final goal was positive freedom only attainable in a particular kind of community.

According to King, the "ultimate aim" of the movement was the "redemptive community" (Meier, Rudwick, and Broderick 306).[8] In a broad sense, this simply meant the brotherhood of all humanity. Yet beyond this, the term refers to a community in which there is "mutual regard" or "empathy" (Carson 23; King, *Stride* 102–06; King, *Where* 101). Love, says King, while necessary for the redemptive community, is not sufficient; there must be empathy, the ability to see things from the point of view of another. Empathy, as opposed to pity, puts one on a level of equality with others (*Where* 101).

This concept of community challenges classical liberalism's assumption that groups represent barriers to individual development, albeit necessary ones. King distinguishes between unity and uniformity (*Where* 124).[9] Rather than crushing its members' autonomy or subsuming them to a race, the redemptive community gives the individual the support necessary for a stronger sense of individuality than he or she could achieve in isolation. In the words of one SNCC representative, "[w]e seek a community in which man can realize the full meaning of the self which demands open relationship with others" (Zinn 37). Or as King put it, evoking Martin Buber, "'I' cannot reach fulfillment without 'thou.' The self cannot be self without other selves" (*Where* 180).[10]

In incomplete form, jazz has often represented such ideas. Jazz has served as an arena for individual expression, one of the few public forums for African-Americans for much of United States history. Archie Shepp, who was involved in the free jazz of the Sixties, made this point and alluded to its political implications when asked what the base of the jazz tradition was:

> Self expression. And a certain quality of human dignity despite all obstacles, despite the enslavement of the black man and then his oppression. And each of the great players has had so distinctive, so individual a voice. There is only one Bird [Charlie Parker], one Ben Webster, one Cootie Williams. That's jazz—the uniqueness of the individual. If he believes in himself, every person is not only different but valuably different. (qtd. in Hentoff, "Archie Shepp" 119)

Although jazz musicians begin by imitating the style of admired players, only by assimilating and transcending those influences can they attain excellence.

The main vehicle for individual expression in jazz has been the improvised solo. In modern (post-1940) small group jazz, a series of solos follows the playing of the written melody of the song.[11] The soloist sometimes refers to the melody of the song but often abandons it completely, developing his or her own themes. Improvisors base their melodies on the harmonic structure of the song—either a progression of chords or, in "modal" jazz, a single scale.

Self-expression through improvisation is not confined to the soloist. As the soloist improvises, the "rhythm section" (usually consisting of piano, bass, and drums) supports him or her by playing complementary chords, basslines, and rhythms. Even accompanying musicians, in their empathic roles, have considerable room for self-expression. The pianist can use different voicings of chords; he or she can substitute appropriate chords and can vary the frequency and rhythm of the playing of those chords. The bass player also has many options as to how to approach a given chord progression. Finally, while it is usually crucial that the drummer keep extremely accurate time, he or she has many options concerning tone, rhythmic patterns, accents, and intensity. Thus, one improvises even as one accompanies.

At the same time that it encourages individual expression, jazz partially embodies positive freedom, freedom as empathic interaction among equals. Good musicians strive to express their individuality in tone and style, but a successful performance, one that "swings," results from empathy within the group. It is essential that each musician listen to the others. Each strives to complement the other harmonically, rhythmically, and melodically. The more sympathetic the rest of the group, the better the soloist is able to develop his or her individual statement.

Pre-Sixties jazz, then, encompassed considerable individual freedom, both positive and negative. However, this freedom was limited in three ways. First, when someone played solo the others either "accompanied" him or her or remained silent. The accompanying musicians were not free to speak as forcefully as the soloist; rarely would all the instruments play equally prominent melodies simultaneously. Second, bass and drums took a clearly subsidiary role, often not playing solos at all, but remaining in the background. Finally, all instruments were bound by a chordal structure, meter, and tempo.

In the 1960s, members of the "free jazz" movement dramatically expanded the freedom inherent in earlier jazz. Free jazz musicians rejected many previous rules of harmony, meter, and song form, giving the individual musician many more choices. In addition, they experimented with polyphony—the simultaneous production of two or more melodic lines—to create a more equal group process.[12] In this essay, I show how the growing musical freedom created by the budding avant-garde was used by Charles Mingus and Ornette Coleman to express rebellion against an unjust society by breaking musical conventions as well as to create new forms that posited an egalitarian alternative to U.S. inequality.[13]

III

One does not have to probe beneath the surface to discover that Charles Mingus saw some of his music as political commentary. The titles of his pieces make the point: "Fables of Faubus" (1957), "Haitian Fight Song" (1955) (which he said could be titled "Afro-American Fight Song"), "Work Song" (1955), "Prayer for Passive Resistance" (1960), and "Meditations on Integration" (1964) (Priestley 78).

Sometimes these politically titled songs had lyrics, as in "Fables of Faubus":

Oh Lord, don't let them shoot us
Oh Lord, don't let them stab us
Oh Lord, don't let them tar and feather us
Oh Lord, no more swastikas!

Oh Lord, no more Ku Klux Klan!

Name me someone ridiculous
[answer:] Governor Faubus!
Why is he so sick and ridiculous?
[answer:] He won't permit integrated schools
Then he's a fool! . . .

Although these lyrics make their message clear, Mingus's purely instrumental works conveyed a more subtle and complex political meaning. Sometimes the music expressed an emotional response to injustice. For example, about "Haitian Fight Song," which features a long, bluesy solo by Mingus himself, he said:

I can't play it right unless I'm thinking about prejudice and hate and persecution, and how unfair it is. There's sadness and cries in it, but also determination. And it usually ends with my feeling: "I told them! I hope somebody heard me." (liner notes, *Best of Mingus*)

And indeed much of the dissonance and emotion in his music mirrors the anger over racism that he often expressed verbally. It is significant that the blues played such an important role in Mingus's music, for it has always communicated a complex mixture of pain and determination. As Richard Wright put it,

[t]he most astonishing aspect of the blues is that, though replete with a sense of defeat and down-heartedness, they are not intrinsically pessimistic; their burden of woe and melancholy is dialectically redeemed through sheer force of sensuality, into an almost exultant affirmation of life, of love, of sex, of movement, of hope. (9)

Although Wright is speaking of blues songs, with lyrics, the same feeling pervades many instrumental blues, or even instrumental music with blues elements.[14]

In addition to its cathartic element, Mingus's music moved toward the representation of a positive alternative by creating a group that supported and encouraged strong individuality. Though he never considered himself part of the "free jazz" movement, in many of his pieces he tried to break down the hierarchy of instruments as well as the strictures on time, note choice, and rhythm that had existed in earlier jazz. As titles like "Percussion Discussion" and "Conversation" suggest, Mingus tried to reproduce in musical form the dynamics of a good conversation or meeting. Bringing about such conversations required the lifting of restrictions on the rhythm section and the creation of structures in which all musicians in the group could improvise together, rather than being confined to a series of solo statements. "Percussion Discussion" illustrates the liberation of the rhythm instruments, and "Conversation" portrays collective improvisation.

"Percussion Discussion," as the title suggests, is a dialogue, a musical interchange between Mingus on bass and Max Roach on drums. To add to the original "conversation," recorded live in a nightclub in 1955, Mingus overdubbed a "three-quarter bass," an instrument pitched between a bass and a cello. The piece consists of various interactions between the instruments—sometimes they all play together, sometimes in pairs, and sometimes alone. Near the end Mingus and Roach have a back-and-forth section in which they trade ideas, Roach often rhythmically and melodically echoing (or contrasting) Mingus's ideas.

By the unprecedented act of banishing all instruments except bass and drums, Mingus liberates those two instruments from their subordinate roles. Each is then allowed to explore its ability to express itself in ways not previously possible. Each instrument steps out of its traditional role, blurring the distinction between rhythm/percussion and melody—Roach plays melodies and Mingus achieves percussive effects by striking the bass with the bow and snapping the strings against the neck. This expansion of expression represents a large step toward true polyphony—bass and drums, instruments which had been primarily supportive, part of the "rhythm section," stepped into the forefront as lead voices.

One can see in this group without musical second-class citizens a reflection, or anticipation, of the movement of African-Americans, a group in the "background," to come forward and be heard as equals.

"Conversation" illustrates the beginnings of the breakdown of solo form and the rise of polyphonic group improvisation. Here collective improvisation grows out of traditional form. After each of the horns has soloed for a chorus, they trade two-measure phrases, which, though not unusual in itself, is usually preceded by "trading fours," the exchanging of four-measure ideas. But what follows is extremely unusual: a chorus of trading one-measure phrases and then half-measure (two beat) ideas. Finally, the dialogue having been taken as far as it will go, the musicians engage in a chorus of collective improvisation. By taking the practice of "trading fours" to its limit to where it turns into a collective improvisation, Mingus shows how the polyphony of the budding avant-garde grew out of, yet transformed, the polyphony within earlier jazz. The early polyphony, most apparent in the New Orleans music that came to prominence in the 1920s, employed collective improvisation within traditional harmony, meter, and song form; in the Sixties, jazz musicians would revive polyphony in the context of an attack on previous conventions and the exploration of musical freedom, giving it a new meaning.

The first full-scale attempt at polyphony, if not entirely successful, took place in January 1956 with "Pithecanthropus Erectus." According to Mingus, this instrumental piece is about domination and conflict:

> [I]t depicts musically my conception of the modern counterpart of the first man to stand erect—how proud he was, considering himself the "first" to ascend from all fours, pounding his chest and preaching his superiority over the mammals still in a prone position. Overcome with self-esteem, he goes out to rule the world, if not the universe; but both his own failure to realize the inevitable emancipation of those he sought to enslave, and his greed in attempting to stand on a false security, deny him not only the right of ever being a man, but finally destroy him completely. (liner notes, *Best of Mingus*)

The applications of this anthropological tale to U.S. race relations are obvious.[15]

How might the music reflect this theme? Certainly the final section of the piece seems to represent the anarchy of unorganized rebellion—saxophones scream into the extreme high register, the pianist pounds out tone clusters, and bass and drums flail away on their instruments. It is as if in the state of war, discourse has been replaced by shouting; individual voices cannot be heard in the melee. Yet within the piece lies an alternative to the state of war, for another section features interactive group improvisation—individual members can be heard "conversing" in a polyphonic manner, playing simultaneous melodies that fit together because of the musicians' responsive listening. Here we can see echoes, in musical form, of the kind of empathic collective process, balancing individual and group, that King and others were beginning to speak about.

Although the piece represented an important step on the road to the musical representation of the beloved community, the polyphony is limited. During the interactive group section, one can hear each voice, but no one makes strong statements, even for a moment. It is as if the group, musical and political, does not yet have a strong enough sense of itself to trust individuals to "speak out" without endangering the whole. During other parts of the piece, the musicians "solo" in the standard manner. Four years later, however, Mingus would create coherent group improvisation featuring strong individual statements.

IV

The album *Charles Mingus Presents Charles Mingus,* recorded in 1960, represents the full flowering of the polyphonic improvisation begun during the previous decade. The album contains one of Mingus's most explicitly political compositions with lyrics, "Fables of Faubus." It also contains his most radical extension of the conversational technique in a piece called "What Love," in which Mingus on bass and Eric Dolphy on bass clarinet engage in a literal dialogue on their instruments, mimicking human voices in a "discussion" free of tempo or bar lines. However, "Folk Forms #1" best embodies the fully realized total group improvisation toward which Mingus had been striving.

What strikes one first about "Folk Forms #1," a twelve minute performance based—significantly—on the blues, is the expressiveness on the part of the individual players. The players use their instrument in every conceivable way, the horn players employing growls, honks, and smears; conventional harmony is stretched to its limits. Yet the piece's real achievement is its polyphony. Each section begins by featuring one of the musicians. Each player's "solo" consists of three sections: at first he plays alone or with a fairly traditional accompaniment. Then he engages in duets with the other instruments, followed by sections of collective improvisation featuring much New Orleans–style counterpoint and call-and-response. Despite this pre-set structure, the effect is one of great collective spontaneity and improvisation: the piece juggles bass, drums, saxophone, and trumpet in every combination while constantly shifting meters, rhythms, moods, and dynamics.

Whitney Balliet's account captures the spirit of the performance:

> It begins with Mingus playing a simple blueslike figure. He is joined by [Dannie] Richmond [drums], in ad-lib time. [Eric] Dolphy enters (on alto saxophone), and is almost immediately followed by [Ted] Curson [trumpet], who is muted. The horns converse, the rhythm slips into four-four time and is interrupted by breaks and out-of-tempo passages. Dolphy and Richmond drop out, and Mingus backs Curson. Richmond and Dolphy return, and all four men swim around and come to a stop. Mingus solos without backing, and Richmond reappears, pulling the horns after him. There is another stop, and Dolphy solos against broken rhythms, and the four take up their ruminations again. After a third stop, Richmond solos and he and Mingus go into a kicking, jumping, unbelievably swinging duet. Mingus falls silent, allowing Richmond to finish his solo, and there is a stop. Mingus solos briefly, and all converse intently until the rhythm slows, Dolphy moans, and they go out. (105)

More than any other Mingus piece up to this time, "Folk Forms" is a truly polyphonic work. Prefigured by "Percussion Discussion," bass and drums transcend their supporting roles and become lead melodic voices. Each instrument constantly vies for our attention as voices in the conversation momentarily take the lead, only to be "answered" by another. A near perfect example of polyphonic group improvisation, "Folk Forms" balances group and individual in a remarkable way. Transcending the confines of the 12-measure blues form, the piece has a sense of risk, as if the musicians are stretching their individual freedom and expressiveness to the limit, yet this individual risk taking is only made possible by an empathic, cohesive group.

Mingus achieved this musical vision of positive freedom, maximizing individual expression and group solidarity, by simultaneously insisting on two apparently contradictory things. First, he demanded that his musicians develop an individual, personal style, that their improvisations come from "who they were"; he was most harsh on those who played standardized phrases ("licks"), especially those derived from Charlie Parker (Blumenthal 29). Another technique that Mingus used for bringing out individuality was to stop the band during a performance and have someone play an unaccompanied solo. According to drummer Dannie Richmond, "[h]e had a theory that if you couldn't play alone first, that you couldn't play with anyone else" (Primack 41). Yet he simultaneously insisted that the ideas his musicians improvised fit into the style, mood, and structure of his often elaborate compositions. Thus, despite the unity of the music, many musicians attested to the fact that they developed their own personal style through working with Mingus. As saxophonist Jackie McLean put it,

[a]fter I left the Mingus band, I really began to be Jackie McLean. I had a more open mind to improvisation and a more individual sound. Prior to that time, I was still very much into Bird. My experience with Mingus really helped me grow.[16] (Primack 40)

Despite the fact that, like any good leader, Mingus had a strong vision which brought order and coherence, his best performances employed a collective process. Instead of Mingus conducting the rather complicated pieces, the group moved together by careful listening. There were cues, but anyone could give the cue if he sensed the group was ready. Like citizens in a classical democracy, people took turns leading, with all the risk and excitement such leadership brings. According to saxophonist Bobby Jones, "[w]ith Mingus you have the freedom to give the cue yourself if you think the group is ready, but you really have to know when. It's exhilarating when you do it, to have everybody jump in with you" (Morgenstern 18). Each had equal responsibility and freedom as long as he paid attention to the group process. Many of the compositions themselves were written collectively; as with Ellington, improvisations that worked were incorporated into the fixed melody of the composition.

Thus, Mingus's mature polyphonic work allowed for both great individual expression and group solidarity, musically representing the community that reconciles them. Through musical empathy, individuals used their increased technical freedom to create coherent structure. What Mingus began, others continued. Ornette Coleman's "Free Jazz," which gave the movement its name, carried "conversational" improvisation to new heights, lifting even more restrictions on individual expression while hoping to preserve group solidarity.

V

Ornette Coleman, unlike Mingus, does not express political sentiments through song titles and lyrics. However, from interviews it is apparent that he has experienced a lot of racism and is passionately concerned with its elimination (Spellman 93–94). One of the themes running through his interviews and his work is his quest to be recognized as a full human being: "I would rather think human first than think of being defeated because I'm black"[17] (Taylor 40–41). His music, we shall see, presented a vision of freedom consonant with this quest for recognition.

Like Mingus, Coleman draws heavily upon the blues. True to his roots playing rhythm and blues in Texas, Coleman's saxophone playing is replete with bent notes and nearly literal "cries." One hears in his playing the mixture of sadness and determination alluded to in Wright's discussion of the blues. However, Coleman goes beyond Mingus in his attack on traditional harmony, especially in "Free Jazz."

"Free Jazz: A Collective Improvisation" was recorded in 1960 with an unusual ensemble: two drummers, two bass players, two trumpeters, Eric Dolphy on bass clarinet, and the leader Ornette Coleman on a plastic alto saxophone.[18] The work consists of one "take" (uninterrupted recording) of 38 minutes. There are brief, partially written, partially improvised ensemble themes which introduce 5- to 10-minute sections of free improvisation, but for the most part the music is collectively created through improvisation.

What strikes one most immediately about the piece is its range of expression: the work encompasses styles from the avant-garde (Don Cherry) to the "straight ahead" (Freddie Hubbard). As with Mingus's "Folk Forms," a chord-playing instrument such as piano or guitar is absent, giving the soloist more freedom in note choice. In fact, as Coleman himself emphasized, the lack of predetermined chords encouraged musicians to create their own melodies rather than play "licks":

> Usually, when you play a melody, you have a set pattern [i.e., chords] to know just what you can do while the other person's doing a certain thing. But in this case, when we played the melody, no one knew where to go or what to do to show that he knew where he was going. . . . I finally got them to where they could see how to express themselves without linking up to a definite maze [i.e., chord progression]. . . . I think it was a case of teaching them how to feel more confident in being expressive like that for themselves.[19] (Litweiler 33–34)

The soloists use this freedom for expressive purposes: in this and later efforts, Coleman and others extended the tonal possibilities of their instruments by such devices as playing extensively in the extreme lower register, playing in the very high register, using squeaks and squawks, playing below the bridge on the bass, and rattling the keys on a saxophone for a percussive effect. Coleman and Dolphy in particular seemed to be striving with their tones to "speak" through their horns, evoking individuality and the metaphor of speech.

But alongside the great diversity and individual expression, the performance maintains a remarkable group cohesiveness. After the theme of each section is played, one instrumentalist begins his solo, accompanied by the bassists and the drummers. The soloist improvises without reference to a set of chords or to a song with a particular meter or number of measures. Obviously, how-ever, there must be some relationship between what the soloist plays and what the bassists and drummers are doing. But this is arrived at in an intuitive and aural manner rather than being de-cided beforehand. The improvisation becomes even more "collec-tive" when the other horn players join in. They may (1) "answer" the soloist; (2) "talk to" each other; (3) play counterpoint (New Orleans style); (4) play background figures ("riffs") or held notes, sometimes in unison or in harmony with others; (5) attempt to play in unison with the soloist; (6) deliberately play against the others; and (7) put forward an idea of their own.

Very quickly, the soloist no longer stands out, and the group conversation takes precedence. Then, the soloist is briefly allowed to play alone again with the "rhythm section," until the members of the group come in again. This back-and-forth process continues until, presumably cued by Coleman, the ensemble plays a written passage again. It is as if the soloist makes a statement that is then bandied about in a group discussion.

The only change in the format comes during the bass solo section, where the bassists have a conversation among themselves without horns, and the drum solo section, where the drums play together without accompaniment. This is perhaps a necessity, a recognition of the fact that because of the drums' relative inability to play pitched notes and the bass's timbre and volume they will not be heard as prominent solo voices if the horns are playing as well. As in any good discussion, the structure is altered to accom-modate those who are not so easily heard, like a meeting which quiets for an elderly person.

This collective improvisation, combining unprecedented indi-vidual freedom and expression with group coherence, carried to new heights the polyphony present in traditional jazz perfor-mances. Without pre-set chords or meter, musical empathy was even more necessary for a successful performance. In the words of the leader Coleman:

> [t]he most important thing was for us to play together, all at
> the same time, without getting in each other's way, and also to
> have enough room for each player to *ad lib* alone—and to fol-
> low this idea for the duration of the album. When the soloist

played something that suggested a musical idea or direction, I
played that behind him in my style. He continued his own way
in his solo, of course. (liner notes, *Free Jazz*)

Not that the individual disappears into the whole; Coleman
says that he played behind the soloist in his "own style" and the
soloist continued "in his own way." He insisted that his musicians
not "accompany" anyone but express themselves in a manner that
contributed to the music as a whole. As he put it,

[w]hat I have always wanted my bands to do is have every man
express *anything*, but yet at the same time show the thing that
is allowing us to make music together, which has something to
do with the person seeing in his mind the difference between
making music total together or trying to make someone sound
good, that's two different things. I don't like to do something
just to make someone sound good because it's giving a false
image of you. . . . As long as they [the other musicians] don't
do anything to make me sound good but they get with the
music, then that's beautiful . . . [Y]ou've got to blend your instrument with other instruments to make music, not to give
support to some other instrument simply because it needs
your support to sound good. (Spellman 143–44)

The distinction between "making someone sound good" and con-
tributing to the music seems to contrast self-abnegation with an
equal, or polyphonic, group process. That is, Coleman suggests
that the way to support other people is not to conform to them,
giving up one's own identity for theirs, for that would represent a
kind of inauthentic role-playing ("giving a false image of you").
Rather, what supports and frees one's fellow individual is to contribute to the whole of which both are a part ("get[ting] with the
music").

In what he calls "free group improvisation," Coleman tries to
go beyond jazz's previous dichotomization of group and individual, where, he says, "the individual is either swallowed up in a
group situation, or else he is out front soloing, with none of the
other horns doing anything but calmly awaiting their turn for *their*
solos"[20] (liner notes, *Change of the Century*). "Free Jazz" strives for a
polyphonic relationship between soloist and ensemble, with a will-

ingness to interact freely, even allowing the soloist to be submerged temporarily. The soloist becomes less of a "star" or a virtuoso striving to outdo the other musicians and more of a "first among equals."

As in any group conversation, some voices are more compelling than others. In "Free Jazz," this is the result of characteristics of the instruments as well as differences in the strength and individuality of the musicians. Perhaps acknowledging his role as a leader, Coleman's solo section is longer than the others. But all in all, it is a very balanced conversation.[21]

We can thus see these free jazz performances as a musical enactment of the ideas of freedom put forward in the growing civil rights movement. Free jazz broke musical conventions to increase individual expression, mirroring the efforts of civil rights leaders to lift rules and conventions constricting the lives of blacks. Musicians like Mingus, Coleman, and Dolphy developed modes of individual expression previously unavailable in jazz, sometimes expressing a relatively unsublimated anger and sadness reflective of the situation of many African-Americans at that time. This is negative, liberal freedom, or liberation; each member of the group could conceivably use this freedom for purely individual ends, creating anarchy.

At the same time, the positive freedom of the redemptive community was represented in jazz performances through the process of polyphonic group improvisation. Much of pre-Sixties jazz was polyphonic in the sense that all instruments improvise simultaneously to some degree. However, "free jazz" took the polyphony inherent in most jazz to unprecedented completeness. A notion of democratic community voiced by King and others before him was musically enacted in a type of interactive group improvisation that is truly polyphonic—individuals can be heard engaging in collective conversation, with each voice sometimes taking the lead and sometimes acting as more of a background, with none simply subsidiary. Musically, as never before in jazz, all the members of the group became equals. Yet such equality did not lead to anarchy; rather, the resulting musical product was remarkably coherent. Musicians achieved coherence not by subordinating individuality to the group but by the kind of empathy and "mutual regard" found in democratic group discussions. While King envisioned the metamorphosis of America's "jangling discords" into a "beautiful symphony of brotherhood" (*Words* 97), jazz musicians created performances that both reflected the dissonance of a society torn by racial strife and offered a model of harmonious brotherhood. As marchers in Selma called for the smashing of racial hierarchy and the formation of the "redemptive community," avant-garde jazz musicians like Charles Mingus and Ornette Coleman sought to overthrow established musical strictures and create musical democracy.

VI

Despite its momentary achievement in music, the redemptive community was not to become a reality in America. The year 1960, when "Free Jazz" was made, was a year of relative optimism for African-Americans. The hope was that white society could be moved by the force of morality, that love could bring about a redemptive community, not only liberating blacks but transforming the U.S. in the process.

The translation into social action of what had been achieved musically by Coleman and Mingus came up against severe obstacles, however. As the decade wore on, the tremendous white resistance to change became apparent; ideals came up against repression, intransigence, and brutality. And many began to realize that the elimination of discrimination was not enough; much of the problem was the entrenched poverty that demanded economic solutions.

In response to some of the perceived limitations of the civil rights approaches of the early Sixties, the "black power" movement emphasized group solidarity rather than the conception of freedom contained in the idea of the redemptive community. The redemptive community's vision of a group that retained individuality ran counter to modern interest group politics. Black power, on the other hand, in calling for African-Americans to unite on the basis of interest, did not challenge but instead implicitly accepted mainstream group politics in which individuals within a group are more or less interchangeable. It was as if the political vision captured in the music of Mingus, Roach, and Coleman had been premature. Though it provided a model of freedom that could be applied to the black community, the U.S. was not ready. African-Americans first had to consolidate their own ranks.

Black power's rejection of the redemptive community was reflected in jazz. Musically, too, the polyphonic balance between group and individual achieved in 1960 failed to hold. "Ascension" typifies the jazz of the mid-Sixties just as "Free Jazz" represented the music of the first few years of the rapidly evolving decade. The piece was recorded by 11 musicians under the leadership of John Coltrane in 1965.[22] Like "Free Jazz," "Ascension" alternates structured ensemble passages with passages of soloist backed by a rhythm section (in this case, a standard one with another bass). In "Ascension," as in "Free Jazz," there is no pre-set meter, harmony, or dynamics for the solo sections.

Here the similarities end, however. First, while during the "solo" sections of "Free Jazz" the soloist alternated between foreground playing and collective interaction with the others, during the solo sections of "Ascension," the other horns stay silent. Whereas in "Free Jazz" the partially written ensemble passages that introduced the "solo"/interactive sections were quite brief, in "Ascension" these introductory passages are equal to or longer than the "solo" sections.

Second, although "Ascension's" introductory ensemble sections featured some "free"-sounding collective improvisation, the group improvisation differs in character from that in "Free Jazz." In the collective passages of "Ascension," one has to strain to hear a particular instrumentalist. During the free improvisation sections, the players tend to repeat one phrase or simply "scream" through their instruments (or pound away, in the drummer's case).[23] Rather than a conversation, it is a collective religious ritual, an act of transcendence ("Ascension") rather than of liberation ("Free Jazz"). One might call it "textural" group improvisation rather than real polyphony.[24] Politically, one might argue, what earlier had been a community became a mass. Prefiguring both the interest-oriented group called for by the emerging black power movement and the subsequent militaristic cadres like the Black Panthers, the individuals are not integrated into the group as individuals but are subservient to the group sound like interchangeable parts.[25] Where "Free Jazz" as the redemptive community overcomes the dichotomy between group and individual, "Ascension" is unable to do so, alternating collective catharsis with individual soloing.

As the decade wore on, the breakdown of the democratic community balancing group and individual, freedom and structure, became more evident, musically and politically. Some chose order over individuality, pursuing an emotionless formalism, heavily influenced by modern European "classical" music. Saxophonist Anthony Braxton, for example, titled his pieces with mathematical formulas and explicitly stated that he wished to remove all feeling from music.

Other developments reflected the opposite, though complementary, trend in African-American politics. For these musicians, democracy became anarchy; "free jazz" became Dionysian "energy music." Political passions had given life to the technical liberation of the early Fifties and led to the collective creation of new forms to embody those sentiments. Now passion exploded all form; dialogue gave way to the chaos prefigured in the "apocalypse" of Mingus's "Pithecanthropus Erectus." There is an incident in a Coltrane concert recorded in Seattle in 1965 where, after several minutes of intense, free-form squealing by Coltrane and saxophonist Pharoah Sanders, the musicians lay down their instruments and begin to wail, as if in agony ("Evolution"). Such an outcome suggests that jazz could no longer find musical forms to express the political sentiments and aspirations of African-Americans as it once had. While the failure of jazz to give form to feeling gave birth to Coltrane's scream in a Seattle nightclub, the failure of the U.S. to give form to black political aspirations brought forth shouting in the streets of Watts the very same year.

VII

It is difficult to pinpoint any direct influence of free jazz upon U.S. race relations, partly because it had so few listeners and partly because such influence by works of art is quite rare. However, it did give aesthetic form to the ideas of the civil rights movement. As Clifford Geertz put it, the arts

> seem specifically designed to demonstrate that ideas are visible, audible, and—one needs to make up a word here—tact-

ible, that they can be cast in forms where the senses, and through the senses the emotions, can reflectively address them. (119–20)

Perhaps because of its direct connection to the senses and the emotions, free jazz allowed its listeners to experience or understand the kind of freedom SNCC and King talked about in a way that words alone could not convey.

Yet the music was no mere "reflection" of preexisting ideas and actions. Some of the early experiments in free jazz seem to have preceded the political developments of the movement, prefiguring the activism of the Sixties. In the words of SDS activist Carl Oglesby,

[in the Sixties] politics itself . . . continued the march formerly begun in art, in the consciousness which the black and white jazz and the white and black poetry of the '50s began to instill and focus. (qtd. in Hodgson 310)

It is as if African-American jazz musicians and black political activists, in different forms, were groping toward similar understandings of their experience, understandings that would soon give birth to the activism of the Civil Rights Movement and the New Left.

Why did free jazz fail to maintain its vision of community in the face of the late Sixties attack on that vision by those opposed to civil rights and by many in the movement itself? Perhaps there was a sense that a limit had been reached: how does one continue to develop a model of freedom, dimly grasped but present in the air, when society turns its back and refuses to create egalitarian social and political structures? In addition, free jazz made extraordinary, perhaps impossible, demands on the listener. In a polyphonic, free performance, there are no fixed key centers, melodies, or lead instruments to hold on to; it is up to the listener to weave out of the various threads a tapestry of his or her own, perhaps a different one upon each listening.[26] Even many jazz musicians disliked free jazz; they argued that freedom requires structure and (incorrectly, I think) saw none in free jazz.[27] They also felt that the music, since it sounded like it required no training, threatened their sense of professional standing.

Contemporary jazz has drawn upon some of the innovations of free jazz, but for the most part remains tied to traditional harmony. What Coleman and Coltrane were to the Sixties, Wynton Marsalis, with his rejection of free jazz and its values, is to the past 10 years. Even formerly avant-garde musicians are making albums of "standards." It is only somewhat of an exaggeration to say that during the Reagan-Bush years, jazz became neoconservative.

Despite the political and musical rejection of free jazz and its values, its performances show that the redemptive community is possible, even if only in a small group, and teach us something about its conditions. Most of all, the successful free, polyphonic works of Mingus and Coleman suggest that empathy is crucial to freedom, for without it individual expression easily becomes anarchy (or the war of each against all), and group solidarity threatens individuality.

Free jazz also teaches us something about the relationship among the arts, political ideas, and social change. These works show us how the arts can "make real" political ideas at the forefront of society, rendering them accessible to the senses. Yet the arts sometimes abandon those ideas in the face of society's resistance to them, in this case reflecting the fragility of egalitarian political ideals. The reemergence of free polyphony to prominence in jazz might have to await the wider acceptance of "polyphonic" politics—a politics of solidarity based on empathic respect for difference. In the meantime, however, we can draw hope from the representation of such politics in music.

Notes

1. For more on the political meaning of jazz, see Jones, Backus, Wilmer, and Ellison. For a purely musical analysis of free jazz, see Jost.

2. Other works by Ellington in this vein included "Creole Rhapsody" (1931), "Black, Brown, and Beige" (1943), and "Tone Parallel to Harlem" (1950) (Budds 99).

3. Thelonious Monk once called bebop "something they can't play," presumably referring to white popular musicians ("The Loneliest Monk" 86).

4. On the beginnings of rhythm and blues in Los Angeles and New York, see Shaw, *Honkers and Shouters* xvi–xvii, and *Black Popular Music in America* 187–92.

5. Coltrane agreed to play a benefit for SNCC at the University of California in 1961, but the concert was canceled after the Chancellor said that students could not raise funds for political organizations (Kofsky 221–22).

6. Proto-avant-garde pianist and composer Thelonious Monk said something similar: "The best thing about jazz is that it makes a person appreciate freedom. Jazz and freedom go hand in hand" (*Esquire's World of Jazz* 202).

7. Of course, there were differences among black political actors and thinkers. While King stressed a national/universalist view, SNCC was more localist (Carson). The role of whites in the movement was controversial, increasingly so as time went on. Despite differences, however, there was a consensus on the need for community and for a reevaluation of American society.

8. SNCC's founding creed also mentions this term (Carson 23).

9. In his critique of Plato, Aristotle also uses a musical metaphor to argue against uniformity, which he saw as undermining real solidarity, necessarily based on diversity: "It was as if you were to turn harmony into mere unison, or to reduce a theme to a single beat" (51; Book II.v, sec. 14).

10. King obviously does not address the postmodern insight that any group marginalizes some individuals. Perhaps he would envision a group that continually recreates its identity in response to the awareness of such marginalization; presumably, politics might then continually strive toward, though never completely achieve, inclusiveness.

11. There is an element of improvisation even in playing the written melody, as the musician can interpret that melody using dynamics, tone, phrasing, rhythm, and embellishment.

12. Polyphony is opposed to homophony or monophony in which there is only one melodic line. "Row, row, row your boat" and other such "rounds" are a type of polyphony in which one melody is staggered at different times (technically, "imitative counterpoint"). The more equal in prominence the different melodic lines are, the closer one gets to true polyphony. Polyphony was a feature of New Orleans jazz, though without the freedom of "free jazz."

Others who have connected polyphony and politics include Theodor Adorno and Mikhail Bakhtin. Adorno emphasized the collective nature of polyphony, seeing its source in the "collective practices of cult and dance," emphasizing its evocation of plurality (Adorno, *Philosophy* 18; *Introduction* 97). Bakhtin sees in Dostoevsky's "polyphonic novel" a kind of political equality that opposes hierarchy and monologic authoritarianism:

> *A plurality of independent and unmerged voices and consciousnesses, a genuine polyphony of fully valid voices is in fact the chief characteristic of Dostoevsky's novel.* What unfolds in his works is not a multitude of characters and fates in a single objective world illuminated by a single authorial consciousness; rather, *a plurality of consciousnesses, each with equal rights and each with its own world*, combine but are not merged in the unity of the event. Dostoevsky's heroes are, by the very nature of his creative design, *not only objects of authorial discourse but also subjects of their own directly signifying discourse.* (Bakhtin 6–7; emphasis in the original)

13. Two other relevant examples are worth noting here, even though they are beyond the scope of this article. First, in 1949 Lennie Tristano recorded two tracks in which the group was told to improvise without pre-set parameters (*Crosscurrents* Capitol M-11060). This early instance of "free jazz," however, sounded nothing like the music to later bear that name; in particular, it lacked the connection with the blues that would characterize the music of the late Fifties and early Sixties. Second, in a series of albums beginning in 1965, Miles Davis's group, though not completely abandoning traditional harmony, stretched it toward its

limits, while simultaneously experimenting with tempo, meter, and, to some degree, polyphony. Though important and influential, this music, coming as it did five years after Mingus's "Folk Forms #1" and Coleman's "free jazz" (analyzed below), is not central to an understanding of the way free jazz came to embody the vision of the developing civil rights movement. (Pekar cites recordings by Django Reinhardt; Shorty Rogers, Jimmy Guiffre, and Shelly Manne; and Chico Hamilton as other precursors of the "free jazz" of the Sixties.)

14. The blues is in one sense a chord progression, usually 12 measures, featuring movement among tonic, subdominant, and dominant. However, blues feeling can be injected into any progression by the use of "bent" or flatted notes, or perhaps even a certain tonal quality. In both his feeling for the blues and his emphasis on polyphony and group improvisation, Mingus was influenced by Ellington. Ellington obviously did not explore the harmonic freedom that Mingus did.

15. According to Ronald Radano, the title of this piece referred to Louis B. Leakey's theory, publicized in 1959, that the human race originated in Africa (65n96).

16. Radano, 40. The article gives evidence that Dannie Richmond, John Handy, and Charles McPherson went through a similar process of development. See also Blumenthal 29; Morgenstern 18.

17. The word "human" shows up repeatedly in his song and album titles. See also Spellman 93–94.

18. The other musicians were Don Cherry (trumpet), Freddie Hubbard (trumpet), Eric Dolphy (bass clarinet), Scott Le Faro (bass), Charlie Haden (bass), Billy Higgins (drums), and Ed Blackwell (drums). Because the name of the performance became the name of a style, I will refer to the composition as "Free Jazz" and the style as "free jazz."

19. It is true that a person could play patterns based on chords or scales even if there was no pre-set harmony, but it is less likely, and even if he did he would have to make sure his implied harmony fit in with that of the rest of the group.

20. Later in the same liner notes, Coleman adds, "I don't tell the members of my group what to do. I want them to play what they hear in the piece for themselves. I let everyone express himself just as he wants to. The musicians have complete freedom, and so, of course, our final result depends entirely on the musicianship, emotional make-up and taste of the individual members. Ours is at all times a group effort and it is only because we have the rapport that we do that our music takes on the shape that it does. A strong personality with a star-complex would take away from the effectiveness of our group, no matter how brilliantly he played . . ."

21. When I use the word "conversation" I am not being totally metaphorical. At one point in Hubbard's "solo" section, there is a musical dialogue between Coleman and Dolphy which imitates speech patterns in the manner of "What Love" (which Dolphy had earlier played with Mingus, although it was not recorded until after "Free Jazz"). The vocalized tone of saxophonists Coleman and Dolphy in general contributes to the air of "conversationality." Dolphy himself said that he tries "to get the instrument to more or less speak" (liner notes, "Free Jazz").

22. "Ascension" features Coltrane, Archie Shepp, and Pharoah Sanders (tenor sax), Dewey Johnson and Freddie Hubbard (trumpet), Art Davis and Jimmy Garrison (bass), Marion Brown and John Tchicai (alto sax), McCoy Tyner (piano),

and Elvin Jones (drums). There were two versions of the piece recorded and released.

23. According to Simpkins, the players were sometimes given four notes to play, and they could play them in any order and rhythmic arrangement (129).

24. Jost makes a similar point about the two works, though without ascribing a political connotation to the difference (89).

25. Indeed, this is stated explicitly in the liner notes by Shepp: "The emphasis was on textures rather than the making of an organizational entity. There was a unity, but it was a unity of sounds and textures rather than an ABA approach. You can hear, in the saxophones especially, a reaching for sound and an exploration of the possibilities of sound."

26. Thus, Coltrane said that "the audience, in listening, is in an act of participation. And when you know that somebody is maybe moved the same way you are . . . it's just like having another member of the group" (Kofsky 226).

27. See statements by Randy Weston, Philly Joe Jones, and Johnny Griffin (Taylor 27, 45–46, 67).

Works Cited

Adorno, Theodor W. *Introduction to the Sociology of Modern Music.* Trans. E. B. Ashton. New York: Continuum, 1988.
———. *Philosophy of Modern Music.* Trans. Anne G. Mitchell and Westley V. Blomster. New York: Seabury, 1980.
Aristotle. *Politics.* Trans. Ernest Barker. London: Oxford, 1976.
Backus, Rob. *Fire Music: A Political History of Jazz.* Chicago: Vanguard, 1976.
Bakhtin, Mikhail. *Problems of Dostoevsky's Poetics.* Trans. Caryl Emerson. Minneapolis: U of Minnesota P, 1984.
Balliet, Whitney. "Mingus." *New Yorker.* 18 June 1979: 100–05.
Blumenthal, Bob. "Mal Waldron." *Down Beat* April 1981: 29.
Budds, Michael J. *Jazz in the Sixties.* Iowa City: U of Iowa P, 1978.
Carson, Clayborne. *In Struggle.* Cambridge: Harvard, 1981.
Cole, Bill. *John Coltrane.* New York: Schirmer, 1976.
Coleman, Ornette. *Change of the Century.* SD-1327. Atlantic, 1959.
———. *Free Jazz.* 1364. Atlantic, 1960.
Coltrane, John. *Ascension.* AS-95 (reissued as MCA-29020). Impulse, 1965.
———. "Evolution." Featuring Pharoah Sanders. *Live in Seattle.* AS 9202-2. Impulse, 1965.
Ellison, Ralph. *Shadow and Act.* New York: Vintage, 1972.
Esquire's World of Jazz. New York: Thomas Crowell, 1975.
Geertz, Clifford. *Local Knowledge.* New York: Basic, 1983.
Hentoff, Nat. "Archie Shepp: The Way Ahead." *Black Giants.* New York: World, 1970.
———. *Jazz Is.* New York: Avon, 1976.
Hodgson, Godfrey. *America in Our Time.* New York: Vintage, 1978.
Jones, LeRoi. *Blues People.* New York: Morrow, 1963.
Jost, Ekkehard. *Free Jazz.* New York: Da Capo, 1981.
King, Jr., Martin Luther. *Stride Toward Freedom.* San Francisco: Harper, 1958.
———. *Where Do We Go from Here?* Boston: Beacon, 1968.

———. *The Words of Martin Luther King.* Ed. Coretta Scott King. New York: Newmarket, 1983.

Kofsky, Frank. *Black Nationalism and the Revolution in Music.* New York: Pathfinder, 1970.

Lambert, G. E. *Duke Ellington.* New York: A. S. Barnes, 1959.

Litweiler, John. *The Freedom Principle.* New York: Morrow, 1984.

"The Loneliest Monk." *Time* June 1964: 86.

McLean, Jackie. "Let Freedom Ring." *Let Freedom Ring.* BST 84106. Blue Note, 1962.

Meier, August, Elliott Rudwick, and Francis L. Broderick. *Black Protest Thought in the Twentieth Century.* 2nd ed. Indianapolis: Bobbs-Merrill, 1971.

Mingus, Charles. *Charles Mingus Presents Charles Mingus.* BR-5012. Barnaby/Candid, 1960.

———. "Conversation." *East Coasting.* 1957. AFF 86. Affinity, 1982.

———. "Fables of Faubus." *Charles Mingus Presents Charles Mingus.* BR-5012. Barnaby/Candid, 1960.

———. "Haitian Fight Song." 1957. *The Best of Charles Mingus.* SD 1555. Atlantic, 1970.

———. "Percussion Discussion." 1955. *Chazz!* F-86022. Fantasy, 1962.

———. "Pithecanthropus Erectus." 1956. *The Best of Charles Mingus.* SD 1555. Atlantic, 1970.

———. "Work Song." *Chazz!* F-86022. Fantasy, 1962.

Morgenstern, Dan. "Inside Mingus With Bobby Jones." *Down Beat* 11 May 1972: 18.

Pekar, Harvey. "Father of Free Jazz." *Northern Ohio Live* May 1994: 16–18.

Priestley, Brian. *Mingus: A Critical Biography.* New York: Da Capo, 1982.

Primack, Bret. "The Gospel According to Mingus: Disciples Carry the Tune." *Down Beat* 7 Dec. 1978: 41.

Radano, Ronald M. *New Musical Figurations: Anthony Braxton's Cultural Critique.* Chicago: U of Chicago P, 1993.

Roach, Max. *Freedom Now Suite.* JC 36390. Columbia, 1960.

Shaw, Arnold. *Black Popular Music in America.* New York: Schirmer, 1986.

———. *Honkers and Shouters.* New York: Collier, 1978.

Sidran, Ben. *Black Talk.* New York: Da Capo, 1971.

Simpkins, C. O. *Coltrane.* New York: Herndon House, 1975.

Spellman, A. B. *Four Lives in the Bebop Business.* New York: Pantheon, 1966.

Taylor, Arthur. *Notes and Tones.* New York: Perigee, 1982.

Tristano, Lennie. *Crosscurrents.* M-11060. Capitol, 1949.

Walton, Ortiz. *Music: Black, White & Blue.* New York: Morrow, 1972.

Wilmer, Valerie. *As Serious as Your Life.* Westport: Lawrence Hill, 1977.

Wright, Richard. Foreword. *The Meaning of the Blues.* By Paul Oliver. New York: Collier, 1963. 9–12.

Zinn, Howard. *SNCC: The New Abolitionists.* Boston: Beacon, 1964.

Technico-Military Thrills and the Technology of Terror: Tom Clancy and the Commission on the Disappeared

Celeste Fraser Delgado

> In drawing up this report, we wondered about the best way to deal with the theme [of torture] so that this chapter did not turn into merely an encyclopedia of horror. We could find no way to avoid this. After all, what else were these tortures but an immense display of the most degrading and indescribable acts of degradation, which the military governments, lacking all legitimacy in power, used to secure power over a whole nation?
>
> —*Nunca Más: The Report of the Argentine National Commission on the Disappeared*

> But who cares if it all seems improbable?
>
> —Review of *The Hunt for Red October* (Alden)

In 1984, two national bestsellers published at opposite ends of the Western Hemisphere made visible the invisible, revealing to readers closely guarded secrets of each nation. In the United States, Tom Clancy's *The Hunt for Red October* inaugurated a new

© 1996 by *Cultural Critique*. Winter 1995–96. 0882-4371/96/$5.00.

genre—the "technico-military thriller"—by reserving the starring role in his first novel for the secret technologies and tactics deployed by the Superpowers at the tail end of the Cold War. Concurrently in Argentina, the National Commission on the Disappeared (CONADEP) released *Nunca Más*, a report sponsored by the newly elected government at the end of what the toppled military regime had called the "dirty war." With the intention of ensuring that the horrors committed and vehemently denied by that regime would happen "never again," *Nunca Más* exposed the tactics of the dirty war: the systematic abduction, torture, and disappearance of nearly 30,000 Argentine citizens. I will argue that each of these disparate texts attempts to neutralize through narrative strategies a postmodern display of power that turns upon an aesthetic of disappearance.[1]

In his "technico-military thriller," Clancy glorifies the technological armor of the Superpowers, producing a sense of improbability that grants the reader permission to take pleasure in the tall-telling of a best-man-wins fight to the death. Marko Ramius, a renowned Lithuanian submarine captain, decides to defect to the U.S. with the Soviet Navy's most advanced submarine, the *Red October*, under his command. The Red October's disappearance mobilizes both the Soviet and U.S. navies and intelligence services, as the U.S. attempts to capture the defecting sub and the Soviet Union attempts to destroy it. An average American turned Central Intelligence Agency analyst, Jack Ryan, rises neatly to the occasion to outsmart the Soviets and bring the heroic captain and his submarine to the land of liberty. Clancy construes the Cold War as a game of high-tech hide-and-seek played by nuclear submarines, in which human bodies meld with machines that extend the senses.

As an "encyclopedia of horror," *Nunca Más* sets out to surmount the sense of improbability provoked by the allegation of a systematic repressive machine by documenting minutely the acts, instruments, and sites of torture deployed in the dirty war. The document presents testimony of survivors of torture inflicted by the Argentine military, portraying the military regime in the words and suffering of the regime's targets. Upping the ante from hide-and-seek to search-and-destroy, CONADEP displays machines that mortify the flesh through the intensification of sensation.

Despite the disparity between the work performed by each of

these texts, I do not intend a kind of ethical critique in which the glamorization of death-dealing technologies is simply wrong (or "bad literature") while the denunciation of such technologies is right (or "good literature").[2] Rather, I am concerned here with how this work is performed. Counterpoising these representations of the tortured- and the techno-body, I describe the schema of embodiment employed by each text as peripheral and central instances of the postmodern display of power. This display takes place within what Donna Haraway has termed the "informatics of domination"—a global system in which the technology of coding (and decoding) has shut down all forms of political action premised upon organic, self-contained entities, such as the isolated human body and the nation-state (80–83). *The Hunt for Red October* and *Nunca Más* contain this postmodern display, injecting the cybernetic recombinants of bodies and machines with organic human consciousness in order either to justify or denounce the power motivating intelligence technologies.

I propose as an organizing principle for this postmodern display of power the concept of the Central Intelligence Agency (CIA). The CIA serves as a historically imprecise but theoretically powerful way of understanding various technologies of surveillance and control within the informatics of domination. The CIA holds a special "central" relationship to the other intelligence organizations in the U.S.—"CIA is, in effect, the nucleus around which some twenty major intelligence organizations operate" (Breckinridge xiv)—as well as a central relationship to the intelligence organizations of allied nations through both the direct sharing of intelligence and the dissemination of intelligence technology. The systematic practice of intelligence-gathering worldwide allows us to use the CIA as a concept where we cannot refer specifically to the perpetrators of particular actions. The CIA represents an epistemology, a way of extracting knowledge from the atmosphere (through satellites, sonar, and other extrasensory marvels of detection) and from the human body (through training, torture, and temptation). The CIA represents a mode of writing, a way of inscribing bodies with the knowledge produced by the policies and the police forces of the central world powers and a way of proliferating that knowledge through intervention in the world media. Most important to this analysis, precisely because the minute operations of the corporate identity called the CIA remain veiled in an elaborate system of secrecy, the concept of the CIA captures the primary element of the postmodern display of power: disappearance.

The paradoxical role of disappearance in display requires a repositioning of Elaine Scarry's analysis of the fundamental dynamics of the contemporary practice of torture in her treatise *The Body in Pain*. Drawing from Amnesty International documents that catalogue the incidents of torture integral to keeping the current world order, Scarry formulates this kind of torture as the making of a fiction of the regime's power on and through the tortured body. Her formulation asserts on an intimate level the function that Foucault attributes to the public spectacle of torture in premodern times, when bodies tortured in public represented sovereign power. To understand the function of this presumably premodern practice in a postmodern age, I enlarge Scarry's frame and situate the tortured body in the context of the informatics of domination.

The informatics of domination operates on cybernetic rather than human bodies, displacing the biopolitics of Foucault onto a simulacra of politics (Haraway 80). According to Foucault, governments in the modern period extended control over the lives of individuals through the professed adoption of the function of maintaining those lives. This function made regimes more dependent upon discursive fiction, as the unmediated transformation of individual bodies into testimonies to power conflicted with the alleged life-giving function: "As soon as power gave itself the function of administering life, its reason for being and the logic of its exercise—and not the awakening of humanitarian feeling—made it more and more difficult to apply the death penalty" (Foucault 138). With the transition to multinational capitalism, the governments of postmodern nations have taken on the function of maintaining the market, the fundamental ideological category of the global economy characterized by an extranational concentration of power and a technological displacement of workers.[3] The brutality of the repression necessary to enforce this transition has pushed many states to the untenable apex of contradiction between the persistent promise of life contained in the legitimation of the modern state and a life-threatening disciplinary system.

In one instance, the military junta that ruled Argentina from

1976 to 1983 brought Argentina through the transition to late capitalism by turning the state into a death-dealing machine. Because
national autogenocide undermined claims to the protection of a
ser nacional—a unified national body disciplined by the state for its
own good—the state needed to conceal the evidence of contradiction. Rather than displayed, the bodies testifying to the state's
power were disappeared. In another instance, the U.S. has used
clandestine operations since 1954—most notoriously through the
CIA—to efface the contradiction between the professed ideal of
protection of a universal democracy and the actual practice of violent imposition of the multinational market. Clandestine operations and secret military technology occlude a vast network of lethal weaponry, maintaining the Cold War illusion of a superpower
predicated on détente. In each case, the postmodern device of disappearance conceals the agency behind the repressive apparatus
while at the same time effectively undermining through erasure
the agency of the object of repression.

Within this dynamic of disappearance, we may reinterpret
Scarry's grammar of torture as a calculus of textual embodiment:
"[w]hat assists the conversion of absolute pain into the fiction of
absolute power is an obsessive, self-conscious display of agency. On
the simplest level, the agent displayed is the weapon" (Scarry 27).
This statement provides an uncanny gloss of *The Hunt for Red October,* as the plot undergirds a spectacular display of weapons that
extends agents' bodies and converts the pain of nuclear warfare
into a fiction of U.S. superpower. With an "obsessive, self-conscious
display of the [Central Intelligence] [A]gency," violence is paradoxically concealed through the display of the weapon. By contrast,
Nunca Más mimics the regime's display of agency with a crucial
difference: not only does the Report make public the intimate theater of torture, but in this publication CONADEP displays the
weapon *as inserted in* the tortured body in order to extract the regime as agent.

Deadly Reading

The meaning of the aerial photo, its *reading,* depends on all
that can be drawn from the rationalized act of interpretation
as a source of military intelligence . . . few pictures, except pos-

sibly in the medical field, are as "free," seemingly, from a
higher meaning than that of their usage.
—Allan Sekula on U.S. aerial operations during W.W.I.

In *The Aesthetics of Disappearance,* Paul Virilio decries a "new
prosthetic synergy . . . that blends motor, eye, and weapon" (56).
Virilio quotes theorist Allan Sekula, who describes a deadly instru-
mentality in the interpretation of aerial photography (57). The
weapon, in this formulation of photography, serves as the instrument of interpretation: reading results in death. The positing of
interpretation as the instrument of death in the field of military
intelligence decontextualizes the act of interpretation: that act can
only be "rationalized" insofar as the interpretation fits within the
rationalization for a particular instance of combat by a particular
military force. Interpretation of any material mobilized in the field
of intelligence assumes a "higher meaning"—a wider interpretive
grid—that allows for the identification of targets based not only on
their physical appearance or geographical location but first and
foremost on the ideological focus of the intelligent eye.

Throughout the Cold War, intelligence gathering worldwide
would fall under the interpretive grid of the struggle between the
Superpowers to control or "center" the world. This struggle coincided with two major reconceptualizations of military strategy at
the end of World War II. In an effort to centralize the gathering
of intelligence (whose fragmentary nature during World War II
government officials held responsible for the unforeseen bombing
of Pearl Harbor), the National Security Act of 1947 created the
CIA. At the same time, technological development in general came
to play an eminent role in military planning. After World War II,
"the quality of military technology, more than the quantity of in-
dustrial production, was widely viewed as the most important pre-
dictor of success in the next war" (Roland 367). This view led to
the burgeoning military technology since World War II, evident in
such industry crossovers as "computers, sonar, radar, jet engines,
swept-wing aircraft, insecticides, transistors, fire- and weather-
resistant clothing, anti-bacterial drugs, numerically controlled machine tools, high-speed integrated circuits, [and] nuclear power"
(Smith 4). In the National Security Council Directive 10/2 of 1948
and again in the National Security Council Directive 5412/1 of

1955, defense policy makers attributed the need for a twin commitment to intelligence and technology to the "vicious activities of the USSR and Communist China and the governments and parties dominated by them (hereinafter referred to as 'International Communism')" (NSCD 5412/1, 146). In a 1954 assessment of the mission of the CIA that led to this assertion, the Doolittle Commission proclaimed that the U.S. would combat these "vicious activities" by joining in: "[the U.S.] must subvert, sabotage, and destroy our enemies by more clever, more sophisticated, and more effective methods than those used against us" (Doolittle 144).

These "clever," "sophisticated," and "more effective methods" represent a combination of covert action and technological advance that corresponds to a split in modes of intelligence collection. The intelligence acronym HUMINT refers to intelligence collected by humans by either open or covert means, whereas other methods of gathering intelligence employ machines and fall under the sign of the kind of the technology in use, for example: COMINT (communications intelligence), ELINT (electronics intelligence), and PHOTINT (photographic intelligence, including instruments ranging from infrared cameras to satellites to overhead reconnaissance planes) (Breckinridge 4). Whether the mode of collection falls to human or machine, the centrality of the anticommunist struggle to the official U.S. conception of national security would determine the methods of gathering and modes of interpretation of intelligence over the thirty-year span from Doolittle's assessment of the Cold War to Clancy's first novel.

Although the proclaimed battle of the U.S. against International Communism supplied the ideology and the technology deployed in the struggle against International Communism worldwide, a kind of division of intelligence labor spread across nations at the center and the periphery. Where technology-intense intelligence methods characterized the central struggle between the U.S. and the Soviet Union, human intelligence (HUMINT)—particularly interrogation and torture—characterized the struggle against alleged Marxist insurgents in the peripheral arenas. This technological division of labor as manifested in the intelligence agencies of the U.S. and Argentina has formal consequence in both *The Hunt for Red October* and *Nunca Más*.

The Hunt for Red October

As an insurance salesman with no access to classified material, Clancy gathered his own intelligence from open sources (information in the public domain). From these sources, Clancy recreated the technical capacity of the U.S. and Soviet intelligence organizations with such accuracy that rumors recount concern on the part of the U.S. government about Clancy's access to classified information. However, public information about the structure of the intelligence community and the heady pace of technology available to the Navy abounds. Rather than discover secrets, Clancy's work animates technologies.

Clancy copiously transcribes naval and intelligence jargon, locking his readers into a bewilderingly complex technological world where systems designated by acronyms like SOSUS and SAPS behave like characters and minute technical descriptions come to function as crucial devices in the plot. Presumably only military experts (who have purportedly made Clancy's novels a bestseller on military bases) can keep the technological pace. Clancy weaves a technological spell for the uninitiated, whose pleasure in the plot depends upon a certain epistemological surrender.

With dizzying detail and apocalyptic stakes in the ultimate Superpower battle, *The Hunt for Red October* capitalizes on the headiness generated by the mere description of the technological possibilities available to the contemporary Navy, such as this one by naval historian David K. Allison:

> The advent of nuclear power made possible a "true" submarine, one designed to cruise under water, not just dive occasionally. Guided missiles have largely replaced guns and bombs . . . Satellites for communications, surveillance, and navigation have extended Naval Operations to outer space . . . Sensors such as monopulse radars and towed acoustic arrays have brought substantial improvements in capabilities for locating targets above and below the sea surface. But as sensors have improved so have the means to counter them, such as chaff, paints that absorb electronic signalling, and radar signal jammers. To meet the ever-increasing need for high-speed information processing, computers now monitor tactical situations and help commanders make rapid decisions. Reliance on

electronic devices has become so pronounced that the Navy has built ships and aircraft equipped with nothing but sensors and computer processors for gathering tactical information or assisting in weapons delivery. (314)

Clancy animates this technological profusion by inserting characters into the machinery. This emphasis has prompted many critics to disparage Clancy's creation of characters, as one reviewer of *The Hunt for Red October* purports: "Clancy is more skilled and convincing writing about machinery—the machinery of underseas warfare and intelligence—than about men" (Setlowe 2). Because Clancy takes up technology precisely as an extension of human senses, the opposition between humans and machines made in criticism of his work has no force. Other critics have suggested that the technology in Clancy's work is a character, but this holds true only insofar as Clancy melds his human characters with his machines. At the extreme, satellites and the "ships and aircraft equipped with nothing but sensors and computer processors" isolate and refine the human senses of hearing and seeing possessed by the military and intelligence personnel. The computer processors accelerate these humans' ability to analyze the information gathered from these sensing machines.

Clancy situates this extension of the senses within the context of human mastery. Human beings fill in for the limitations of technology, making infinite the potential to accrue ever greater power as resourceful operators rig up new methods for mastering space and sea. One such character is the talented young enlisted sonar operator Jones. Kicked out of a master's degree program in engineering because of a prank that backfired, Jones spends his time in the Navy outwitting and modifying machines. He discovers the unique "acoustical signature" of the *Red October* as he plays with a strange sound on his sonar, then plots the course of that sound on his captain's charts. This discovery requires a clever circumvention of the machine:

> There was a considerable amount of surface noise. The signal processors filtered most of it out, and every few minutes Jones switched them off his channel, getting the sound unimpeded to make sure that they weren't filtering too much out. Machines were dumb; Jones wondered if SAPS might be letting

some of that anomalous signal get lost inside the computer chips. That was a problem with computers, really a problem with programming: you'd tell the machine to do something and it would do it to the wrong thing. (260)

Here the signal algorithmic processing system (SAPS) maintains a relationship with human hearing in which the sonar does not simply substitute for or even necessarily improve upon the human ear, rather human programmers determine the mode of operation of the machine in relation to their own desires and capacities. The assurance that "machines [are] dumb" serves to confirm the corollary: people are smart. In the technician, Clancy creates a nerd-cum-Superhero, a kind of Clark Kent who doesn't change clothes to become Superman—more impressively perhaps, he changes algorithms.

In the process of leading every reader into the technological wonderland of the modern military, Clancy allows every man to envision himself in the role of Superman. While the novel's nearly 500 pages cut from Soviet sub to the Pentagon, from SOSUS to SAPS, the hunt and discovery of the *Red October* revolves around the capabilities of CIA analyst and Everyman Jack Ryan.[4] As an Everyman, Ryan works at a desk, gets seasick and airsick in Navy contraptions, and desperately wants to finish this mission in time to get home to his wife and kids for the holidays. As an analyst, in the estimation of his superiors at the CIA:

> Ryan had the ability to sort through a pile of data and come out with three or four facts that meant something. This was too rare a thing at the CIA. The agency still spent too much money on collecting data and not enough on collating it. Analysts had none of the supposed glamor—a Hollywood-generated illusion—of a secret agent in a foreign land. But Jack knew how to analyze reports from these men and data from technical sources. He knew how to make a decision and was not afraid to say what he thought, whether his boss liked it or not. (55)

Despite the valorization of the analyst in this passage, Clancy has Ryan cross over from analyst to operative. A strand tying together analysis and action, Ryan leaves his desk to deliver a top-secret message to a British admiral, to engage in a shoot-out amidst nuclear missiles with an agent of the KGB, and ultimately to pilot the *Red October* during a Soviet submarine attack. As an analyst, he makes both human intelligence (HUMINT) and the various forms of technical intelligence meaningful. As an operative, he makes intelligence exciting. As a figure combining the CIA analyst and operative, part nerd, part secret agent, Ryan serves as the humanizing center of technology.

Clancy's depiction of human consciousness at the center of a world filled with artificial censors seems designed to assuage the kind of anxiety about prosthetic mediation that Paul Virilio expresses in his nightmare description of "our technical future":

> the abandonment of the vehicular speed of bodies for the strangely impressive one of light vectors, the internment of bodies is no longer in the cinematic cell of travel but in a cell outside of time, which would be an electronic terminal where we'd leave it up to the instruments to organize our most vital rhythms, without ever changing position ourselves, the authority of electronic automatism reducing our will to zero . . . somehow the vision of light moving on a screen would have replaced all personal movement . . . The development of high technical speeds would thus result in the disappearance of consciousness as the direct perception of phenomena that inform us of our own existence. (104)

Rather than abandon the "vehicular speed of bodies for the strangely impressive one of light vectors," Clancy transmutes bodies into vehicles whose speed heightens the stakes in both time and consciousness. In the structure of the fiction, Clancy obsessively tracks the movement of the submarine through space and time by dividing *The Hunt for Red October* into chapters labeled chronologically both according to the time of the novel and the date on the calendar. Clancy splits the chapters into smaller sections labeled according to location as plotted by either vehicle, architectural site, or geographical location. The speed of the submarines and the method of propulsion determines the ability of the various sensing machines to track their movement. The capabilities of the sensing machines circumscribe the possibility of the *Red October's* disappearance. The "development of high technical speeds" here, whether in the submarines or the supercomputers, licenses a hyper display of human consciousness (which we might also call intelligence) as augmented by machines and centralized by Jack Ryan. The closer the *Red October* comes to vanishing, the more developed become the senses engaged in the hunt; the closer the *Red October* comes to vanishing, the more visible Clancy makes human consciousness. This hyperhumanism in a sea of technology invites the reader to partake in the pleasure of mastery over a nature made more treacherous by the inventions of man.

The humanization of technology facilitates the displacement of guilt in the central power's tactics of disappearance by displacing the representation of death from human bodies onto technological bodies. In portraying human bodies as coextensive with technology, Clancy departs from the old trope of equating ships with women. Before sacrificing the aging submarine *Ethan Allen*, which serves as a double for the *Red October*, one Admiral Gallery returns to the sub once under his command to pay a last tribute, a moment he shares with the submarine's present crew:

> He'd recognized some of the senior chiefs and asked them if the old girl had any life left in her. To a man, the chiefs said yes. A ship becomes more than a machine to her crew. (247)

The making of the ship "more than a machine," that is, the humanizing of the machine, informs Clancy's manner of describing the "life" and the demise of the technological wonders he creates.

In contrast, Clancy treats the death of human bodies with relative economy, integrating those bodies into the body of the submarine as so many no-longer-working parts. When a Soviet sub engaged in the hunt for the *Red October* goes under, Clancy devotes scant lines in the eight pages cataloguing the destruction to the agony of the crew on board:

> In the *Politovskiy*'s reactor, the runaway fission reaction had virtually annihilated both the incoming seawater and the uranium fuel rods. Their debris settled on the after wall of the reactor vessel. In a minute there was a meter-wide puddle of radioactive slag, enough to form its own critical mass. The reaction continued unabated, this time directly attacking the

tough stainless steel of the vessel. The uranium mass dropped
free, against the aft bulkhead.
　　Petchukocov knew he was dead. He saw the paint on the
forward bulkhead turn black, and his last impression was of a
dark mass surrounded with the blue glow. The engineer's
body vaporized an instant later, and the mass of slag dropped
to the next bulkhead.
　　Forward, the submarine's nearly vertical angle in the water eased. The high-pressure air in the ballast tanks spilled out
of the bottom floods and the tanks filled with water, dropping
the angle of the boat and submerging her. (194)

Clancy portrays Petchukocov's death not in terms of his own physical sensations, but in terms of his perception of the destruction of
the ship: the paint on the bulkhead, the "blue glow." Petchukocov
appropriately vanishes or is "vaporized" into the bulkhead, as
Clancy slides his demise into the collapse of the slag introduced
in the previous paragraph. Clancy goes on to refer briefly to the
screaming and scrambling of the men on the ship as they attempt
to escape, but this description too slides back into the body of the
submarine. The senses of the submarine displace the senses of the
human bodies in Clancy's representation of the Superpowers'
death-dealing technology.
　　The one exception to this treatment of human and technological bodies occurs in the missile room shoot-out between Ryan and
a secret agent of the KGB stowed away on the Red October:

[The Soviet agent] was in his early twenties, if that, and his
clear blue eyes were staring overhead while he tried to say
something. His face was rigid with pain as he mouthed words,
but all that came out was an unintelligible gurgle . . .
　　The blue eyes fixed Jack's face. Whoever he was, he
knew death was coming to him. The pain on the face was replaced by something else. Sadness, an infinite sadness. . .He
was still trying to speak. A pink froth gathered at the corners
of his mouth. Lung shot. (352–53)

While Clancy does depict the death of a human body here, that
process occurs not as a representation of the dying man's sensations but of the perception of the man who killed him, CIA analyst
Jack Ryan. Ryan analyzes the Soviet agent's death both in terms of

the cause ("lung shot") and as an attempt to speak. Blood, not words, emerges from the young agent's mouth, an emission matched by Ryan's reaction to the killing:

> He dropped on all fours and threw up violently, his vomit spilling through the grates onto the lower deck ten feet below. For a whole minute his stomach heaved, well past the time he was dry. He had to spit several times to get the worst of the taste from his mouth before standing. (353)

Only Ryan's physical sensations receive the kind of treatment Clancy otherwise reserves for the destruction of military hardware. His reaction to killing portrays him as the "guilty agent"—not in the sense of an agent whose responsibility for the death of another should be condemned, but in the sense of an agent whose sense of guilt takes on an embodiment as vivid as that of the death of the man he killed. Ryan's "heaving stomach" expels the human pain that the melding of man with machine in high-tech warfare cannot entirely subsume.

As a last resort, Clancy removes that pain from view by expelling the bodies in pain from his plot. This metatextual disappearance follows the disappearance of the *Red October* within the realm of the story. Because the U.S. Navy must return the *Red October* to the Soviet Union if the Soviets discover the capture, Admiral Greer, Ryan's boss at the CIA, and consultant Skip Tyler discuss the clandestine options for keeping the sub:

> "Next you'll ask if we should arrange for the crew to disappear."
> "The thought had occurred to me," Tyler said.
> "It's occurred to us, too. But we won't. Murder a hundred men? Even if we wanted to, there's no way we could conceal it in this day and age. Hell, I doubt even the Soviets could. Besides that, this simply is not the sort of thing you do in peacetime. That's one difference between us and them." (183)

Although Tyler plans an ingenious and rather innocent sleight-of-hand to retain the *Red October*, the ethical distinction between the Soviet Union and the U.S., between "us and them," collapses in the final pages. As the ultimate battle for the *Red October* ensues, peacetime protocol prohibits the U.S. vessels from firing until fired upon. At the helm of a submarine for the first time, Ryan miraculously rams the *Red October* into the hostile Soviet sub and breaks her "watertight integrity" (457). When Ryan appears squeamish at leaving the entire crew presumed dead, Greer joins Deputy Director of Operations (DDO) Robert Ritter in dismissing any effort at rescue: "'It's a war, Jack,' Ritter said, more kindly than usual, "a real war. You did well, boy" (468). The definition of the encounter as "a real war" erases what Ryan might otherwise have had to consider as murder and the "hundred men" who served on the V. K. Konovalov disappear from the plot.

This contradiction in the depiction of the nobility of "our" mission as opposed to "theirs" not only bursts the "watertight integrity" of the Soviet sub, but also leaves a hole in the "integrity" of an otherwise airtight plot: the comforting words of the CIA directors give no indication of how the disappearance of a second submarine along with the Soviets' second star commander will be explained in the wake of the capture of the *Red October.* The persistent presence of the human body in the war machine can only be eliminated by a disappearing act that leaves a lacuna in Clancy's plot.

Deadly Writing

Where is the vast quantity of written material which must have been in the hands of those who made such a huge and sinister machine?

—*Nunca Más* (264)

In a localized counterpart to the Cold War, the Argentine armed forces waged the dirty war against alleged Marxist insurgents on their own soil. As the U.S. National Security Act prescribed mimicking the methods of International Communism, the Doctrine of National Security in Argentina authorized the adoption by the armed forces of the urban guerrilla tactics and procedures of their insurgents or "enemies" (Grecco and González 132). The derivation of the Doctrine of National Security from the U.S. National Security Act touches upon a deeper relationship between the Cold War and the dirty war. In 1983, Junta member General

Camps credits the U.S. and France as being the "main source of counterinsurgency training. [These countries] organized centers for teaching counterinsurgency techniques (especially in the U.S.) and sent out instructors, observers, and an enormous amount of literature" (qtd. in Sábato 443).

This training in technique coincided with training in ideology, as evidenced by General Camps' description of Argentina's place in the struggle against International Communism:

> We [the rulers of Argentina] have to look at this globally and strategically, since Argentina is merely one theater of operations in a global confrontation between Moscow and the United States. What the Soviet Union wants is not to destabilize Argentina but to destabilize the United States, and for this it needs the help of other governments in the region. (qtd. in Sábato 443)

General Camps places his own country on the periphery as the Superpowers' struggle for the center. This allows the military regime to interpret attacks against their own right-to-rule as foreign to Argentina's own national interest, while at the same time aligning domestic interests with those of the U.S.

The Doctrine of National Security partakes of the Cold War rhetoric but in waging the dirty war, the Argentine generals adopted a very different strategy of technological development in the context of the peripheral struggle of counterinsurgency. Coronel Francisco Cervo explains why technological advances in artillery and satellite surveillance did not apply in the dirty war:

> Even the internal organization of the Army had to change, now that Divisions that are important in traditional combat, like Artillery and tanks, don't work in this war. It was necessary to privilege the formation of individual combatants, of the men of the Infantry, the Division that took the forefront in the majority of actions. Furthermore, the circumstance of having to operate in big cities, among a lot of civilians, where innocent people sometimes fell under the bullets, where it was nearly impossible to identify precisely who was the enemy, provoked confusion among the troops that translated into psychological effects. (Grecco and González 134; my translation)

Military officers returned frequently to the dilemma of discovering the enemy among countrymen and women; one officer corrected a U.S. military adviser, asserting that the search was not like "finding a needle in a hay stack" but like finding "[a particular piece of] hay in a hay stack" (Grecco and González 133). The military needed to develop a method to determine not so much what the enemy was doing, but who among the general populace that enemy was.

Rather than resorting to the high-tech surveillance tools used to monitor Soviet military activities, the Argentine military undertook to separate the insurgent from the citizen by taking prisoners and making them talk. Aldo Rico, former leader of the First Corps of Special Services and Commando Company during the dictatorship, contends that counterinsurgency requires the gathering of intelligence not just by human beings but directly from human beings, without consideration for constitutional or human rights:

> It is necessary to make the prisoner talk one way or another. This is the issue that must be confronted. The war of subversion is a special kind of war. There are no ethics. The issue is that either I permit guerrillas to take refuge in their constitutional rights or I obtain information rapidly in order to avoid a greater harm. (Grecco and González 138; my translation)

For military strategists, the dirty war authorized a substitution of "ethics" by a technique of rapid information retrieval: the technology of interrogation.

Reliance on interrogation forms the cornerstone of intelligence collection in the counterinsurgency struggle worldwide. At the 10-year meeting of the Consortium for the Study of Intelligence to devise the "Intelligence Requirements of the 1980s" for the U.S., speakers Schlomo Gazit and Michael Handel, members of the Israeli intelligence service, outlined the methods most appropriate in combating insurgency. The speakers rank "collection sources on terrorist organizations," dismissing methods such as open sources (unclassified material, such as newspapers, from which the majority of intelligence is gathered), aerial photography, and the interception of communications as inappropriate to insurgent organizations. Rather the speakers highlight the need for the collection of "technical intelligence" regarding the kind and location of weapons used by these organizations. In meeting that need, "the most important source of information on terrorist activities is what is normally referred to as human intelligence (HUMINT)." Of the three methods of HUMINT—recruiting agents, planting recruits, and interrogation—the speakers proclaim the third most effective:

> (c) The "cheapest" and easiest source of information available is an immediate, thorough, and systematic interrogation of a captured terrorist. In such cases, there is always a race against time between the capacity to gain an immediate advantage from the information obtained by interrogation and the precautionary measures taken by the terrorist organization immediately receiving the news that one of its members has been captured. An obvious conclusion is, of course, to delay as long as possible the publication of the capture or detention of a terrorist member. (137)

The emphasis on timing, linked here to a need to keep hidden the capture of a person to be interrogated, takes on particular significance in the Argentine refinement of the technology of interrogation as "disappearance."

U.S. intelligence expert Robert Chapman considers Gazit and Handel's talk "a much-needed text on the insurgent's tactical use of terror, and it should become, I believe, a reference work for all military and all intelligence organizations in this country." Like most of the representatives of the U.S. intelligence community at the Consortium, Chapman criticizes the constitutional constraints on effective interrogation methods. Chapman reviews counterinsurgency struggles around the world, attributing to Uruguay the only total defeat of an insurgency movement, because "the primary weapon was intelligence obtained through interrogation." Chapman goes on to lament the discontinuation of "counterinsurgency assistance" to these countries by the U.S. at the time of the conference. Throughout the 1980s, however, the Republican administrations undid, covertly and overtly, most of the restrictions on this assistance imposed by the Carter administration. Chapman's mention of Uruguay is significant both because of the documentation of U.S. assistance in that "successful" counterinsurgency struggle and because of the close working relationship between the repressive military apparatus of Uruguay and that of neighboring Argentina (Gazit and Handel 143).

Manuel Hevia, a Cuban exile working for the U.S. Public Safety Mission (police assistance) in Montevideo, Uruguay, describes his education under U.S. instructor Daniel Mitrione, in what the CONADEP Report terms a "diabolical technology" (3)—torture as a method of interrogation:

> He used to say, "Precise pain in the precise place at the precise time. You must be careful. You should avoid excesses." Another phrase of his, "Remember that the death of the prisoner constitutes the failure of the technician." Because he considered himself a technician. (Poelchau 67)

Supported by the U.S. government and often under the direction of operatives in the CIA, police assistance programs based both in the target countries and within U.S. borders have disseminated systematic, uniform techniques of torture throughout the world. Despite the crucial ethical reversals and release of individuals effected by international human rights groups such as Amnesty International, the ideology of counterinsurgency continues to legitimate torture and other forms of terror in the struggle toward progressively more centralized control of material resources throughout the world.

Nunca Más

The Report from the National Commission on the Disappeared (CONADEP) identifies this systematization across the Argentine expanse:

> From the huge amount of documentation we have gathered, it can be seen that these human rights were violated not in a haphazard fashion, but systematically, according to a similar pattern, with identical kidnappings and tortures taking place throughout the country. (3)

The 450-page report documents minutely this systematic repression, relaying the testimony of survivors, recreating the Secret Detention Centers, recounting the acts of resistance and compliance by various social organizations domestically and internationally, and providing a detailed demography of disappearance.

In contrast to the efforts by Clancy's novel to obscure the pain inflicted in the name of promoting U.S. democracy around the world, it is tempting, perhaps imperative, to applaud CONADEP's efforts to expose the torture practiced in the name of protecting Argentine democracy. At the same time, it is important to keep in mind the limits to the effectiveness of exposure as an epistemological enterprise. Both *The Hunt for Red October* and *Nunca Más* rely upon the Enlightenment assumption that knowledge is power. From opposed global standpoints, each work emphasizes human consciousness as a check against technological terror. Where Clancy's fantasy presents intelligence as the instrument that controls and justifies Superpower violence, CONADEP's denunciation depends upon the premise that making state terror public knowledge will, by itself, bring that violence to an end.

Despite the performative intent of the document's title, "Never Again," the transition to democracy in Argentina has suffered from the concurrent transition to privatization and the "free" market that has institutionalized a permanent economic "crisis" and swift repression of protest. Many of the perpetrators and directors of the terror under the fallen regime have either never been convicted or were released by the general amnesty granted by the administration of President Carlos Menem. Many currently hold positions of political power. The belief that making state terror visible will make it end ignores the contradiction between the life-affirming legitimation of the modern nation and the life-threatening disciplinary system of the postmodern state.

The horrifying material presented under the heading of "Torture" in the first section of *Nunca Más* makes that contradiction most evident. The relentless recitation of incident upon incident of torture has a numbing effect of horror directly opposed to the wonder excited by Clancy's catalogue of technologies of surveillance. The ironic naming of one method of torture referred to in the testimony printed here indicates the distance between the technologies portrayed by Clancy and those portrayed by CONADEP: the "submarine." The following fragments, taken from sep-

arate testimony by survivors of disappearance, relate the procedure:

> Another method was to tie us to a board and put a container
> full of water at one end. The victim's head would be sub-
> merged in it and they wouldn't pull him out until he let out
> the last bubble of air; as soon as he took a mouthful of air they
> submerged him again. (43)

> I tried to kill myself by drinking foul water in the tub which
> was meant for another kind of torture called *submarino*, but I
> did not succeed. (39)

> They tied me up and laid me down on something made of
> metal, they hit me and put me head-first in a container of wa-
> ter until I was drowning. (51)

> He was also subjected to the *submarino*, in a 200-liter tub. While
> he was in it they banged on the sides of the tub and applied
> electricity. (35)

Unlike the monopulse radars and towed acoustic arrays found in
Clancy's submarines, the submarine as method of interrogation
does not extend the senses but overwhelms them. The underwater
submersion cuts off oxygen until the final fatal moment and leaves
the ears with a long-lasting ringing. The method occurs in both
"wet" and "dry" forms; in the dry forms, the interrogators sub-
merge the victims in dry materials, such as human feces. What
"technicians" such as Mitrione might term the "precision" of the
method lies in pinpointing the amount of time the victim can sustain life underwater. Theoretically, when used as a method for
gathering intelligence, precise timing will coincide with questioning of the victim. The method lacks a certain technological so-
phistication, however, as the area of application is restricted to the
victim's head and the method of immersion remains the same despite variations in material. Perhaps for this reason, the "submarine," although mentioned many times by those testifying before
CONADEP, appears less often than methods involving electric
shock.

Believed by some commentators to have developed from the availability of military telephones for the application of electric shock in the field, the use of electricity in interrogation takes many forms. The testimony of one woman reveals an application similar to the one to which many attribute the method's origin: the use of "an instrument of torture known as the 'telephone' (an electric prod applied simultaneously to the ears and teeth)" (28–29). The torturers applied electric shock to all the surfaces of the body, particularly to the genitals and the teeth, as well as to the inside of the body, as in the case in which the victim was forced to swallow a string of electrodes that then "seemed like a thousand crystals were shattering, splintering inside one and moving through the body, cutting everywhere" (30). The instruments for applying shock take a number of different forms, from the "'helmet of death' (a horrendous device full of electrodes placed over the head), which doesn't even allow you to say no" (32) to a device called "the machine," a "kind of underpants . . . which had several electric terminals in them. When they were connected, the victim received electric current in several places at once" (36). "The machine" as described here maximizes the potential for subjugation of the subject under interrogation; the "master" of the machine has no sensory interaction, making "the machine" on the "technician's" end an instrument but not a prosthetic device. In contrast, "the machine" impacts the victims' senses absolutely, making prostheses too weak a word for the fusion of electrode and flesh.

Where Clancy's submarine collects intelligence by extending human senses outward through the ocean, the torturer's submarine as reported by CONADEP immerses the victim, overwhelming the senses. Rather than extending outward toward the atmosphere, the technology catalogued in *Nunca Más* moves along the surfaces and into the orifices of the victims' bodies, purportedly in an effort to extract intelligence from the flesh.

Virilio takes the electroshock torture of individuals as an emblem of "the active prostheses of intelligence" characteristic of the current direction of technological development in general, contending that the substitution of electronics for the senses enacts a "transparency" or disappearance of individual consciousness on the level of social experience:

The confession by way of the political-military interrogation, extorted from the suspect by electro-shock torture, is important also as a social or rather technico-social experience, a new effort towards transparency. (Virilio 48–49)

Virilio creates a slippage here between the extension of the senses in the technology of surveillance at the atmospheric level and what we might consider the intensification of certain senses produced by the technology of torture on the level of the human body. Sensation mediates between the experience of human bodies and consciousness, organizing that experience as intelligence. Even the use of prosthetic intelligence complicates sensory mediation, but does not replace it. Unlike the sonar or computer technician who can access information through senses not otherwise available using human capacity alone, the technician of torture can presently only intensify human sensation. While advanced instruments of torture may allow for control over the timing, intensity, and location of pain on the victims' bodies, the technician cannot guarantee that pain will access directly the victims' consciousness, allowing for no direct control over the extraction of any information the victim might possess.

The Report blames this endemic imprecision for the abduction of random citizens:

[b]ecause of these indiscriminate methods, not only members of armed groups but also their relatives, friends, colleagues at work or school, political party activists, priests and laymen committed to the problems of the poor, student activists, trade unionists, neighborhood leaders and—in a remarkably high number of cases—people with no kind of trade union or political activity at all, were all rounded up and tortured. It was enough to appear in somebody's address book to become a target for the notorious 'task forces.' (60–61)

The testimony presented in the Report supports this assertion. One man testifies to his abduction and extensive torture after a casual acquaintance mentioned his name while under torture herself. She "cracked, tried to save herself, or was driven to the edge of insanity and began to invent the most far-fetched things. She

sent over fifty people to prison" (32). Control over the victims' bodies in no way allows the technicians control over the intelligence
contained or not contained in the victims' consciousness. By high-
lighting the horror resulting from the "indiscriminate" nature of
the military's methods, CONADEP conveyed the message that Every Body could become a Tortured Body at the mercy of the military machine.

As portrayed here, the systematic repression practiced by the
military regime puts Every Body at risk for what Elaine Scarry calls
"world dissolution" or the "obliteration of the contents of consciousness" (54). Testimony to the overwhelming of consciousness
by the intensity of sensation recurs frequently in *Nunca Más*, often
figured as a loss of a "sense of time":

> If when I was set free someone had asked me: did they torture
> you a lot? I would have replied: Yes, for the whole of the three
> months . . . If I were asked that same question today, I would
> say that I've now lived through seven years of torture. (20)

> I was in that position, literally hanging at a distance of about
> 30 centimeters from the floor, for a period of time which is not
> possible to determine in hours, only in terms of pain. Because
> of the great suffering induced by this form of torture, one loses
> all track of time. (39)

> As I continued to answer in the negative, they increased the
> frequency, duration, and intensity of the discharges, which
> were always to the head. I lost track of time, although several
> hours seemed to have gone by. (40)

> [They] hung me by the throat, until I passed out. I began to
> lose track of time and my memories became confused, so that
> I can't be sure of the order of events, but I'm almost certain
> that they took a photo of me and then used the electric prod
> on me on the floor. (42)

> As she had those convulsions and her body writhed about,
> they would get more annoyed. The doctor would come and
> examine her, but time went by, until she lost all track of it. (48)

The intensification of sensation leads to a loss of the ability to organize sense; rather than becoming "transparent" as Virilio suggests, consciousness assaulted by electric shock retreats. The HUMINT technician cannot look through the tortured body to read the intelligence contained in the victim's consciousness, as the PHOTINT technician can read the shifting positions of enemy formations in a photograph taken by satellite. As Clancy celebrates the heightening of human consciousness through sensory prostheses, CONADEP attempts to make visible the consciousness disappeared by torture in interrogation, a disappearance made redundant by the disappearance of opaque bodies.

According to survivors, the retreat of consciousness during torture is counterbalanced by a heightening of the senses in between acts of interrogation. Maintained blindfolded or under "the hood" in order to keep the prisoners from identifying their captors or place of captivity, survivors recount attempts to divine their surroundings using other senses: from ambient sounds, from shifts in direction they feel when transported from one location to another, and from the architectural space through which they moved in captivity. One man recounts his efforts in this respect:

> Also the sounds of movements (together with my previous idea about the route we had taken) gradually led me to believe that the detention center must be police premises. Piecing together the clues (there was also a police station close by, and a school—I heard girls singing—and a church, from the sound of the bells) it appeared that the place was the detective squad headquarters in San Justo. (87)

The analytic piecing together of atmospheric clues crudely approximates the puzzling out of the *Red October's* location with technologized sense performed by Clancy's analyst Jack Ryan and radar reader Jones. The mundane clues pack none of the technothrills afforded by the aerial photography and oceanic algorithms of *The Hunt for Red October*, but the stake in a personal narrative heightens the sense of urgency in a hunt for self.

CONADEP attempts to "piece together the clues" on a magnified scale, drawing together the testimony of survivors, with that of employees of the military regime, and of witnesses to abductions and to the workings of the secret detention centers that housed the victims. CONADEP drew intelligence from the bodies of the survivors not through torture but through re-member-ing their experience, traveling with them to suspected secret detention centers where the survivors, often in blindfolds, invoked from their bodies memories of the spaces of their captivity. The Report devotes 31 pages to "Abduction" and "Torture" and the bulk of the book, 158 pages, to a recreation of the location and structure of specific secret detention centers. Where Clancy superimposed a shifting grid of time and place to create the illusion of the movement of human consciousness in pursuit of the *Red October,* CONADEP departs from the bodies described in the opening section of "Torture" to recreate in detail the times and places that slipped away from the consciousness of the people disappeared.

Knowing North and South

When I worked briefly on a military intelligence base in Europe—flipping hamburgers for a clientele whose mission, identity, and condiment choice I can neither confirm nor deny—the most chilling moment of a chilly summer came while I watched a human interest story on the Armed Forces Network that announced a name switch in U.S. military war games from Teams West and East to Teams North and South. Coincidentally, perhaps, this realignment of the games took place shortly before the military stance taken by the U.S. against Iraq after the invasion of Kuwait. *The Hunt for Red October* and *Nunca Más* seem to me anticipatory moments on the axis of this realignment, describing a relationship whose apotheosis in the Gulf War Robert Stam has theorized as a split between first world spectatorship and third world suffering: "while one side lived the war as a simulacral video-war or miniseries, with only minimal suffering, the other lived it as a real war replete with death, dismemberment, and disease" (112).

The North and South readings of history oppose war as techno-thrill to war as techno-terror. *The Hunt for Red October* engages readers as spectators who watch as the unlikely omnipotence of family man and analyst-turned-operative Jack Ryan makes visible the hidden omnipresence of the CIA as the superpower agent of history. *Nunca Más* engages readers' vigilant watch, as the unbelievable first-person accounts of hidden torture at once mark the military government as guilty agents and make imperative relentless guard against the repetition of history.

The rendering *in writing* of the spectacle of the techno- and the tortured-body anchors the postmodern display of power etched on these bodies within an anachronistic Enlightenment narrative of progress. Extension of the senses through postmodern weaponry licenses Clancy to displace the physical suffering exacted by the struggle for control over late capital onto a myth of mastery over deadly technologies. The restoration of the senses dulled or disappeared by the military regimes allows CONADEP to reposition physical suffering in an ethical intervention that promises an end to the instruments of torture. The evolution of human consciousness proclaimed by each text marches meagerly across the North/South topos that stands in for the reconfiguration of social relations mapped by multinational capitalism. These texts sketch the imaginative limits of resistance to the relentless logic of late capitalism as, respectively, a fantasy of omnipotence and an impotent denunciation, whose urgent attempt and ultimate failure marks a necessary first step toward more powerful imaginings and more material transformations of bodies, senses, and machines.

Notes

For helpful suggestions on earlier drafts of this essay, I would like to thank the members of the Tech/Lit Collective at Duke University; the Penn State Cultural Studies Collective; and, especially, Cathy N. Davidson.

1. I borrow here from Paul Virilio's title. My application of the term is more specific than his.

2. I must confess I take great pleasure in reading Clancy. Pleasure is precisely not the point of *Nunca Más*.

3. On the market, see Jameson 260–78.

4. I use the masculine exclusive here deliberately. While my own experience confirms the possibility of pleasure in cross-gender identification within Clancy's plot, Clancy's construction makes that crossing necessary. Of the two women appearing as military or intelligence officers, one, "a female yeoman first class" (197), opens the Pentagon door for Skip Tyler once before the door closes on her character forever, and the other serves as the seductive snare for a double agent. A subplot supporting Ryan's position as Everyman has him as anxious to find a "Surfing Barbie" as a Christmas present for his daughter as he is to find the Red October, emphasizing the proper objects of desire for each gender in Clancy's rigidly heterosexual world. For further consideration of the conjunction of masculinity and "managerial heroism" in Clancy's novel *The Sum of All Fears*, see Jeffords.

Works Cited

Alden, John R. "The Cold War at 50 Fathoms." Rev. of *The Hunt for Red October*, by Tom Clancy. *Wall Street Journal* 22 Oct. 1984: 28.

Allison, David K. "U.S. Navy Research and Development." Smith 289–328.

Breckinridge, Scott D. *The CIA and the U.S. Intelligence System*. Boulder: Westview, 1986.

Doolittle, J. H., William B. Franke, Morris Hadley, and William D. Pauley. "Report of the Special Study Group [Doolittle Commission] on the Covert Activities of the Central Intelligence Agency, Sept. 30, 1954 [Excerpts]." Leary 143–45.

Foucault, Michel. *History of Sexuality: Volume I: An Introduction*. New York: Vintage, 1980.

Gazit, Schlomo, and Michael Handel. "Insurgency, Terrorism, and Intelligence." Godson 125–47.

Godson, Roy, ed. *Intelligence Requirements for the 1980s: Counterintelligence*. Washington: National Strategy Information Center; New Brunswick: Transaction, 1980.

Grecco, Jorge, and Gustavo González. *Argentina: el ejército que tenemos*. Buenos Aires: Sudamericana, 1990.

Haraway, Donna. "A Manifesto for Cyborgs: Science, Technology, and Socialist Feminism in the 1980s." *Socialist Review* 80.15.2 (1985): 65–108.

Jameson, Fredric. *Postmodernism; Or, the Cultural Logic of Late Capitalism*. Durham: Duke UP, 1991.

Jeffords, Susan. "The Patriot System or Managerial Heroism." *Cultures of United States Imperialism*. Ed. Amy Kaplan and Donald E. Pease. Durham: Duke UP, 1993.

Leary, William M. *Central Intelligence Agency: History and Documents*. Birmingham: University of Alabama P, 1984.

National Security Council. "National Security Directive 5412/1, December 28, 1955, on Covert Operations." Leary 146–49.

Poelchau, Warner, ed. *White Paper/White Wash: Interviews with Philip Agee on the CIA and El Salvador*. New York: Deep Cover, 1981.

Roland, Alex. "Technology and War: A Bibliographic Essay." Smith 347–80.

Sábato, Ernesto. *Nunca Más: The Report of the Argentine National Commission on the Disappeared*. Trans. Ronald Dworkin. New York: Farrar, in association with *Index on Censorship*, 1986.

Scarry, Elaine. *The Body in Pain: The Making and Unmaking of the World*. New York: Oxford UP, 1985.

Setlowe, Richard. Rev. of *The Hunt for Red October*, by Tom Clancy. *Los Angeles Times Book Review* 9 Dec. 1984: 2.

Smith, Merritt Roe, ed. *Military Enterprise and Technological Change: Perspectives on the American Experience*. Cambridge: MIT P, 1985.

Stam, Robert. "Mobilizing Fictions: The Gulf War, The Media, and the Recruitment of the Spectator." *Public Cultures* 4.2 (1992): 101–26.

Virilio, Paul. *The Aesthetics of Disappearance*. Trans. Phillip Beitchman. New York: Semiotext(e), 1991.

Literary History and the Problem of Oppositional Practice in Contemporary Poetry

David Kellogg

> Like everybody else at the time, he wrote a treatise on the sub-
> lime and the beautiful.
> —Bertrand Russell on Kant (706)

> I take it, in some sense, one looks abt for forbears, simply to
> find some kind of approbation for the immediate expenditure
> of time & energy. A sort of approval. That is, unbearable to be
> altogether outside.
> —Robert Creeley to Charles Olson
> (Olson and Creeley 2: 46–47)

Past and Present in Literary History

With the collapse of poetic Modernism as a coherent aesthetic and the uncertain status of the avant-garde in its wake, American poetry's much-discussed inward turn in the decades fol-lowing World War II participated in, and contributed to, a Roman-tic rewriting of literary history. This rewriting has had conse-

© 1996 by *Cultural Critique*. Winter 1995–96. 0882-4371/96/$5.00.

quences not limited to theory or the academy but also impacting current poetic practice. Much—perhaps most—criticism of contemporary American poetry still takes that poetry's Romantic origins for granted. Contemporary poetry does not always represent itself, nor is it always represented by others, as Romantic in aims, ambitions, modes of perception, or formal resources, but Romanticism remains, as John Koethe says, "the context in which [contemporary] poetry has to locate itself" (72). It is the historical current that poetry either rides or swims against.

Only recently has the academy begun to rediscover the varieties of poetry produced in the early part of this century, a poetry previously stabilized, and then left for dead, under the normative sign of Modernism. Ongoing works of historical recovery force a reconsideration of contemporary poetic practice as well, giving today's most difficult and challenging works contexts dramatically increasing their readability. But even as the heterogeneity and vitality of Modernist practice is reasserted, prevailing models of literary-historical change remain bound by developmental assumptions caught up in the very Romantic thinking otherwise challenged. In explicitly Romantic terms, one might say that, while the content of historical investigation for contemporary poetry is being radically rewritten, its form is still plagued by Romantic preconceptions; to adopt more contemporary language, its *vocabulary* has expanded, while its *syntax* resists change.

It is arguable that Romanticist assumptions are integral to historical thinking as such, forming one conceptual limit for historiography. I shall not address this larger issue, though it is an interesting, if probably unresolvable one. I shall concentrate, instead, on the especially strong link between historiographic models and Romantic assumptions in recent Anglo-American literary, and especially poetic, critical history. It results, at least in part, out of a critical transference that took place in this Romantic rewriting of literary history in the fifties, a transference critical-historical thought is still experiencing.

Characteristically, histories of poetry that lead to, or "explain," contemporary literary productions distinguish between a historical "origin" of a period and its literary-cultural manifestation. A second distinction, which reads a variety of literary projects as attempted reconciliations between subject and object, accompanies this first. These two splits implicate and support each other:

the literature/history binary bears marked correspondence to the subject/object division. This is not a particularly novel observation. Less obvious is the way these distinctions play into certain assumptions about the different jobs that a critic performs when addressing the contemporary and when addressing the historical; less obvious, in other words, is the link these two binaries have with the distinction between practice and theory. More fully articulating the relations among these distinctions demonstrates why, as has often been noted, it is so very difficult to extract one's own narrative from those being critiqued.

What follows, therefore, considers the problem of literary history and its roles in and for a contemporary American poetry whose historical embeddedness is rarely recognized. I seek to inscribe literary history in an understanding of the constraints and possibilities of current literary practice, extending one critic's suggestion that "literary history constitute[s] a system of discourse," and that "[t]his system imposes a definition of literature according to a given era and by virtue of a chain of redundant effects" to the social field of contemporary American poetry (Moisan 692). More specifically, I understand literary history to play an authorizing role in the contemporary economy of poetic value. My immediate focus is on the kinds of representation readily available to histories of modern poetry, especially representations of key transitional stages (Romantic to Modern, Modern to contemporary) as explanatory tools; however, this focus will eventually be broadened to implicate contemporary literary and educational institutions in a dynamic of literary history and contemporary poetics.[1]

In approaching this issue, I was first struck by the dearth of general historical studies of contemporary poetry. Most literary histories of modern poetry stop before the advent of any moment that might be called contemporary, rarely taking living writers into account. Critical works on contemporary poetry, on the other hand, most often take the form of collections, sometimes extended, of review-essays. What histories there are, such as Robert Pinsky's *The Situation of Poetry*, Robert von Hallberg's *American Poetry and Culture 1945–1980*, and James E. B. Breslin's *From Modern to Contemporary*, by their functional explanations of a present which is taken for granted, may commit themselves to teleological frameworks that could be critiqued on their own grounds.

I will return to historical accounts of contemporary poetry

later. First, however, I would like to look briefly at Jerome McGann's *Romantic Ideology* for its assumptions about the differences between the criticism of historical and contemporary works, and then consider Robert Langbaum's 1957 book *The Poetry of Experience*. I find significant continuities between Langbaum's presentation of historicity and various more current histories of modern poetry; I also question the abiding separation of literary history and an ongoing poetic practice. So, despite appearances, this essay is indeed "about" contemporary American poetry, in the sense that it attempts to clear a space in which it is possible to rethink that poetry's relation to history.

The link between the commitment to a literary tradition and a certain conservatism remains a recurrent theme in twentieth-century American poetics. Those poets who write in traditional verse forms, or who invite a return to previous concepts of the proper role of the poet in society, must, so the argument goes, perceive a continuity between the present and the past. Avant-garde poetics, on the other hand, emphasizes breakage and rupture, has no use for the past, and is intentionally amnesiac. The remarkable intensity of recent debates in literary journals between and about the two critical poles of American poetry, the New Formalism and "Language" poetry, can be understood when the debates are seen as struggles, not merely between two forms of poetic stylization, but over the role of history in contemporary American cultural practice. However, the issues are surely more complicated than that, when the New Formalism loudly proclaims its newness, when avant-garde poets as well as more traditional poets construct complex poetic ancestries, when radical stylistic gestures have been connected so often in recent history to far-right political extremism, and when American avant-garde poetry can itself be seen to form a tradition.[2]

Jerome J. McGann writes about both historical and contemporary literary productions, but his aim in each case is markedly different.[3] For instance, in his introduction to *The Romantic Ideology*, a book emphatically *not* focused on the contemporary but rather on what Clifford Siskin calls "the Romantic nature of criticism written about the Romantics" (5), McGann carefully maps out the road not taken, noting that "[w]ere this book concerned with contemporary literary products (say, the poems of James Merrill) its procedures would be quite different" (2) from one that examines, as his does, already distant historical texts.[4] McGann argues for an "essential difference" separating "the journalistic and polemical criticism whose focus is the present from the scholarly and historical criticism which operates in the present only by facing (and defining) the past" (2–3). Though he does not say so explicitly, McGann indicates that the difference is one of value: "contemporary" works of literature (and by implication, other forms of cultural production) are expected to be evaluated; "historical" works, on the other hand, must be described with the question of value suspended "to arrest [the] process of reification" accompanying the institutional transmission of past texts (3). Thus conceived, McGann's own work on Romantic ideology is just one of "two distinct types of criticism which ought not to be confused in practice" (3); distinguishing these types in practice is an act of liberation, while conflating them perpetuates, for McGann, "the crippling illusion that such a past [as represented in criticism] establishes the limits, conceptual and practical, of our present and our future" (3).

McGann, then, wants past works to be studied "in the full range of their pastness" for political, among other, considerations (2). Emphasizing the difference of the past frees the present from that past's shadow, and paradoxically recovers value (albeit a "different" one) for past works: their value is to remain where they are:

> The works of Romantic art, like the works of any historical moment, "transcend" their particular socio-historical position only because they are completely incorporated to that position, only because they have localized themselves. In this fact we observe that paradox fundamental to all works of art which is best resolved through an historical method of criticism: that such works transcend their age and speak to alien cultures because they are so completely true to themselves, because they are time and place specific, because they are—from our point of view—*different*. (2)

The distinction between past and present here asserted brings new meaning to other distinctions that have histories almost as long and complex as that of literary theory itself. While McGann falls clearly on the side of breakage rather than continuity, of separation rather than tradition, the separation of history and poetic practice is a long-standing principle of poetic theory, as is the separation of internal and evaluative from external or social/historical methods of approach. The concept of poetry as imitation has long been both a means for the separation of poetry and history and a vehicle for history's reinscription into poetry. This concept and its implications have taken different forms, however, in different historical and institutional contexts, as literary criticism and literary practice variously define their own relations to, and reflections of, historical and social pressures.

One could ask whether individual projects operating under these assumptions succeed—McGann's concept of "grace under pressure," for instance, by which he recovers value in past works, certainly owes as much to an aesthetic ideology as to McGann's self-evident humanism (2). The distinction between internal and external methods of approach can be challenged pragmatically, as well, by attempting to find avenues for the introduction of sociological methods into the analysis of contemporary culture (the focus of much of the postmodernist debate).[5] From another perspective, it is possible to question the very availability of vocabularies and procedures distant enough from "literature" not to be implicated already in its construction. Tony Bennett has persuasively argued that such vocabularies and procedures—those capable of describing literature yet independent of it—do not as yet exist and, thus, that the possibility of describing literature from "outside" is severely limited (6). He further makes the point that most literary histories, in addition to being hamstrung by definitions of and procedures for analyzing literature that are already aestheticized, find themselves caught in a dyad of literature and history "by displacing the [Marxist] metaphorics of base and superstructure on to the literature/history couplet" (45) and granting one term primacy over the other.

In other words, McGann might be seen as aestheticizing literature in order to give it a humanizing power over an unstable, because textualized, view of history. A complementary approach might find, in history, a stabilizing force in an otherwise renegade and uncontrollable process of literary interpretation.[6] In either case, one element of the dyad is granted explanatory power, as Bennett suggests, by being separated ontologically from the other, more fully textualized element (46–52). McGann would surely

protest my connection of their work to such a view, but this absolute division between historical and contemporary works, and between correspondingly different possibilities for conceptualization,
is enmeshed in precisely this logic. Literature and history, by such
a move, are assigned to different categories of Being, and, thus,
literary history, a discipline that might attack problems common
to them, becomes a literary historiography concerned solely with
unifying a dyad which should never have been created in the first
place, and to the terms of which most forms of attempted reconciliation still, at some level, subscribe.

Returning to the separation of past and present that McGann
and many others vigorously assert, we can see such separation—
between literature as history and literature as practice—as implicit
in the institutional project of literary history. However, it seems to
me inescapable that, as they are read in, modified by, and absorbed
into later contexts, works of the literary-historical project help constitute the field of the literary, and thus the (historical) project par-
ticipates in the shaping and determination of the (contemporary)
practice and production of literature. Contemporary literary productions, including poetic ones, establish themselves—gaining
meaning, value, and significance for contemporary audiences—by
their entrance into a field that literary history has already helped
to determine. Even if in a largely differential sense, contemporary
poetry and poetics must relate to historical poetries for legitimacy
and authority; the lines between poetry and history are nowhere
secure.

To write any literary history that assumes or implies an ontological or historically invariant definition of the literary is necessarily to circumscribe the possibilities for poetic action in the present
while writing about the past. Literary histories must, however, inevitably engage in these struggles—struggles not merely confined
to the relations of past literary practice to past representations of
power or history or some such abstraction, nor indeed limited only
to the effect of past on present critical representation. In fact, literary history may be seen as an agent in struggles over present
literary practice even—perhaps especially—when it declares otherwise.

If my argument thus far is accepted, the interpretive frames
of literary history may be seen to enter the field of contemporary

literary practice along with "poetic" works themselves. If not obviated, then, the distinction between history and practice is here developed differently, and the problem of interpretation is replaced by the problem of strategy. Tony Bennett extends an analogous and, I think, suggestive framework in *Outside Literature:*

> [T]he question to be posed in relation to literary texts is not how to *understand* them but what to *do* with them—that is, how to modify their forms of deployment within contemporary social relations. And this requires a literary history that will seek not to distil the meaning of literary texts by referring them to a history which is conceived as providing an interpretive key to their meaning. . . . It suggests a literary history that is less concerned with the hermeneutic interlacing of past and present within an overarching horizon of meaning than with establishing the discontinuities and differences which have characterised the forms of deployment and uses of literary texts in different historical circumstances. (68)

Bennett's formulation of history denies both traditional humanist or Marxist terms of explanation and totality—what I would call history as describable trajectory (a metaphor to which I will return). It bears considerable relation to McGann's methodological statements on the pastness of the past, though it is, I think, more skeptical about the possibilities for historical explanation. To see use rather than understanding as the purpose of reading is to start "severing the aesthetic connection," in Bennett's phrase (117); additionally, such a perspective recognizes the political and institutional forces particular readings have always served.

Literary history, then, is never merely historical: to define literature at one point is indeed to help describe the limits of its possible future. If this can be claimed generally, it holds even more for poetry, which is almost always defined formally rather than sociologically, and which currently has far closer relations to the aesthetic ideology than does the novel, not to mention most forms of popular culture.[7] Further, contemporary reading and teaching practices mean that poetry will be encountered almost entirely within the confines of the school, and there it will be viewed largely as history—something people used to do. It would be neither desirable nor possible to fix the formation of the aesthetic in a certain point of origin; however, it seems clear that poetry is, among literary forms, currently a major focal point for a fairly direct articulation of aesthetic ideology. One does not need to posit a hierarchy of forms, or approve of the situation, to recognize that in practice poetry is seen as a more aestheticized, and thus less obviously socialized, genre than, for instance, the novel. "Severing the aesthetic connection" in the case of poetry, then, might have significant effects in more obviously (I do not say more actually) socially determined forms of cultural production, as well as in the practice of poetry itself.

It may be objected that since poetry has less direct social force than the novel or film, tracing its deployment is nearly impossible—an objection I grant. But with this caveat: "the situation of poetry" is still purely social and should not be defined in aesthetic terms, even if the resulting description risks acquiring the messiness and shifting boundaries of social life itself. Examples are cited constantly and enviously in North American poetry journals, as Hank Lazer notes, of poets—Latin American, Irish, Eastern European, African—whose impact is directly political (125).[8] One could also find examples in the United States, especially among feminist, African-American, Native American, Hispanic-American, and gay and lesbian communities, as well as alternative local poetry scenes all over the United States, in such cities as San Francisco, Washington, D.C., New York, and Chicago, with their nightclub "poetry slams." The presence of such locally effective poetry communities suggests that the problem of social effectivity in poetry lies not with "poetry" as such nor with individual poets, but with the institutions that maintain and disseminate poetry—that is, with de facto definitions of poetry found in education, anthologies, patronage systems public and private, little magazines, M.F.A. programs, and elsewhere. And literary history is implicated in all these institutions.

Oppositional poetics in our time, therefore, must look both forward and backward, both toward the diverse and contentious arenas of contemporary poetic production and toward the institutions and rhetorics that seek to define and delimit such practice. Such poetics takes multiple shapes in alternative histories, anthologies, magazines, writing programs, affiliations, and self-definitions, as well as the promotion of certain forms of writing over others.

All of these forms of opposition exist in practice, yet little has changed in the most authorized representations of poetry and its histories. Indeed, Modernism itself has been subsumed into a rather dreary Romantic aesthetic, the effect (not to say the point) of which is to cripple the social and historical possibilities of poetry. Dismantling this aesthetic is partly a problem of reading—of describing a certain event in literary history or historiography in order to destabilize those representations that have come down to us. To this project, McGann's work is a welcome contribution. However, its aims and distinctions must be expanded.

Some scholarly works on contemporary poetry seek explicitly to define it within rhetorical, epistemological, or social traditions, and such works, which clearly seek to place contemporary work in an exhaustive historical framework, also clearly establish monological hierarchies of form and achievement.[9] My contention here, on the other hand, is that even literary-historical works unconcerned with contemporary poetry may participate in establishing the space in which contemporary poetry arises, by their partial constitution of the available cultural memory. The hotly debated issue of the canon and its formation must enter my argument at this point, though I have little interest in adding to the noise level of the debate. I would merely propose that, in the complex feedback loop between literary history and contemporary poetic production, the canon operates as an unstable reference point, limiting but not determining the interplay of all the elements that go into the making of the poem. Or as Cary Nelson rather more dramatically puts it, "canon formation and writing literary history . . . feed into each other and become conservative, even reactionary, political forces" (*Repression and Recovery* 39).[10] To pretend that such limiting representations do not exist or to cordon off the literary past from the literary present, as Jerome McGann allows, is to uphold a revised separation of literature from history—the very thing McGann claims not to do. When the contemporary practice and production of literature are admitted into the historiographic model, that model becomes complex indeed, and the traditional form of literary history as a "celebratory chronological staging of the canon," in Nelson's words, is more difficult to sustain (53). The dismantling of reductive histories requires reading them in order to read *through* them, to a different literary present as much as to a different past.

The Shape of Subjectivist History: Robert Langbaum

The year 1957 was a good one for literary study. The New Criticism had confirmed the hegemony it gained after the war, and the major principles of reading were being refined rather than generally questioned. It was expanding its territory, as well; that year Ian Watt's monumental *The Rise of the Novel* not only applied New Critical principles to the relatively neglected genre of the novel, but applied them in the service of *history.* By the late 1950s, in fact, New Criticism had so consolidated its victories on the critical battlefield that history, previously a marginalized area of its project, became a significant subject for inquiry. Histories of literary criticism that propose sharp divisions between formal and historical approaches during this period display by this same formal, rather than historical, division the inroads New Criticism has made into literary history. In fact, "criticism" and "history" were complexly intertwined: historical criticism was largely absorbed in, but not eliminated by, its putative enemy in (New Critical and Chicago school) formalism.[11] Concurrent with this shift was a revaluation of a Romanticism vilified by earlier New Critics and proponents of modernism. Cleanth Brooks' *The Well Wrought Urn* was only the first (1947) in a series of postwar attempts to develop an approach to poetry in a New Critical framework that would be inclusive of Romanticism. Though hardly a New Critical work, Northrop Frye's *Anatomy of Criticism,* also published in 1957, may be seen as a product of these two shifts, as may Robert Langbaum's *The Poetry of Experience: The Dramatic Monologue in Modern Literary Tradition.*

Reading *The Poetry of Experience* in the 1990s is a strange experience, a combination of amused hindsight and sometimes shocked recognition. For though its ideological implications have surfaced with time and the collapse of a common vocabulary, many of its operative procedures still obtain. Here Langbaum defines the central concerns of the poetry he examines: "That essential idea is, I would suggest, the doctrine of experience—the doctrine that the imaginative apprehension gained through immediate experience is primary and certain, whereas the analytic reflection that follows is secondary and problematical" (35). A quarter of a century later (1983), M. L. Rosenthal and Sally M. Gall similarly see their own *critical* project on the modern poetic sequence in this light, originating out of direct experience of the poem as against the "analytic reflection" dismissed by Langbaum: "In short, what is called for is a critical method and theory congruent with and reflexive from poetic practice—a poet's poetics" (5). And Albert Gelpi, in *A Coherent Splendor* (1987), a collection of readings that doubles, to an extent, as a history of Modernist poetics, uses analogous language when defending the purity of his project against social and ideological criticism:

> The [American modernist] poets discussed in these pages are all individualists, all white, educated, bourgeois, all but a couple of them male. My commentary will call attention, from time to time, to the ways in which elitist, individualist assumptions about gender, race, and class limit and even distort the work under discussion. But I shall be more concerned with what the poetry *does* rather than with what it does not do—in part because the most illuminating criticism, in my view, arises and develops from the inside (that is, from inside the work and from inside the critic) and in part because this poetry, whatever its distortions and omissions, addresses issues critical to the psychological and moral life of those who wrote it and those who read it. (6)

There is much to consider in a comparison of these passages. Most interesting to me are (1) that what Langbaum calls a *doctrine* Rosenthal/Gall and Gelpi seem to see as merely the natural and obvious, if difficult to realize, goal and (2) that what Langbaum discovers in the *poetry* has filtered down to become, by the 1980s, a major principle of the historical *criticism* of this poetry. (It should also be clear from the context that Gelpi's conception of what poetry *does* is a far cry from Bennett's focus on the *use* of literary texts in specific social and institutional instances.)

To take another instance, here is Langbaum on the underlying causes of the development of Modernist poetry:

> Whatever the difference between the literary movements of the nineteenth and twentieth centuries, they are connected by their view of the world as meaningless, [and] by their response to the same wilderness. That wilderness is the legacy of the Enlightenment . . . bequeathing a world in which fact is measurable quantity whose value is man-made and illusory. Such a world offers no objective verification for just the perceptions

by which men live, perceptions of beauty, goodness and
spirit. (11)

Now Rosenthal and Gall:

> The modern sequence goes many-sidedly into who and where
> we are *subjectively:* it springs from the same pressures on sensi-
> bility that have caused our poets' experiments with shorter
> forms. It, too, is a response to the lyrical possibilities of lan-
> guage opened up by those pressures in times of cultural and
> psychological crisis, when all past certainties have many times
> been thrown chaotically into question. (3)

And now Gelpi:

> For all its personal idiosyncracies [*sic*] and elitist biases, then,
> Modernist poetry . . . constitutes an often valiant, sometimes
> last-ditch effort to validate poetry as a psychological and moral
> activity in an increasingly insane and amoral world. (7)

Clearly, some common views of history are at work here. All three
narratives locate an invisible catastrophe at some point in the eighteenth century—invisible in the sense of immaterial, though Langbaum identifies it more precisely than the others: "The thing
which happened was . . . Newton, Locke and the Enlightenment"
(38).

That *The Poetry of Experience* locates the self-blinding split between subject and object in what is called the Enlightenment
should come as no surprise. Langbaum's particular reading of history since that "event" performs similar rhetorical reversals in several other cases; his operative categories—experience, the particular, the individual voice and its history—are utterly emptied, and
the social possibilities of a focus on quotidian experience, supposedly the strength of the poetry he examines, excluded from consideration:

> It is at the point where the life established by the particular
> perspective becomes so strong a surge as to lose its form, that
> the speaker reaches his apotheosis of perception and self-
> perception, becoming more himself than ever only to dissolve

his own particularity and the particularity of what he sees in
the general stream of being. (209)

By such reversals, Langbaum can have his experience and eat it
too. As for meaning, "[u]ltimately, of course, the same thing is
learned in all dramatic monologues. . . . They all mean the same
thing—the greatest possible surge of life" (208). This is the case in
spite of the "genius of the dramatic monologue, the thing to be
worked for," what Langbaum calls its "disequilibrium," that effect
when each element of the poem is thrown "on its own to be judged
intrinsically; while *their meaning,* their relation to each other, *remains in question*" (188; emphasis added).

Earlier in his argument Langbaum has defined the "meaning" of the dramatic monologue as "character in its unformulated
being, in all its particularity"—that is, before its mediation in language (181). But if the particulars of character are unmediated,
they cannot mean anything, as Langbaum realizes, and certainly
cannot be apprehended in their prelinguistic particularity. For all
the exuberance of Langbaum's "general stream of being" rhetoric,
his presentation takes on an elegiac tone, as with the French exis-
tentialists he sometimes resembles—after all, Langbaum is left neither with the particulars that make up characters, nor even with
particular characters themselves, but merely with the *idea* of character coupled with the *idea* of nonmediation and direct experience—pure subjectivity.

He attempts to avoid this trap dialectically. One must read, he
argues, both sides of the Romantic tradition, only one of which
is the poetry of sincerity and autobiography—in fact, the "more
enduring contribution" of Romantic poetry has been "Keats, the
pre-Raphaelites, and the aesthetic and symbolist movements . . .
the poetry of art, even of artifice and insincerity" (34–35). In this
body of literature, "sincerity and autobiography," loaded terms in
naive Romanticist poetics, "are encoded, written backwards" (35).
A poetry of the object as well as of the subject, then, turns out to
be a product of Romanticism seen in a humanist dialectic:

> Romanticism is both idealistic and realistic in that it conceives
> of the ideal as existing only in conjunction with the real and
> the real as existing only in conjunction with the ideal. The two

are brought into conjunction only in the act of perception when the higher or imaginative rationality brings the ideal to the real by penetrating and possessing the external world as a way of knowing both itself and the external world. (24)

Thus known "organically," the external world is "imbue[d] . . . with life," and we find in the contemplated object "the counterpart of our own consciousness" (25), which is elevated by the process.

The "romanticist," however, as Langbaum conceives such a subject attempting to *be* an object, "never forgets that he [*sic*] is playing a role. The result is that the experience makes him more acutely aware than ever of his own modernity and his own distinctness from the external world" (25). The dialectic of Romanticism inevitably leads back to a subject in crisis; Langbaum wonders whether literature since the Enlightenment, "whatever its program, can be anything but romantic," and suggests that "[t]o bridge the gap between knowledge and value we ought to require . . . an even more extreme and articulated romanticism" (28) of the literature in our own day. Subject swallows object, the dramatic is effaced by the lyric, and so the history of literature since Keats tends inevitably toward Robert Lowell.[12]

Or rather, it tends toward a particular reading of Robert Lowell—the psychological interpretation, which gains in force over the course of Langbaum's work and "isolates character from the external motivations of plot (such as money, love, power). It makes of character an autonomous force, motivated solely by the need for self-expression" (177). Political, religious, social, gendered, ideological, and other readings, including more complexly mediated psychological and phenomenological interpretations than the ones Langbaum offers, are excluded not only from Lowell, but from the entire post-Enlightenment literary corpus—a literature that, in Langbaum's terms, manages to pay attention to everything while noticing nothing but itself.

Elsewhere Langbaum notes that "the whole truth" of the dramatic monologue, the truth "about the speaker," "lies outside the facts, in an area of existence where all contradictions are resolved" (203). The particulars of experience are, like Wittgenstein's ladder, used once and thrown away in the service of self-expression. Such a Romanticism tries to heal the split of subject and object by a dialectic that annihilates both. Langbaum's "particularity," like Gelpi's "what poetry does," serves a fundamentally conservative and static general understanding. Other ways of attacking the problem of the authority of subjective experience do not seem to enter Langbaum's formulation—certainly not in the case of poetry, which for Langbaum seems barely to exist before Romanticism, and impossible to continue without it.

No historical ruptures of comparable significance are discerned after the intervention of the Enlightenment, and so modern post-Enlightenment literary history is represented in relatively continuous and unbroken terms. As a consequence, all that follows is a sort of postlapsarian response, and Modernism becomes by definition merely an extension and intensification of nineteenth-century Romanticism. Such continuous, curiously unhistorical models of literary-historical change explain the curious internationalism of books like Robert Pinsky's *The Situation of Poetry*, concerned almost solely with contemporary *American* poetry yet finding its originating instance in Keats' "Ode to a Nightingale" (47–61). Pinsky's discussion of tradition never refers to American social history, but instead views the "current moment" in contemporary poetry as an epistemological and (to a lesser degree) rhetorical, rather than a historically constituted, one (vii). History in these narratives serves as an abstract and distant point of origin; to extend the metaphor of the trajectory introduced earlier, social history is the explosion that sets the cannonball of subjective history in flight. Subsequent to that initial impulse, however, and after a moment of stabilization into formal categories, literature would seem to proceed along subjective rather than social lines, developing in a linear, describable, and predictable course, following its own internal formal laws of evolution. The reification of historical forces into formal principles creates a seeming inevitability about the posthistorical period of genre development.

Langbaum's narrative shares with Pinsky's, and to a lesser degree with Rosenthal and Gall's, a debt to Romantic poetics for its explanation of contemporary poetry. Langbaum recognizes more than these others the extent to which his explanation of *history* relies on Romantic assumptions. Romantic explanations of contemporary poetry may have gained in force during the late fifties and sixties as a way for poets to evade the burden of Modernism.[13] With

Harold Bloom's categorical dismissal of Modernism in the seventies as "exposed as having never been there" (*A Map* 28), the subjective teleology of contemporary poetry seemed assured. In the last decade or so, the tide has begun to change: poetic modernism is being exposed in the work of scholars such as Cary Nelson and Marjorie Perloff as both more vital and more varied than had previously been thought; historical critics such as Lisa M. Steinman and Gregory S. Jay are interrogating the connections between visions of American literature and visions of American history in new and interesting ways;[14] the dialectics of modern and postmodern are finally being thought through in poetry as well as elsewhere (Silliman, "Postmodernism"); and the social context of modern poetry is being explored in detail.[15] For the historian of contemporary poetry, the opportunity and the challenge is to think the history of poetry while admitting "external" considerations into their narratives at multiple levels. The early strain of this burden is evident in Pinsky's work, which maintains multiple debts to Romantic theory in its commitment to poetry as a particular form of knowledge, in its formalist, developmental historiography, and in its allegiance to the subjectivist stance of much contemporary poetry, but the main thesis of which is that contemporary poetry does and should admit extraliterary, abstract, and discursive elements into its construction.

James E. B. Breslin's *From Modern to Contemporary* tries even harder than Pinsky's work to extract itself from the dominant historical narrative, arguing against Roy Harvey Pearce's classic study *The Continuity of American Poetry* that "[t]he history of American poetry forms . . . a series of discontinuities, eruptions of creative energy that suddenly alienate poetry from what had come to seem its essential and permanent nature" (xiii). This principle applies to contemporary poems, too, which "contain cracks, fissures; they are heterogeneous" (61). Against the emphasis on rupture, discontinuity, and breakage is a deep skepticism about the usefulness of historical periodization.

But some periodization seems necessary if the emphasis on breakage is to avoid losing all hope of generalization. Breslin is explicit about not wanting to transform "critical fictions" of historical periods into "critical myths," and notes wryly how easily "ostensibly historical terms become covertly evaluative" (55). His solution to this dilemma seems to smuggle continuity back into his model in another guise, in terms of "history as a dynamic *process*" (57). "Contemporary poetry," Breslin asserts, "is not an exactly surveyable field but an ongoing process" (58). The authority of external, historical interpretation thus both asserted and undermined, the concept of history as process returns critical authority to an inductive criticism constituted explicitly from within the literary field, with "form . . . understood as an unfolding process of discovery" (60). In Breslin as in Pinsky, the model of interpretation seems taken directly from what is seen to be the main achievement of the poetry in question; form in postmodern poetry "is best discussed in particular works by particular poets" rather than within some generalized external model of history or representation (60). Breslin sees contemporary poetry, like his own criticism, as an inductive form of knowledge: it "ground[s] itself in a sharply observed physical present," it is a "poetics of immediacy," and it "seek[s] nontotalizing literary forms which relate to familiar realities in a way that is not appropriating" (61–62). Now, I am not suggesting that Breslin's particular observations about contemporary poetry are *wrong*, but his work fails to extract itself from an internally constituted theory of poetry. Its *critical* authority is thereby undermined, and Breslin's memorable characterization of the contemporary American poetry scene as resembling "a small affluent town in Northern California" loses some of its force, if none of its charm (250).

Robert von Hallberg also seeks to admit social history into his examination of the formation of contemporary American verse, though his strategies are almost directly opposed to Breslin's. His basic critical move is entirely to deny the division of poetry and social history, and to read for social life in what he calls culturally "centrist poets" (4), poets who have not "written from an adversary perspective" (228) but rather "have looked . . . searchingly and fairly at the national culture" (244). Instead of forming literary-historical models in terms constituted within the literary field, von Hallberg reads poetry as a direct function of social history. This strategy privileges a writing of poetic history in terms of its social content; aside from a few suggestive comments, von Hallberg proposes no general model of the dynamics of change and continuity in the history of poetry.

Representing contemporary American poetry as culturally

centrist, von Hallberg's way of opposing the prevailing view of that poetry as marginal relies on a conflation of *centrist* and *central* unworthy of the book as a whole but indicative of its shaky dual identity as evaluative close reading and social history. It is finally more satisfactory as the former and tends to read the poetry as a reflection of history rather than an engagement with it. After giving due consideration to the cultural context of contemporary poetry, von Hallberg's analysis mainly devotes itself to close readings of the works of individual poets and to particular cultural themes in contemporary poetry. Historical and social content is given considerable weight, but the dynamics of history themselves are evaded. While this strategy produces searching examinations of specific works of poetry in terms of their relation to, for instance, systems analysis (36–61) or the tourist culture supported by global American hegemony (62–92), von Hallberg finally spatializes rather than historicizes the contemporary poetic scene.[16]

We could continue comparing Langbaum's narrative with other reconstructions of the advent of modern and contemporary poetry ad nauseam, from Rosenthal/Gall through Gelpi to David Perkins, whose two-volume *History of Modern Poetry* is clearly a major attempt to totalize the field.[17] Such a comparison shows, with rare exceptions, almost entirely psychologized versions of history, few attempts to clarify modern poetry that do not reach back to the psychological and epistemological crises of the Romantics for justification and explanation, and a general displacement of historical forces onto the content or form of the work. They all display what Clifford Siskin calls the "lyric turn"—"that feature by which creative and critical narratives, from the past and from the present, veer from the generic and historical to the natural and transcendent, metamorphosing all analysis into claims for Imaginative vision" (12). It matters little whether the narrative in question is humanist, dialectical, or (as in Langbaum) some combination of the two—the arrangement of historical origin and literary/formal response still holds. Nor is it a question of tracing "influence," though I suspect that could be done, especially in the case of Langbaum's influence on Rosenthal and Gall (Harmon 182). Indeed, attempting to account for influence from book to book would merely repeat for criticism what all these works do for poetry. We should rather find in Langbaum merely a more easily dissected version of the crisis implicit in all these other histories, but whose commonality should not be traced to a simple case of "influence": the problematic of the centered subject.

In each of these accounts, the organization and place of subjectivity holds both a central and marginal place in discussions of literary history: central, because the historical originating moment is often one in which new conceptions of individuality, personhood, character, subjective articulation, and the like come into being; marginal, because representing the evolution of literary forms after this moment requires a relatively stable and essentialized human nature. Decentered, and then restabilized in representation—Langbaum et al. enact at a critical distance the same dialectic they note in the literature examined, and thus aestheticize historical change.

It is perhaps anticlimactic, at this point, to have recast Langbaum's narrative in such familiar terms. One might make similar claims for virtually any book of literary criticism or theory published 35 years ago. Still, Langbaum's work is significant for at least recognizing the crisis as one of subjectivity, even if his project is itself as much a symptom as a description of that crisis. Also, it remains worth reading, as I suggested above, for being explicit and unabashedly ideological whereas more recent accounts hide their allegiances, paying lip-service to possible alternative narratives while remaining deeply conservative. Turning from Robert Langbaum to Rosenthal/Gall, Gelpi, Breslin, or von Hallberg, a critical reader does not so much rejoice at how far we have come as stand amazed at the persistence of the aestheticization of history in its strongest forms. Indeed, the new versions of this aesthetic might be more pernicious, as what were mere theses in *The Poetry of Experience* have become axiomatic more recently.

Alternative Genealogies

History as trajectory implies a present. If the human subject has a single, linear history that evolves and develops over time, then narratives of that development in a recent past may lay claim to having some authority over our own action and articulation as present subjects. This is especially the case if the narrative is one of the increased vesting of authority in subjective experience, as it is in Langbaum and others, though the eventual coincidence of this historical narrative and our own practical, active subjectivity provides a point of indeterminacy and a possible escape. *We* are the targets of the cannonball of subjective history. The question for me, at least, is how to get out of its way.

I have mentioned above some forms of opposition to the received and authorized histories of poetry, forms that cover institutional, theoretical, and pragmatic grounds. As tactics, strategies, and attitudes, all of these forms of resistance disturb either the trajectory or the target of subjective history: that is, they all work either by the fragmentation of linear narrative, or by the multiplication of subject-positions. What are needed for an alternative theorization of the literary past and present are, first, a way of describing the problematic of the modern subject's history and construction without repeating that problematic in its own account, and second, a way of understanding the field of literature in a nonhierarchical and nonreductive relation to this problematic. A number of attempts have been made to meet this first need, from Charles Taylor's return to external moral sources in his (otherwise sympathetic) account of modern Western identity to Paul Smith's appropriation of French feminism toward a heterogeneous and nontheoretical conception of agency.[18] The most forceful attempt at a revised history of the subject so far remains, to my mind, that of Michel Foucault. Especially in his later "genealogical" phase, certain of Foucault's methodological strategies, in addition to his historical observations, can usefully be employed in a contemporary understanding of the dynamics of change and continuity in poetic history as well.

In order to explain this suggestion, I should elaborate on just what I am appropriating from Foucault, as well as how my use of Foucault's work differs from that of some other literary critics. As is well known, Foucault's historical method relies on the description of the transition of multiple levels of a society, including its discourses, practices, institutions, and knowledges, into new forms; but it does this without resorting to the causal explanations or hierarchical relations favored by Marxists and humanists. The changes described accompany new forms of subjectivity, though Foucault did not write histories of subjectivity per se. In Anglo-American literary criticism, elements of Foucault's work have found sympathetic audiences among historical critics, and his writing has been instrumental in the renewal and revitalization of historical criticism in a number of fields. The main impact of Foucault in literary criticism so far has been toward understanding literature in relation to, as a reflection of, or as a critique of the various regimes of power/knowledge that Foucault has examined at length, such as medical practice, disciplinary institutions, or sexuality; or, alternatively, in relation to areas of discourse, practice, and subject positioning not explicitly analyzed by Foucault but potentially susceptible to Foucauldian critique. This dominant method of appropriating Foucault for literary criticism can lead, strangely, to the reassertion of a field of literature separate from, interacting in a limited way with, or transcending the discourses of power and domination in a given society.

The direct examination of literature *itself*—its practices, institutions, self-definitions, and histories—as a diffuse regime or field of power and knowledge in terms extending Foucault's analyses of medicine, prisons, and sexuality, is still in its infancy. Yet the production, practice, dissemination, transmission, and reproduction of literature, perhaps especially poetry, precisely resembles what Foucault calls a *technology of the self;* such technologies, as he describes them, "permit individuals to effect by their own means or with the help of others a certain number of operations on their own bodies and souls, thoughts, conduct, and way of being, so as to transform themselves in order to attain a certain state of happiness, purity, wisdom, perfection, or immortality" ("Technologies" 18). A direct rather than indirect Foucauldian genealogy of contemporary poetry would attempt to determine the shape of that poetry as a technology of the self and as a form and object of particular knowledges, practices, and discourses. It would, however, sidestep the evolutionary model of Langbaum and the "lyric turn" of others examined here; as Foucault notes of genealogy in general,

> it must record the singularity of events outside of any monotonous finality; it must seek them in the most unpromising places, in what we tend to feel is without history—in sentiments, love, conscience, instincts; it must be sensitive to their

recurrence, not in order to trace the gradual curve of their evolution, but to isolate the different scenes where they engaged in different roles. (*Language, Counter-Memory, Practice* 139–40)[19]

It certainly can be and has been argued that Foucault's genealogical work proposes binary oppositions, such as that between sex and bodies, no less ontologically invested than those he attempts to overthrow. It has also been argued by various Enlightenment-descended perspectives from Taylor to Habermas that Foucault's work goes too far, though I find such arguments unconvincing.[20] Still, the genealogical strategy of reinscribing abstract concepts and terms into a social field, which I take to be Foucault's major analytical move, remains salutary and important. Indeed, the problem of poetry and the problem of subject-formation are by now so intertwined that we may connect without too much resistance Langbaum's narrative of modern poetry and Foucault's discussion of "sex" in his *History of Sexuality, Volume 1.*

At this point, I would not like to make overly strong claims regarding the relationship of poetry to sexuality in Foucault's sense. Certainly Foucault, among others, has noticed a new conception of literature accompanying new organizations of subjectivity in the social field; however, his own scattered remarks on the subject are more suggestive than rigorous.[21] Speculations are possible, of course, and multiple points of connection, resemblance, and resistance between the two can be located. It is fairly easy to see how the "extreme and articulated romanticism" called for in Langbaum's *The Poetry of Experience* strikingly resembles the cry for sexual expression, the "institutional incitement to speak about [sex] . . . and to cause *it* to speak through explicit articulation and endlessly accumulated detail" that Foucault sees as one of the hallmarks of modernity (18). This incitement, in Foucault, results from an ontologically empty creation given the name *sex:*

> Sex . . . is doubtless but an ideal point made necessary by the deployment of sexuality and its operation. We must not make the mistake of thinking that sex is an autonomous agency which secondarily produces manifold effects of sexuality over the entire length of its surface of contact with power. On the contrary, sex is the most speculative, most ideal, and most in-

ternal element in a deployment of sexuality organized by power in its grip on bodies and their materiality, their forces, energies, sensations, and pleasures. (155)

Foucault's *History of Sexuality* has led to confused readings by some, such as Allan Megill, who argue that Foucault has not proved, or even given evidence for, the thesis that sex is on the upswing. Were Foucault to have held such a thesis, it would be utterly meaningless—what would it mean that "sexuality has proliferated" in Megill's terms (237), what measures or evidences would be acceptable as support for a statement of this type? In any case, such is hardly Foucault's thesis in the *History;* indeed, he avoids addressing that question entirely.[22] His purpose, rather, is to put "the repressive hypothesis," as he terms it, "back within a general economy of discourses on sex in modern societies" (11). Foucault elaborates:

> The central issue, then (at least in the first instance), is not to determine whether one says yes or no to sex, whether one formulates prohibitions or permissions, whether one asserts its importance or denies its effects, or whether one refines the words one uses to designate it; but to account for the fact that it is spoken about, to discover who does the speaking, the positions and viewpoints from which they speak, the institutions which prompt people to speak about it and which store and distribute the things that are said . . . What is at issue, briefly, is the over-all "discursive fact," the way in which sex is "put into discourse." (11)

Here lies the distinction, crucial to Foucault and a stumbling block to readers such as Megill, between "sex" and "sexuality." Foucault refuses a history of sexual practices, *mores,* behaviors, beliefs, codes, and the like, in favor of a genealogy of the discursive field in which sex comes to be seen as providing an essential key to human nature. This is Foucault's way of exposing, so to speak, this "nature" of "sex" as a constructed, historically contingent, unstable object that nonetheless appears to function as one of the most immutable and important, if elusive, indices of life itself.

It should be noted that in the narrative of subjectivity thus far described, "sex" has exactly the same relation to material bodies in

Foucault as "poetry" has to the particulars of time-space experience in Langbaum. Indeed, Langbaum finds in "poetry" the same power of truth and life that Foucault views as being sought in the endless articulation of "sex." A crude periodization would find multiple parallels of history and use, with both "sex" and "poetry" gaining similar functions and authorities, during roughly the same time period, regarding the construction, affirmation, and maintenance of an essentialized self. What in one account might be seen as merely the beginning of a "Romantic" view of poetry might in another view be seen as the rise of "poetry" as an empty ontological category, the way "sex" has for Foucault a certain unchartable origin. (I put them both in quotes to emphasize this and to undermine their integrity as discrete categories.) In fact, the creation of "literature," of which "poetry" as such is the most idealized form, resembles the history of sexuality in our time enough for both to be seen as involved in the making of our modernity. It is also important to note the similarity, in both fields, of the possibility for resistance through the multiplication of centers; for Foucault, the power-relation between "sex," on the one hand, and bodies, on the other, needs to be attacked "through a tactical reversal of the various mechanisms of sexuality" in order to affirm "the claims of bodies, pleasures, and knowledges, in their multiplicity and their possibility of resistance" (157). Resistance must counter the ontological priority of the thing resisted, whether it be "sex" or "poetry," even and especially if such resistance operates on the same plane as that which had formerly claimed absolute right.

Toward the Poetic

The institutional deployment of "poetry" should not be fought on the level of definitions because such a fight is bound to lose once it allows the ontological claim to proceed unchallenged, or to be challenged indeed on its own level. We need to distinguish between the practical constraints put on contemporary literary production through the diffuse action of history and the tendency of historical narratives to explain contemporary literary production by a retrogressive authorization. This is one major difference between historical explanation and contextual genealogy;[23] the former attempts to locate origins that lose their history and neatly explain a naturalized and unchallenged present, while the latter is, as Foucault notes, "gray, meticulous, and patently documentary" (*Language, Counter-Memory, Practice* 139). Tony Bennett is surely correct about the paucity of vocabulary available to us here; we need a term that will serve for *poetry* the same function *sexuality* serves for *sex* in Foucault, so that we can understand the deployment of what might be called the *poetic* function in the construction of the modern self.

Cary Nelson has approached this issue in *Repression and Recovery*, perhaps the most successful revisionist history of Modern(ist) American poetry. Noting at the outset of his study that "no single story can be told about modern poetry and its varied audiences that is even marginally adequate" (7), Nelson works by the method of what I have above called contextual genealogy, seeking to represent both the explosion of socially aggressive poetry during the period investigated and that poetry's subsequent expulsion from authorized history. Pursuing this goal while maintaining a reflexive stance toward his own critical practice, Nelson expands both the canon and the concept of poetry, thinking poetry "as a field of discourses displaying an intelligible (though shifting and contested) range of aesthetic variations" (129), and "a cultural domain that is constantly being reformed and repositioned" (244). This expansion leads him to model the relations of power, poetry, and literary history around the "virtual space" of an "expanded canon" (57). This, in turn, prompts Nelson to rethink the concept of what he calls "literariness" and "the poetic" in a manner that, while not fully theorized, still constitutes an important step toward an adequate theory of the poetic.

According to Nelson, poetry is "a formation constituted not only by the subject matter and style of poetry, by statements about poetics, and by the struggle over the changing social functions poetry serves, but also by all alternative efforts to define and co-opt the other social domains poetry addresses" (129). Poetry, then, is constituted within a social field and determined in part by its discursive Others, hegemonic discourses that claim the representation of multiple social domains for themselves and deny poetry's involvement with those domains. Nelson further argues that the poetic is implicated in the historical construction of subjectivity:

"[O]ne cannot think the concept of the poetic without asking how the culture's available forms of idealization feed into and relate to one another. These forms are the idealized subject positions offered to us . . ." (130). These and other comments on the poetic begin to frame it as an organizing principle of the literary field, one which takes into account the multifarious and variable relations of power, subjectivity, literary and nonliterary knowledge, and institutional constraints in particular discursive formations. Nelson investigates, in addition to individual poems, such evidence as little magazines, cover and internal art in poetry books, order and arrangements of books, publishers and publishing practices, musical accompaniment to poems, and audiences real and implied. He also is able, through a shrewd historical sense, to relate the coexistence of traditional and modernist poetics in leftist poetry (21–25).

If adequately realized, a fuller understanding of the poetic would go a long way toward enabling historical considerations of contemporary poetry to move away from historical explanation and toward contextual genealogy. Nelson does not develop a theory of the poetic in terms of discursive formations beyond these and a few other remarks; his goals lie elsewhere, and are for the most part realized. He does, however, mention the role(s) played by the poetic as an ideology in academic criticism. Nelson rightly notes that this criticism transmits and authorizes "the longstanding general insistence that poetry has no relation to 'the popular'" and "works hard to reinforce the separation between the poetic and the everyday" (67). The reasons for this form of the ideology of the poetic are not hard to imagine: "As a discipline, English gets a good part of its self-image and its ideology from an idealized notion of the poetic" (246). For Nelson, it seems, the ideology of the poetic is the poetic tout court.

Nelson's critical stance is authorized in part by Marxist theory and may gain still greater authority in the context of his study by challenging an idealized view of the poetic in favor of an ideological one. Following Foucault, I find the use of ideology to explain the organization of discursive fields inadequate.[24] It seems to me that a theory of the poetic can help model the organization of the field of contemporary poetry *only* if it is seen in a nonexternal relation to a productive, rather than repressive, view of the operations of power. Nelson holds a similar view when he describes power as a "constitutive structuration of literariness that gives it meaning" (56). An analysis of the poetic in history would search out the local centers of the poetic's deployment, uncover their genealogy and principles of operation, and trace the dynamics and effects of the poetic at multiple levels, in multiple domains, and without totalization. Otherwise, we are left merely with genre history.[25] Genre histories may make us more secure when facing an unfamiliar or threatening terrain, but they do so by displacing that which contests them, and by clearing an illusory space for a "natural" literature.

Alternative forms of literary history could be proposed, of course, and are in fact necessary. Indeed, as Clifford Siskin notes, "to say that historicizing enables the past to be of value to the present is no longer to be forced, by the Romantic logic of sympathy/judgement, into fetishizing that past into parts with various independent values" (62). But to write such histories requires that we trace the *deployment* of "poetry," not its being; that we think always in terms of multiple rather than singular histories; that we trace such histories through their institutions as much as through "practitioners"; and that we seek a new descriptive vocabulary for the task.

Notes

1. S. J. Schmidt proposes four major requirements of a "constructivist" approach to literary history: (1) that literary historiography make *"explicit* acknowledgement of the fundamental *constructivity* of literary history and the resulting consequences" (296); (2) that, conceiving literature as a social system, "literary history should be oriented towards agent-text-context-syndromes instead of (more or less) autonomous works of art whose relations to 'society' must then be constructed ex post" (296); (3) that the range of study of the literary be expanded to "take into account not only literary texts but the whole range of communicative means that are supposedly available in a particular society whose literary system is under investigation" (298)—in other words, that *"literary history has to be a history of media, too"* (299); and (4) that literary historians "reflect upon the possible application of the knowledge they produce in domains outside the academic sphere" (299).

2. See, e.g., Perloff, "Avant-Garde or Endgame," *Radical Artifice;* Kalaidjian, "Transpersonal Poetics"; and Hartley, 1–25.

3. See McGann's "Contemporary Poetry, Alternate Routes" for his discussion of contemporary avant-garde poetry. The opposition between the historical and

the contemporary invoked occasionally here should not be taken as one to which I subscribe, but rather as shorthand for the point of view I am critiquing. The unspoken hero of *The Romantic Ideology*, though nods are made to Heine and the Frankfurt School, is Paul de Man, especially his "Literary History and Literary Modernity" (*Blindness and Insight* 142–65) for the discussion of history in the Introduction, though McGann's version of the Romantic ideology itself owes most to de Man's "The Rhetoric of Temporality" (*Blindness and Insight* 187–228).

4. See also Siskin's critique of McGann in *The Historicity of Romantic Discourse*, 56–62.

5. See Jameson, *Postmodernism*, especially the conclusion (297–418); Laclau and Mouffe; and David Harvey's rigorous *The Condition of Postmodernity* for sympathetic discussions of the possibilities of social theory in the postmodern context.

6. Jameson's absolutist representation of History as "last instance," "absent cause," or "untranscendable horizon" becomes a powerful means of explaining and interpreting individual literary phenomena, as Jameson knows full well. See Jameson on the value of a new hermeneutic (*Political Unconscious* 21) and the accompanying footnote, which is virtually a litany of by now classic poststructuralist critiques of interpretive processes.

7. See, for instance, the comments of Mikhail Bakhtin on social language's absence from poetry (*The Dialogic Imagination* 287–88). Bakhtin's work on discourse as the dialogic, which has proved remarkably fruitful for the admission of new, relatively unaestheticized, methods of analysis into the study of the novel and popular culture, has been largely ignored by scholars of poetry. However, this is not to say it has no potential here as well. See Emerson and Morson, 319–25. See also Davidson, "Discourse in Poetry."

Also see Kristin Ross, *The Emergence of Social Space: Rimbaud and the Paris Commune*. Ross notes that her own project has an ambiguous position in Marxist theory, since "Marxist literary critics from Lukács through Sartre and on up to the current generation . . . have continued to reassert the traditionally dominant concern with narrative and the novel genre" (11). Ross's work reads what might be called the late symbolist French poetic in a manner similar to Cary Nelson's investigation into "modernist" poetry (discussed below); she refuses the explanatory hermeneutic role for literary history, reading instead the poems as historical events and neither separating those poems from their social contexts nor conceiving the poem/context relation in terms of bases and superstructures.

8. See the issue of which Lazer's essay is a part, a special issue of *Poetry East* dedicated to "Art and Guns: Political Poetry at Home and Abroad" (Winter 1982–Spring 1983). While about half the issue is devoted to international political poetries (conveniently divided by region—Central America, Germany, Hungary, Ireland, Japan, Poland, Scandinavia, South Africa), the first half discusses and prints domestic varieties of political poetry.

9. I am thinking especially of the historical schemas of Harold Bloom (begining with *The Anxiety of Influence*) but also of more pluralistic works, such as Robert Pinsky's seminal *The Situation of Poetry*, Lynn Keller's *Re-Making it New: Contemporary American Poetry and the Modernist Tradition*, and Mutlu Konuk Blasing's sophisticated anti-Bloomian *American Poetry: The Rhetoric of Its Forms*. In different ways, each of these works defines a historical, epistemological, or rhetorical situation into which contemporary works are variously slotted, meeting or failing to meet the particular demands set up at the outset.

10. See Clément Moisan, "Works of Literary History as an Instance of Historicity." Moisan's conclusion is worth quoting at some length:

We teach literature then because, in a changing world, literature constitutes, by its historicity, stability. Thus, we confront the entropy of the system. The past is transfixed; it immobilizes the present and heralds the future. When the system destabilizes and its elements enter into a conflict that precludes any possible mediation, a split occurs which takes up the works as exemplary models of prevailing issues and situations. Changes in mentalities and in conceptions tend then to destroy the past and substitute the ideology of the present, to substitute new values for outdated ones. In both cases, the act of historicizing results in canonization. It is this function of conservation that society, consciously or not, confers upon historians. The works themselves ensure the illustration of this function through a constant reactualization of the literary canon. . . . The instance of historicity and its result, canonization, are perhaps the twin avatars of a comedy of manners in which he who loses, wins. (693)

11. See R. S. Crane, *Critical and Historical Principles of Literary History,* for one of the most sophisticated pre-poststructuralist discussions of the relations between historical and formal interests in literary history, by a leader of the Chicago formalists. For a discussion of the complications of formalist and historical criticism, see Graff, *Professing Literature,* 183–94.

12. Lowell is the only younger poet Langbaum cites as poet (though he does mention a lecture of Randall Jarrell); "Robert Lowell's latest volume (*The Mills of the Kavanaughs,* 1951) consists entirely of dramatic monologues . . ." (76).

13. Cary Nelson argues: "The oppressive weight of the past that many poets [of the fifties] felt was not something that the past did to us but rather something we, as a culture, did to ourselves. We were driven, it seems, to preserve our past in an intimidating and attenuated form" (*Repression and Recovery* 36).

14. See Steinman, *Made in America,* for a fascinating discussion of the implication of modernist American poetry in particularly American models of social progress and technological achievement; and Jay, *America the Scrivener,* for a more general theoretical discussion of the cross-pollination of models for American history and American literature.

15. See Marjorie Perloff's "Pound/Stevens: Whose Era?" in *The Dance of the Intellect,* 1–32, for a clear, if partisan, summary of the opposing camps in the debate over poetic modernism.

16. My language here draws broadly from William Spanos's essay, "Modern Literary Criticism and the Spatialization of Time." The impact of this article, and of others making similar points about the antihistoricist aesthetic of much modern literary criticism, have yet to be felt in most of the "historical" criticism of contemporary poetry.

17. But Perkins' work, I must admit, is somewhat anomalous. Though its assignation of space to individual poets more or less follows canonical lines, it allows historical ("external") factors in at multiple points. I attribute this to the encyclopedic, rather than narrative, character of the books, which seem designed to be referred to as much as read. Perkins's recent *Is Literary History Possible?* can very easily be interpreted as both a defense and qualification of the claims made in the *History.*

18. See Taylor, *Sources of the Self,* and Smith, *Discerning the Subject.*

19. Here I avoid the distinction sometimes made between Foucault's "genealogical" and "ethical" phases. His late work on self-construction and technologies on the self does not, for me, repudiate his earlier work in *Discipline and Punish* and the first volume of the *History of Sexuality*. Foucault never, to my knowledge, dismissed the concept of agency, though his late work on ethics was his first attempt to conceptualize the issue.

20. See especially Jürgen Habermas, *The Philosophical Discourse of Modernity*, 238–93 and passim; and Peter Dews, *Logics of Disintegration*, 170–220. See also the debate beginning with Charles Taylor, "Foucault on Freedom and Truth," and William Connolly, "Taylor, Foucault, and Otherness," and Taylor's rebuttal in the same issue, "Connolly, Foucault, and Truth."

21. See his "Language to Infinity" in *Language, Counter-Memory, Practice*, 53–67; and *The Order of Things*, 300.

22. Megill acknowledges, but refuses to legitimate, the reading I would take, which rigorously distinguishes between Foucault's use of the terms "sex" and "sexuality." Though he wisely admits that Foucault employs such a distinction while "articulating an antinaturalism" in the *History of Sexuality*, he claims that this distinction cannot hold up (253). Megill seems here not to grasp the extent of Foucault's playfulness in his assertion that sexuality came into being in recent centuries. This leads him to reduce Foucault to a classic false choice: either Foucault's argument must hold to the idea of a natural sex, or it must commit to a spurious historical narrative.

23. Foucault allies himself in an interview with "the methodical precaution and the radical but unaggressive skepticism which makes it a principle not to regard the point in time where we are now standing as the outcome of a teleological progression which it would be one's business to reconstruct historically" (*Power/ Knowledge* 49). This distinction also seems to bear resemblance to Clifford Siskin's not altogether clear division between the history of genre and "generic history"; the former sees genre as a "Romantic developmental tale," while the latter views it as "a family concept" (10).

24. "The notion of ideology appears to me to be difficult to make use of, for three reasons. The first is that, like it or not, it always stands in virtual opposition to something else which is supposed to count as truth. . . . The second drawback is that the concept of ideology refers, I think necessarily, to something of the order of a subject. Thirdly, ideology stands in a secondary position relative to something which functions as its infrastructure, as its material, economic determinant, etc." Foucault, *Power/Knowledge* 118.

25. But see Ralph Cohen's defenses of genre criticism in "History and Genre," and "Do Postmodern Genres Exist?"

Works Cited

Bakhtin, Mikhail. *The Dialogic Imagination: Four Essays*. Trans. Michael Holquist and Caryl Emerson. Ed. Michael Holquist. Austin: U of Texas P, 1981.

Bennett, Tony. *Outside Literature*. London: Routledge, 1990.

Blasing, Mutlu Konuk. *American Poetry: The Rhetoric of Its Forms*. New Haven: Yale UP, 1987.

Bloom, Harold. *The Anxiety of Influence: A Theory of Poetry*. New York: Oxford UP, 1973.

184   *David Kellogg*

———. *A Map of Misreading*. New York: Oxford UP, 1975.

Breslin, James E. B. *From Modern to Contemporary: American Poetry 1945–1965*. Chicago: U of Chicago P, 1965.

Cohen, Ralph. "Do Postmodern Genres Exist?" *Postmodern Genres*. Ed. Marjorie Perloff. Norman: U of Oklahoma P, 1989. 11–27.

———. "History and Genre." *New Literary History* Winter 1986: 203–18.

Connolly, William. "Taylor, Foucault, and Otherness." *Political Theory* 13.3 (Aug. 1985): 365–76.

Crane, R. S. *Critical and Historical Principles of Literary History*. 1967. Chicago: U of Chicago P, 1971.

Davidson, Michael. "Discourse in Poetry." *Code of Signals*. Ed. Michael Palmer. Berkeley: North Atlantic, 1983. 143–50.

De Man, Paul. *Blindness and Insight: Essays in the Rhetoric of Contemporary Criticism*. 2nd ed. Minneapolis: U of Minnesota P, 1983.

Dews, Peter. *Logics of Disintegration: Poststructuralist Thought and the Claims of Critical Theory*. London: Verso, 1987.

Foucault, Michel. *Discipline and Punish: The Birth of the Prison*. Trans. Alan Sheridan. New York: Vintage, 1979.

———. *The History of Sexuality, Volume 1: An Introduction*. Trans. Robert Hurley. New York: Vintage, 1990.

———. *Language, Counter-Memory, Practice: Selected Essays and Interviews*. Ed. Donald F. Bouchard. Trans. Bouchard and Sherry Simon. Ithaca: Cornell UP, 1977.

———. *The Order of Things: An Archeology of the Human Sciences*. New York: Vintage, 1973.

———. *Power/Knowledge: Selected Interviews and Other Writings 1972–1977*. Ed. Colin Gordon. Trans. Gordon, Leo Marshall, John Mepham, and Kate Soper. New York: Pantheon, 1980.

———. "Technologies of the Self." *Technologies of the Self: A Seminar with Michel Foucault*. Ed. Luther H. Martin, Huck Gutman, and Patrick H. Hutton. Amherst: U of Massachusetts P, 1988. 16–49.

Gelpi, Albert. *A Coherent Splendor: The American Poetic Renaissance 1910–1950*. Cambridge: Cambridge UP, 1987.

Graff, Gerald. *Professing Literature: An Institutional History*. Chicago: U of Chicago P, 1987.

Habermas, Jürgen. *The Philosophical Discourse of Modernity: Twelve Lectures*. Trans. Frederick G. Lawrence. Cambridge: MIT P, 1987.

Harmon, William. Review of *The Modern Poetic Sequence*. By M. L. Rosenthal. *Georgia Review* 38.1 (1984): 182–84.

Hartley, George. *Textual Politics and the Language Poets*. Bloomington: Indiana UP, 1989.

Harvey, David. *The Condition of Postmodernity: An Enquiry into the Origins of Cultural Change*. London: Blackwell, 1989.

Jameson, Fredric. *The Political Unconscious: Narrative as a Socially Symbolic Act*. Ithaca: Cornell UP, 1981.

———. *Postmodernism; Or, the Cultural Logic of Late Capitalism*. Durham: Duke UP, 1991.

Jay, Gregory S. *America the Scrivener: Deconstruction and the Subject of Literary History*. Ithaca: Cornell UP, 1990.

Kalaidjian, Walter. "Transpersonal Poetics: Language Writing and the Historical Avant-Gardes in Postmodern Culture." *American Literary History* 3.2 (Summer 1991): 319–36.

Keller, Lynn. *Re-Making it New: Contemporary American Poetry and the Modernist Tradition*. New York: Cambridge UP, 1987.

Koethe, John. "Contrary Impulses: The Tension Between Poetry and Theory." *Critical Inquiry* 18.1 (1991): 64–75.

Laclau, Ernesto, and Chantal Mouffe. *Hegemony and Socialist Strategy: Towards a Radical Democratic Politics*. London: Verso, 1985.

Langbaum, Robert. *The Poetry of Experience: The Dramatic Monologue in Modern Literary Tradition*. 1957. Chicago: U of Chicago P, 1985.

Lazer, Hank. "Poetry and Politics: A Naive Approach." *Poetry East* 9–10 (Winter 1982–Spring 1983): 125–34.

McGann, Jerome J. "Contemporary Poetry, Alternate Routes." *Critical Inquiry* 13.3 (1987): 624–47. Rpt. *Social Values and Poetic Acts*. By McGann. Cambridge: Harvard UP, 1988. 197–220.

———. "Laura (Riding) Jackson and the Literal Truth." *Critical Inquiry* 18.3 (1992): 454–73.

———. *The Romantic Ideology: A Critical Investigation*. Chicago: U of Chicago P, 1983.

Megill, Allan. *Prophets of Extremity: Nietzsche, Heidegger, Foucault, Derrida*. Berkeley: U of California P, 1985.

Moisan, Clément. "Works of Literary History as an Instance of Historicity." *Poetics Today* 12.4 (1991): 685–96.

Morson, Gary Saul, and Caryl Emerson. *Michael Bakhtin: Creation of a Prosaics*. Stanford: Stanford UP, 1990.

Nelson, Cary. *Our Last First Poets: Vision and History in Contemporary American Poetry*. Urbana: U of Illinois P, 1981.

———. *Repression and Recovery: Modern American Poetry and the Politics of Cultural Memory 1910–1945*. Madison: U of Wisconsin P, 1990.

Olson, Charles, and Robert Creeley. *The Complete Correspondence*. Ed. George F. Butterick. 8 vols. to date. Santa Barbara: Black Sparrow, 1980–.

Perkins, David. *A History of Modern Poetry, Volume 1: From the 1890s to the High Modernist Mode*. Cambridge: Harvard UP, 1976.

———. *A History of Modern Poetry, Volume 2: Modernism and After*. Cambridge: Harvard UP, 1987.

———. *Is Literary History Possible?* Baltimore: Johns Hopkins UP, 1992.

Perloff, Marjorie. *The Dance of the Intellect: Studies in the Poetry of the Pound Tradition*. New York: Cambridge UP, 1985.

———. *Radical Artifice: Writing Poetry in the Age of Media*. Chicago: U of Chicago P, 1991.

Pinsky, Robert. *The Situation of Poetry: Contemporary Poetry and Its Traditions*. Princeton: Princeton UP, 1976.

Ross, Kristin. *The Emergence of Social Space: Rimbaud and the Paris Commune*. Theory and History of Literature 60. Minneapolis: U of Minnesota P, 1988.

Russell, Bertrand. *A History of Western Philosophy*. New York: Simon and Schuster, 1945.

Schmidt, Siegfried J. "On Writing Histories of Literature: Some Remarks from a Constructivist Point of View." *Poetics* 14 (1985): 279–301.

Silliman, Ron. "'Postmodernism': Sign for a Struggle, the Struggle for the Sign." *Conversant Essays: Contemporary Poets on Poetry*. Ed. James McCorkle. Detroit: Wayne State UP, 1990. 79–98.

Siskin, Clifford. *The Historicity of Romantic Discourse*. New York: Oxford UP, 1988.

Smith, Paul. *Discerning the Subject*. Theory and History of Literature 55. Minneapolis: U of Minnesota P, 1988.

Spanos, William V. "Modern Literary Criticism and the Spatialization of Time:

An Existential Critique." *Journal of Aesthetics and Art Criticism* 29 (1970): 87–104.

Steinman, Lisa M. *Made in America: Science, Technology, and American Modernist Poets.* New Haven: Yale UP, 1987.

Taylor, Charles. "Connolly, Foucault, and Truth." *Political Theory* 13.3 (August 1985): 377–85.

———. "Foucault on Freedom and Truth," *Political Theory* 12.2 (May 1984): 152–83.

———. *Sources of the Self: The Making of the Modern Identity.* Cambridge: Harvard UP, 1989.

Von Hallberg, Robert. *American Poetry and Culture 1945–1980.* Cambridge: Harvard UP, 1985.

Disney World and Posthistory

William F. Van Wert

This study deals primarily with Disney World and is presented, at least in places, in narrative form, following a linear time frame, an actual walk-through analysis of Magic Kingdom and EP-COT, and, most importantly, the retention of my two sons as participants and speakers. The study intends to show the skewed history, ahistory, or posthistory of Disney in theme parks that have eradicated all sense of shame from history. It also will show that Disney World is based upon an elaborate and highly successful blueprint of high modernism (and assembly-line capitalism), whose major trope, I contend, is metaphor, while the actual experience of the park must necessarily follow a postmodernist line of thinking/experiencing, whose major trope is metonymy. Thus, the experience of the park is often at odds with the blueprint. Further, I want to show that the major critics of Disney's theme parks (excluding Max Apple in fiction and the *South Atlantic Quarterly* issue devoted to Disney), Louis Marin and Jean Baudrillard, have given an aerial view of Disney, with no actual proof that either one ever set foot in the park or went on any rides. Their analyses rely on blueprints, conceptual thinking, and figures of resemblance (meta-

© 1996 by *Cultural Critique*. Winter 1995–96. 0882-4371/96/$5.00.

phor, analogy, simile). From de Tocqueville to Baudrillard, it is my belief that it cannot be otherwise: to be a critic of a foreign culture means having recourse to metaphor and figures of resemblance. Were I to presume to do cultural analysis of France, I too would use metaphor and not metonymy. Of the two, metonymy is the more appropriate trope to deconstruct a master narrative like Disney World. In fact, Disney has moved to France in the form of Euro Disney and with disastrous results, results that can easily be understood in the context of this study.

"Then we must be posthistoric creatures."

This was spoken by my 10-year-old son, David, on the occasion of his first visit to Disney World. We had just completed two marathon days at Magic Kingdom and EPCOT, and we were back at the Day's Inn, sitting in the Denny's Restaurant next door: the hotel, the restaurant, the visits to Disney World, all part of a prepaid package back in Philadelphia. And part of that package, which seemed attractive at the time I bought it, was the promise that kids could eat for free at Denny's. But what they could eat for free turned out to be a highly restricted "juniors" menu, with no more than five choices at any given time, the same choices day after day, meal after meal, portrayed on a plastic-coated menu of garish pictures with a *prehistoric* theme: Stone-Age spaghetti, saber-tooth chicken, brontosaurus burger.

"What do these foods have to do with prehistoric creatures?" asked my 9-year-old son Daniel, who was getting tired of the Stone-Age spaghetti.

"It has to do with packaging," I mumbled.

"Prehistoric creatures ate each other," Daniel said, answering his own question. "If these are prehistoric creatures . . ."

"Then we must be posthistoric creatures," David said.

I hear David respond, not to what Daniel said, but to what Fredric Jameson wrote: "History is what hurts, what refuses desire" (102). This is what they should have stamped on our prepaid tickets: "Hurtful history avoided at all costs." And this is an impossibility, of course, for we are inscribed in a history, by a history, and as a history at birth, history being synonymous with an entire array of interrelated things: language, ideology, culture, the mirror stage, Oedipus complex, and so forth.

So why the provocation? Precisely because, in the overall condensed master narrative of Disney World, we are given the illusion of being posthistoric creatures by avoiding all consciousness (struggle), all ambiguities and complications (when consciousness is always complicating), by repressing all vital and potentially shameful moments in American history (words like "war" and "slavery" are not mentioned), and by suppressing names and dates, anything that might be remembered, altogether. The result is a master narrative that seems contentless (lacking all of the above), but in fact serves as voice drek, a balm to numb the thinking mind, an invitation to accept the replacement of real figures and history with puppetry, holography, and simulacra, and, finally, an invitation to ride passively into the future with nothing to do but be swarmed with progress fed to us by big corporations, whose motives are never questioned.

Disney World dwarfs Orlando, its host city, to one side and Cape Canaveral and the Kennedy Space Center to the other side. It is a monster whose appetite knows no satiety, whose pretense is to provide the very history it conceals, a monster of excess and economy, outrageous expenditure and assembly-line efficiency.

Magic Kingdom

Here, "the map precedes the territory," as Baudrillard has remarked, and we enter "the desert of the real itself" ("Precession" 253). But, whereas Baudrillard confines himself to an opposition between inside (the crowd flow, the technology of rides, and exhibits bonding people together) and outside (the abandonment of the parking lots, with overtones of concentration camps), I would argue that his opposition is too simplistic and needs to be extended far beyond the parking lot to all the TV and newspaper ads for Disney World, to a wide range of institutions and technologies (restaurants, hotels, airlines, rental car agencies) that make themselves available, even subservient, to Disney World. The map precedes the territory, not just in the architecture and simulations of Disney World itself, but because all these institutions of the real conspire to become satellites of the "hyperreal," Baudrillard's term for the age of simulacra.

The parking lot represents, not so much the abandonment Baudrillard describes, but the moment of surrender, the moment of the slave becoming the slave in the Hegelian dialectic, a moment of self-humiliation, to be sure, but compensated for, even temporarily erased, by the lure of the master's kingdom ahead.

More than any prepaid tickets, this moment of giving up one's will is the price of admission, the guarantee of being admitted. Dozens of young attendants (all under 30) in barber-pole–striped coats or shirts precede us, as though they knew we were coming and had anticipated our every move. We move through them, and eventually one of them, with a pointed finger or a wave of the hand, guides us to our individual place, even as hundreds of other cars are being treated in *exactly* the same way, and our entire row (more than 50 cars) is filled before we have locked all our doors. The parking lot is a proof of the master's mastery, a blend of excess and efficiency, the excess of so many cars with license plates from all over the country, the efficiency of assembly-line parking: not a single place left vacant, the whole lot strung like beads, nothing left to chance. Having come this far, we cannot resist, can we? Surrendering the will is easy. It's so easy it's frightening.

We walk to the end of our row and board the tram. Here, we are reminded several times that we are parked in Minnie 43. All parking spaces are a mixture of the proper name of a Disney cartoon character (Mickey, Pluto, Donald) and a number. Even the asphalt is anthropomorphized, preceding us, not as metaphor, but as metonymy, an absence that works like a promissory note, that propels us forward, the assurance already given that the real Minnie, or at least an actor promoting the myth of Minnie, awaits us inside.

We ride the tram to the designated drop-off point, and then we must choose between a monorail or a ferry boat to get to Magic Kingdom, which conforms to a model of a medieval kingdom, the five man-made lakes surrounding the kingdom as a moat would, the admission gates serving as fortress walls, and Cinderella's castle as major icon within. We chose the monorail, because David and Daniel thought it would be faster. It wasn't. The monorail goes faster than the ferry boat, but takes a more circuitous route, so that both converge at the admission gate at the same time. Their mutual convergence emphasizes the fact that the two modes of crossing are more than spatial conveyance, the monorail representing the future and the ferry boat the past, for they put the lie to temporality, which evades history and which lie contaminates all of Disney World: not only is the future not faster than the past, but also both exist simultaneously with assigned values that have nothing to do with temporality. The ferry boat departs to the left, just as inside Magic Kingdom, the "past" of Frontierland, Tom Sawyer's boat ride, and all the cowboy paraphernalia go to the left. The monorail departs to the right, just as inside Magic Kingdom the "future" of Space Mountain and its satellite rides are off to the right.

From an aerial perspective, the one perspective denied to us, but precisely the one the French critics take, the whole of Magic Kingdom would look like a grid of temporality in the shape of a spread fan, Cinderella's castle as the point or pivot, the past to the left, the future to the right, encompassing the expanse of the fan. Splayed/displayed in this way, temporality ceases to be: no relationality, no causality, no vicissitudes, no ethnicity, no cultural difference, and no death, which is perhaps the culminating feature of the master's mastery. What replaces them are excesses and efficiencies, simulacra-shopping, endless lines (you either queue up and "belong" to the queue, take life from the line and move with it, or you are literally nowhere), unsettling metaphors and disguised metonymies, stripped of historical existence and functioning as autonomous tropes.

Disney World has much in common with synthetic Cubism: the convergence of front, back, and profile on one plane; the strippage of the edges for more charge at the center; the assumption of temporality one cannot see, but can know conceptually; the use of addition in the power of subtraction: the nonvisual representation of a fourth dimension collapsed into two-dimensionality.

We move through the admission gates and have to cross four blocks of streets and shops called Main Street, USA, to get to Cinderella's castle. Main Street is not for children. It's there for the parents who bring them, and nostalgia (*la mode retro* for Jameson) is the lure to shopping. The guidebooks tell us this is an authentic reenactment of any small American town at the turn of the century, and, contrary to a museum reenactment, these shops are very much alive. The old-time movie theater shows an old-time movie. The old-time barber shop gives haircuts. Everything is for sale. The only flaw in this ointment is that the soda-pop shop doesn't give original-formula Coca-Cola, and the aisle to the bathrooms is an arcade of pinball machines and video games, none of which existed at the turn of the century.

Once more, temporality is belied. No Main Street ever looked like this, except perhaps in movie musicals like *State Fair* or *Meet Me in Saint Louis.* Yet this Main Street does a lively business, surviving its supposed death and disappearance through ongoing sales. No signs of decay anywhere. No signs of change. No real vitality either, because there are no vicissitudes:

> an operation to deter every real process by its operational double, a metastable, programmatic perfect descriptive machine which provides all the signs of the real and short-circuits all its vicissitudes. (Baudrillard, "Precession" 254)

Baudrillard contrasts the "murderous capacity of images" with the "dialectical capacity of representations as a visible and intelligible mediation of the Real" ("Precession" 256), simulation set against representation, and he describes the killing capacity of simulation this way:

> Simulation . . . starts from the utopia of this principle of equivalence, from the radical negation of the sign as value, from the sign as reversion and death sentence of every reference. ("Precession" 256)

What is scandalous here is that there *is* in fact a murder, an assassination of referentiality, and, perhaps more outrageous, that it goes unnoticed. There once were a thousand Main Streets in small towns all across America, and they have died, not of natural causes. These Main Streets existed in harmony with their surrounding agrarian economies, which they serviced and which have also largely disappeared, both replaced by expanding cities and suburban shopping malls, by the colonialism of municipalities seeking a larger tax base by annexing farm lands and rural tracts, and by big business and agribusiness. The original Main Streets died because of telephone wires, automobiles, the gas and oil industries, murdered by the very conglomerates (AT&T, General Motors, Exxon, etc.) who have conspired to bring us EPCOT in Disney World. I find it cruel and ironic that killer and killed should coexist here for profit, the real death erased by the resurrection of the victim, the erection of this whitewashed simulacrum, a false-town for tourists, whose outrage is mitigated by excess and efficiency, whose longing is short-circuited by shopping, whose nostalgia is incited and then immediately fed by purchase.

And when we finally get to Cinderella's castle, itself a Disney misappropriation of many Eastern European myths (the bloody feet and poked-out eyes have been repressed), I am surprised it is nothing more than an archway which serves as a rite of passage: Main Street before it, the rest of Magic Kingdom beyond it. This is literally metonymy of colossal proportions, for the castle is meant to be viewed from a distance, a directional icon for entry and exit, never actually entered or thought about. Part for the whole, the hollow archway fills and empties, fills and empties, while the gigantic castle itself lies largely vacant.

My boys sense none of this. Instead, they steer me to the 3D movie theater, because they have heard from friends that Michael Jackson is in the movie (this was before Jackson's bad publicity and "fall from grace"). They, too, are shoppers in the culture, sensate shoppers, experience-mongers, already versed and rehearsed in what's *cool* to do: 3D movie, Space Mountain, Big Thunder, Haunted House. It is as though they see nothing in between. They want not so much to encounter these things as to be on the other side of that encounter, to be able to go home and report to their friends that they, too, have now done these things. We have all day to see the movie and go on the rides, but they are in a hurry, and I sense their panic that they won't be able to complete their mental checklist, and I feel their acceleration, not only as the correct response to Disney World's grid of atemporality, past and future reduced to a walking tour of spatial contiguity, but also as the mediating limit to their experience, as though the faster they go, the less they will experience (see, feel, and know), fulfilling some kind of Andy Warhol–like sense of pleasure. Perhaps this is built-in and anticipated. Perhaps this is the secret of sequels, the reason why so many American families go back again and again, until repeatability cancels out acceleration: until, like memorized time tables, they know the rides by rote and are bored.

My sons are disappointed. Instead of Michael Jackson, what we get is an old Chip 'n' Dale cartoon, historically the only 3D cartoon ever produced by the Disney Studios. There are 500 people in the theater watching this cartoon at any given moment while the park is open. The attendants wait for the seats to fill up, and they announce the attendance each time, like they do at ballparks. I am a film teacher by profession, and, unlike my boys, I am old enough to remember going to 3D movies on Saturday afternoons in my childhood and not turning in the special glasses afterwards. But here the master narrative incorporates two interdictions as part of the special viewing conditions: you can't take off the glasses inside or you will hurt your eyes, and you can't leave them on outside or you will hurt your eyes. Oedipal interdictions. Orpheus and Eurydice. Lot's wife. The threat of blindness informs the conditions of viewing, cathecting them, voyeurizing them, making us forgetful that this is an old cartoon, not especially funny or interesting, not even very well made.

I find it strange that we must endure the 3D movie, again like a rite of passage, almost as a precondition for seeing the rest of Magic Kingdom. And what 3D glasses give us, after all, is heightened depth perception, the illusion that the flat horizontal screen can extend vertically and perpendicularly beyond the frame, so that we all duck or reach out to touch, even feeling vertigo when we haven't moved at all. Almost at the point of permitting a vicissitude, the master narrative regains control and promises, like postmodernism, to attack depth perception everywhere else in the park. In other words, the crudity of a 3D movie is only permitted in order to prove a technological triumph over depth elsewhere in the kingdom, specifically through the use of holography. Permit the past only long enough to expose its crudity and show the triumph of technology over it. The effect is not unlike the obsession in museums, upon finding partial bones of dinosaurs or prehistoric humans, with dressing them up, filling in metonymy, building up a full face or body, in order to anthropomorphize them, tame them, feel superior to them. It is as though we need them *whole* to know we've survived them. The popularity of a film like *Jurassic Park* speaks to this perception.

We leave the 3D movie, and I notice that David has not turned in his 3D glasses, and I claim him internally, something genetic perhaps in not heeding interdictions. The sun is blinding, there is massive crowd-flow in all directions, and I am already well behind my boys, who veer to the right. We pass the merry-go-round and flying Dumbo ride, Jules Verne's Twenty Thousand Leagues Under the Sea, and the loud roar of the go-cart speedway before getting to Space Mountain. If I have enumerated the various rides, it is to show that the closer we are to Cinderella's castle, the younger the orientation and simpler the degree of motion and difficulty of the ride. The farther back we go, the older the kids. It is also to show once again the master narrative of technological triumph-in-excess, moving from wooden horse and slow submarine to the automobile and finally to this bizarre simulation of space travel called Space Mountain, which was far and away the most popular ride in Magic Kingdom at the time of our visit.

David and Daniel know ahead of time that this ride is "radical," their experience diminished by the word-of-mouth accounts of their friends. They have no patience with my fear of heights, and they leave me outside. And this is exactly what I am left with, the *outside*, like a hulking white observatory. Space Mountain. What a strange metaphor, the two terms so apparently opposite that they defy rapprochement, the simulacrum of a mountain housing (and concealing) its impossible opposite, the lift-off and escape from gravity. But here what counts is the descent, the crash-landing. In fact, this is Baudrillard's principle of equivalence again at work, one simulation masking another, neither rooted in any real history.

Provisionally, metaphor is the "desire for conceptual rapprochement between human subject and historical continuum . . . or a dispersive ordering of sense, with history deemed synonymous with ideology" (Singer 57). Faced with the deconstructionist postulate that all language is metaphorical, we can see that "metaphor . . . devolves to the vacuum of irony into which all reality is mercilessly sucked and stripped of the illusion of being" (Singer 58). Such an evasion of history can only point to the limits of metaphor as a trope of desire. What is scandalous about the metaphor of Space Mountain is not just the evasion of history, but evasion, itself, used as a strategy to rewrite history, the hurtful history that makes it impossible for us ever to be posthistoric creatures. Less than an hour's drive away, the space shuttle Atlantis is being readied for launch, but there, at least, all the metaphors of naming imply a survival. Here, the thrill of Space Mountain is in the descent, the real tragedy of Challenger stripped of its depth. As Baudrillard remarks, "it is the social itself which, in contemporary discourse, is organized according to the script for a disaster film" ("Precession" 268). Indeed, the billboards announcing the opening of Universal Studios in 1990 depicted a scene from the film *Earthquake*. The simulation of an earthquake was suspended for a day after the real earthquake in San Francisco.

The irony attendant in metaphor can be used very powerfully as long as it is a register of partial forgetting, which is to say, with temporality still possible. For example, in Alain Resnais' film *Night and Fog* (1955), the idea of tourists having themselves photographed in the ovens of the defunct concentration camps is as chilling as archive footage of the victims. In his film *Hiroshima mon amour* (1959), the image of tourists viewing Hiroshima from a bus entitled "Atomic Tours" works the same way. Both examples are ironic. Both work with a whiplash effect, making us responsible for such partial forgetting, throwing us back into historical existence and the need to posit ourselves in that existence and through the determinate contradictions of discourse. At Magic Kingdom, the forgetting is total on a grid of atemporality. And, if temporality is the first prerequisite of history, then referentiality must be the second. With Space Mountain, referentiality is obliterated, like the desexed synonymous bathroom doors in Lacan, so that we have no time frame, no contexture, no shifting positionality, no determinate contradictions, no referent in any real mountains or in the nearby space launch. There is only one simulation concealing another, an inside and an outside, concealment and containment.

And, whereas Space Mountain triumphs over death (surviving the crash) through atemporality and nonreferentiality, the Haunted House achieves the same result through holography. We ride in carts on a conveyor belt through a series of dark gossamer rooms, replete with spider webs, moving sheets, caught bugs, even a talking head under glass, until, at the very end of the ride, we see ourselves in mirrors, always to the left (so that we don't look at the arc projectors to the right), and projected in the cars with us are full-figured ghosts. Of interest here is the spatial positioning of each ghost. The carts are designed for two people, who would normally sit to each side, so that the ghosts are projected onto the center of each cart. I can see the ghost appear between David and Daniel in the cart in front of me. This is remarkable, not so much for the ghost, but for the fact that this is the first and only time I can see my sons in this ride, and they can see that I can see them: the Disney people have anticipated whole families watching each other. I sit alone in my cart, and I sit in the center, so that in the mirror to my left the ghost is projected on top of me, a superimposition, both of us competing for visibility in the mirror. After we go outside, my boys tell me that they were not afraid of the ghost between them, but of the image of me and the ghost merged behind them. The hologram triumphs over the crudity of the 3D glasses (technological history), even as it evades real history, specifically the pain and grief of real dying, the repressed of all such hauntings.

We move from the Haunted House to Big Thunder, a runaway mining car, located at the extreme left end of Magic Kingdom, at the opposite pole from Space Mountain. To get there, we have moved through Frontierland, where they sell coonskin caps and flintlock pistols converted into cap guns. No Indians or Mexicans in sight. We have bypassed Tom Sawyer's boat ride, where a boat replaces Tom's raft, and racial prejudice is repressed (Jim is gone) in favor of looming pirates. I go on Big Thunder with my boys, and once again I am thinking of the naming in/as metaphors. Thunder here does not come from the sky, but rather from the absence of sky. It comes from the rumble and roar of the runaway cars over the tracks, which is echoed and magnified in each cave-tunnel we go through.

I discover something, beyond the fact that I am too old for these rides. I discover that I cannot see my boys in the car in front of me, and I cannot hear them either. I scream their names; they don't hear me. We are all attached to this train of cars, and yet we are completely isolated from each other. The acceleration of the ride only emphasizes that isolation. And I begin to realize the purpose of participation at Magic Kingdom. If you sit outside, as I did at Space Mountain, you can think critically, even as you are literally nowhere in the park, an anonymous body taking up space that nobody wants. But, if you participate, you cease to think critically, and you lose the sense of claustrophobia and crowd-crunch. I came away from Big Thunder disagreeing with Baudrillard about the bonding with other people. In fact, the purpose of participation is to escape otherness, to be swept away in the air-conditioned darkness and stimuli of simulacra by the illusion that no other consciousness stands in the way of our desire, and so no Hegelian struggle is necessary.

I decide to test this hypothesis. My boys have now finished their checklist of major rides, and they are disappointed, still hungry for something to happen. At $28 per person admission price, I agree. They are ready now for Dumbo and the other rides that they had considered too easy, beneath them. As they queue up for Dumbo, I go to sit in one of the pavilions where they serve overpriced drinks and shade from the sun. To discover what a system represses, one must look askance, off to the side, not direct-center. As Jacqueline Rose has pointed out, "[i]t is often forgotten that psychoanalysis describes the psychic law to which we are subject, but only in terms of its *failing* . . . looked at obliquely, it can always be seen to contain its moments of unease" (233). And so it is, that if I look directly at the ride, I see the many Dumbos go round flawlessly, and I see the queue inch forward in apparent silence, motion and rest, motion and rest, and I remember from Plato's *Sophist* that motion and rest are not the qualities of things finally, but the qualities of the perplexed mind. If I look around me under the umbrella of the pavilion, I see those moments of unease and all the otherness that participation in the rides strives to avoid. Nuclear families around me, hot and disgusted: fathers with cameras or full-size camcorders rearranging the right side of their bodies; mothers, sitting, smoking, holding bottles, diapers, souvenirs; children fighting, blowing bubbles in their Coca-Colas with straws, spilling french fries, wandering off. Some 40 people around me and not one serene human being among them.

This is risky territory. There is chaos and change here, struggle and competing consciousnesses. Fathers want to leave or stay only long enough under the pavilion to reload. Children want to buy souvenirs or go on this or that ride again. Mothers want to sit there and be left alone. I realize the risk of gender stereotypes in my description, so I keep looking, but I find no exceptions. The same drama goes on at table after table. Away from the rides and exhibits, away from the air-conditioned darkness and anonymity, away from the map that precedes the territory, temporality returns with otherness.

After nine hours in the kingdom, we leave through Cinderella's castle archway, go by ferry to the tram, which drops us off at Minnie 43, and I drive the rented Ford Tempo to our Day's Inn.

EPCOT

The next morning at breakfast, we wonder if we are ready for EPCOT. Like skiers on the second day, our muscles ache with tourism. From the highway, we can see the big white golf ball, the logo for EPCOT, the equivalent of Cinderella's castle at Magic Kingdom. They call it Spaceship Earth in the guidebook, so why, then, not a rocket? Why this enormous white golf ball? An allusion to the astronauts playing golf on the moon? Maybe it has to do with size and trajectory, the drive of the golf ball likened to the orbit of the earth. Maybe it's like the ending of *The Incredible Shrinking Man*, miniature enjoined with the gigantesque, where the man, shrunken to the size of a dust speck, merges with the cosmos of night stars overhead.

Obviously, I am still not jaded enough. The real answer awaits inside.

Here the parking lot's various sections are named, not after cartoon characters, but after the various exhibits inside: Imagination, Energy, Motion, Harvest. And once again the metaphor in/of naming disturbs me. Concrete called Imagination? Asphalt named Harvest?

We park the car in Motion 20 and board the tram. At EPCOT the tram goes right to the gate, no ferry boat or monorail necessary, because there is no water outside. All the water is inside: one large man-made lake, fronted by all the various houses (House of Imagination, House of Energy, etc.) and surrounded by the pavilions of different countries. The differences between EPCOT and Magic Kingdom go beyond the placement of water. Whereas Magic Kingdom is loud with rides for little children, EPCOT is quiet, serene, and full of massive architecture and foliage, and directs itself to older children and adults. Whereas Magic Kingdom presents us with pie-wedges of supposed Americana, EPCOT aims

more seriously to be, first in the front, a history of various technologies, and, then in the back, a kind of Embassy Row, a world zoo
of different cultures. But, as with a masquerade, EPCOT hides
something, even while revealing the basic terms of that obscuring. And what is concealed, of course, is history, the terms of concealment amounting to a bogus alternative history and a self-
congratulatory showcase.

Here we have a choice: we can enter EPCOT on foot by walking through the archway, or we can ride through the big white ball
of Spaceship Earth. I convince the boys to go through the ball. We
queue up, and I notice the lines move much faster than they do
at Magic Kingdom. This is because, I discover inside, all passage
through the preliminary Houses is by assembly-line carts on a conveyor belt. You cannot walk or stop or take a second look as you
might do in a museum. The escalators move, the carts move, we
must catch them and seat ourselves "on the fly." The same is true
for getting off.

We know the routine now, and we submit to air-conditioning,
the darkness of the interior, the fact of riding in cars on a conveyor
belt, and looking to the left at tableaux depicting the various ages
and stages of communication. The voice of the narrative belongs
to Walter Cronkite, the retired patriarch of evening news, reading
the script that precedes the territory, a narration timed and synco-
pated, so that I can hear the voice repeat what I have just heard
to those people five cars behind me.

And what is scandalous about this narrative is its grandiose
tone, its preference for summary over depth, its apparent lack of
content, concrete details, erudition. We learn that there were cave
drawings, but Lascaux is never named. The Greeks are shown
staging a play, but we don't know which play or whose play. The
birth of the printing press is depicted, but no date is given, and
Gutenberg's name is suppressed. The lack of any concrete data
feels deliberate, in accord with assembly-line observation and the
lack of any fixed specular gaze, as though any dates or proper
names might somehow impact on the mobility of the ride and jar
us out of passivity, into some sort of thinking. Indeed, many adults
told me before we left Philadelphia that these rides through the
various Houses were a good chance to rest up, close the eyes, and
get ready for more rigorous walking elsewhere in the park.

Things change abruptly and radically when we get to the Electronic Age, represented by a series of television sets, which are crowded together and squeezed between the telephone and the computer. Where before there were comfortable lapses into darkness and a kind of rhythmic spacing between tableaux of people figures, here the people disappear, only to reappear as faces boxed in television sets, and now the comfortable tableaux of before become confrontational constructs, located, not off to the left, but directly ahead, in our path, and we veer away at the last minute, seemingly avoiding collision. The passive spectator is mobilized, Walter Cronkite's voice rises to a crescendo, and the masks are taken off.

On those various TV screens: Ed Sullivan, Ozzie and Harriet, and, placed side by side, separated only by the boxes which contain them, the faces of the two Walts: Disney and Cronkite. I yelled to my boys in the car in front of me, naming the faces in the sets, especially those of the two Walts, the creator of this park and the narrator of this ride, metonymically placed, looking very much like a double dose of God the Father (my boys thought they were the same person), but they couldn't hear me.

I am drowned out by the text that rises, even as the trajectory of the cars ascends, ready now to give a proper name to it all: AT&T. The giant white ball in which we are housed is actually the miniaturized logo for AT&T. I now imagine it as the ball that bounced above the words, from word to word, in those old Mitch Miller sing-a-longs.

All proper names and dates have been suppressed to get us to this moment of a fluid American present. The names that have been suppressed, in fact, are foreign names, and the dates that have been suppressed precede American history. The contentless narrative ends with a single naming—AT&T—as though the entire history of communication were but an anticipation, some sort of pagan awaiting of this global, multinational titan god with *American* for a first name. Put another way, the formula is the same as that of public television: an educational program, without commercial interruptions, enhancing the spectator's belief in the "integrity" of the program, but always book-ended, preceded or followed by the claimer: "Brought to you with funds from the ____ Corporation." But here the roles are reversed, because the pro-

202 *William F. Van Wert*

gram is subservient to the claimer: AT&T both authors the history and inherits it, and program succumbs to commercial, so that there is nothing left at the end but the claimer, itself.

But the ride is not quite over. There is one more strategy to be deployed, which successfully diverts the rider's attention away from the transparency of the masquerade by implicating the rider, threatening him/her with fear and unknowing, then providing the immediate reassurance, resulting in a justification for all the self-aggrandizement of AT&T. We leave the television monitors of the Electronic Age, we pass the PCs which follow, and then our cars are rotated, turned around, and we go up a steep incline on the conveyor belt backwards. We thus enter the "future" (the steep incline) blindly, with our faces and bodies turned toward the "past." And when our cars are turned around again so that we face forward, we are in the huge domed ceiling of the ball, the celestial heavens, a cosmos of shooting stars and asteroids created by strobe lights and laser technology. The rider is implicated with fear and unknowing, because this artificial planetarium depicts an imaginary configuration of stars and sky. No Orion, no Dipper, no Pleiades, no Southern Cross. No *familiar* markings. It is as though future time necessitated a radical alterity in spatial coordinates. But then we are immediately reassured by the voice of Walter Cronkite, who tells us that, whatever the challenges the future holds in store for us, AT&T will be there to bring us the Information Age and beyond, well into the next century (similar to the TV ads announcing future "miracles" that AT&T will bring to us).

The strategy works in two ways. We have to think beyond our own life expectancies: that is, think beyond our own deaths, reassured that AT&T will be there to take care of those who survive us. The second way the strategy works is to free AT&T from the past and real history (both deemed inadequate) and, leap-frogging the present, to install itself in the falsified future of posthistory as that which will guarantee our lives to the point of making us forgetful of our deaths.

The domed ceiling of the cosmos, then, defies not only death, but also containment as well, for that which we provisionally called Spaceship Earth when we entered can now be seen to contain the universe as well: that which we know to exist *outside* of any spaceships in existence. This defiance of containment, the illusion of holding the outside inside, explodes the structure of the spaceship as well as the metaphor of Earth. We are left with the big ball, a logo in gigantesque (which is not a spaceship, not the Earth, not even a golf ball), whose only referent is another logo in miniature, the ball of AT&T.

I wonder: why explode the structure and the idea of a center to this circle at the very end of the ride? The answer lies, not in the structure of the ball itself, but outside, in the two-humped halls of excess called Communicore East and West. The ride to the ceiling of the ball establishes a conceptualized trust and serves to prep the rider for Communicore East and West, which are the trade fairs of the future: telephones, computers, hands-on holography, interactive games, a labyrinth of technology that does not estrange or alienate, because of the trust built up in the ball between passive rider and omnipotent AT&T.

The same formula is played out at all the other Houses: concealment; a ride in the air-conditioned darkness with illuminated tableaux to the left; a contentless narrative that hurries through the centuries, names no names, offers no dates, only to rise to a crescendo at ride's end, revealing both the inadequacies of the past and the large corporation that is *already* seeing to our needs in the future; and, finally, a showroom or display to make us forgetful of the past and seduce us into the future. The House of Motion begins with the wheel (Archimedes is never mentioned) and guides us to the great unmasking, the revelation of General Motors as all-powerful agency, dumping us into a Buick showroom: eight late-model Buicks revolving without drivers, as though they, too, were capable of agency. The House of Energy ends in Exxon, providing for all our future needs. The Story of the Land and Harvest comes to us courtesy of Kraft.

I sense an invisible patent at work, as though these big corporations were not content to mass-produce commodities, but felt compelled to mass-produce their generic categories as well (communication, energy, motion, harvest). And, with the uncommon arrogance of the present, they felt further compelled to lay claim to the past as well, so that they are now in the unprecedented business of selling, not just the commodities, but atemporality too.

In the case of the History of Motion, I felt that I was being produced as a commodity as well. If Baudrillard is right, in "The

Ecstasy of Communication," that there has been a shift in the relationship between car and driver, so that the driver has become part
of the screen, then the History of Motion uses its visitors in much
the same way. The transit cars are the assembly line, leading directly to the showroom. But the cars of the assembly line are already operational, as are the display models in the showroom, so
that what is being mass-produced is the passenger, who no longer
drives the cars, but is driven by them and to them. In fact, the
transit cars and showroom models *precede* our visit, so that "late
model" can only refer to the visitors. And I suspect that all of these
Houses mass-produce spectators in the same way. Louis Marin explains the phenomenon this way: "In order to utter his own story,
the visitor is forced to borrow these representations" (59).

The ball in the center, Imagination and Land/Harvest to the
right, Motion and Energy to the left, these Houses occupy the front
of EPCOT's lake. On the left bank: Mexico, China, and Scandinavia. On the opposite shore: Germany, Italy, Japan, Morocco, and
France. On the right bank: England, the United States, and Canada. Visitors can walk around the lake, or they can take a boat
across to any of the other banks.

What do these Houses have to do with the various "history"
Houses in front? What do they have to do with each other? Where
is Russia? Australia? India? Africa and South America? Eastern Europe? Why is the geography so askew? Provisionally, I have only
one answer, and it has to do with the name of this place. EPCOT:
Environmental Prototype Community of Tomorrow. Just as each
of the "history" Houses in front offers the visitor one brief glimpse
of the future, only enough to repeat the name of the big corporation at work in the future, supposedly for our sake, so too here the
T for Tomorrow allows for absolute license with geography.

David has recently been on an exchange program with his
school to Cuernavaca, so he wants to go to the Mexico House first.
All around the lake, the architecture looks authentic: the pink cantina of Mexico, the red pagoda of China, the dark brown temple
style of Japan, the outdoor cafe with tricolor umbrellas for France.
I have been to all these countries, I even speak the languages, and
I am excited to expose my sons to all of these different cultures.

We learn that there is a brief historical movie for Mexico and
decide not to wait the extra half-hour for the next showing. In-

stead, we go inside to the *mercado*. What we find inside is a bizarre form of shopping. The commodities are all authentic enough (pinatas, serapes, sombreros, dolls, jewelry), but they are being sold American-style: compartmentalized shops, salespeople accepting credit cards, fixed high prices on everything, sparkling black floors we could skate across. What David remembers with nostalgia about the mercados in Mexico is missing here: open-air stalls, dust, people in front of goods instead of behind them, talking, lots of talking, bartering in Spanish, taking a drink, going away, coming back—shopping across time. Here it's as though Saks Fifth Avenue or Bloomingdale's had thought up a theme week called "Mexico."

We go across the street to have a drink at the cantina, while a mariachi band plays in the street. The drinks are authentic enough. I order them in Spanish, but the woman counts my change in English. I say "thank you" in Spanish; she answers "you are welcome" in English.

At all of the Houses we visit, we reproduce the experience we had at Mexico. From the outside, there is authentic architecture transplanted; on the inside, shopping replaces culture. A Japanese doll I bought in Tokyo in 1972 for $75 here costs $375. I buy some postcards of Kinkakuji, the Temple of the Golden Pavilion in Kyoto. I speak Japanese to the cashier. She answers in English.

I feel sorry for poor Morocco, the sole representative of the entire African continent, not for its inclusion in EPCOT, but for its half-existence. Only the left half of its House is for shopping. The right half is made up of bathrooms, the only restroom facilities on this side of the lake.

Each House has an authentic cafe or restaurant, and these are packed with tourists, their purchases on their laps. I buy croissants for my boys at the French pavilion, and I approach a young woman selling Coca-Cola who wears a name tag of "Betsy." I ask her in French if her name is Elizabeth, and she answers me in English, a British English with French intonation: "This is not my real name. We don't use our real names. We wear uniforms with American names."

It has taken me three times to understand. I have spoken Spanish, Japanese, and French, I have been understood all three times, and I have been answered in English. Now it makes sense. Where Magic Kingdom avoids otherness, EPCOT pretends to flaunt it, but this alterity has been reduced to a single utterance (including the repression of real names, the wearing of false uniforms, the assumption of American identities), and that utterance is English.[1] The Environmental Prototype Community of Tomorrow mocks heterogeneity, homogenizing every culture into a metaphor of shopping, a universal system of exchange (no bartering), whose currency is the dollar and whose language is English. The false Betsy may speak French with other French workers at the French pavilion, but she may not speak French with me.[2]

I suddenly realize that they have anticipated our every move again. They expect the visitor to choose a clockwise path, going around the lake from left to right, and the entire right side of the lake reinforces what the false Betsy told me. This side of the lake is occupied by Great Britain, the United States, and Canada: the *prototype* of an English-speaking world of tomorrow. Together, they embody the consolidation of all the world's languages into a single language.

I can now provide an answer to my first question about geography. This geography of the world does not include Russia, India, Australia, South America, or Africa, despite the token inclusion of Morocco as a bathroom site; it separates China from Japan, so that Asia is represented only in a segmented (nonthreatening) way. If we count the "history" houses as American, then what we witness here is most of North America laid out as a massive technological power, with Mexico to the left, Canada to the right, congruent and geographically correct. If we then include the separate pavilions of Great Britain and the United States, we can see that North America and its English-speaking ally occupy more than half of the terrain. What remains is a NATO-style slice of Europe, Japan, and China. Clearly, this environmental prototype was built before *detente* was achieved, before the fall of the wall and most Communisms, before many recent border wars and *jihads* and ethnic cleansings. I suspect that the omission of Spain, for example, had originally to do with the inclusion of Mexico, the regime of Franco in Spain, and the fact that Spain was originally excluded as well from the Common Market. Louis Marin has remarked: "Sometimes, if not always, edges and borders have the precise and concealed function of indicating the center" (50). And so it is at EPCOT that a walk around the lake reveals not the independence, diversity, and heterogeneity of foreign countries and cultures, but rather their complementarity, their satellite status. The center of the circle should be the lake, but it is not. The lake is ambiance, a showcase effect, what fountains are to Versailles or how water serves to quiet the masses in Huxley's "Waterworks and Kings." The real center is the big white ball. From whatever position we look, the big ball is always in view, daunting, as though we were standing on the moon looking back at Earth. In this Community of Tomorrow a trick has been played on real history, in which all the roles have been reversed. Here the United States is the commonwealth, the Empire, and all the other countries are its colonies, connected by a placid lake, which might be the imaginary collapse of all oceans into one, by a common language and by a dominant ideology.

My sons are frustrated and tired. They complain. There are no good rides at EPCOT, no arcade games, no predominance of other children, no good souvenirs to be had. They got the autographs of Chip and Dale, but these autographs do not justify the seven hours we have spent in the park. They will tell their friends that EPCOT is a rip-off, not nearly as much fun as Magic Kingdom. They will say that they walked around a lake and nothing happened.

Overview

Peter Wollen once remarked that Andy Warhol held a lifelong fascination with false celebrity (those made famous by staged media events and those made famous by knowing the famous) and with being an impresario. In Warhol's notebooks Wollen found this odd notation: Warhol's dream of becoming Walt Disney, that is to say, of becoming a brand name.[3]

This dream does more than typify the Oedipal bond that exists between high modernism, of which Disney is certainly an example, and what has been called Postmodernism, with Warhol as example. In the loss of affect that informed Warhol's work (and metawork), Wollen notes the twinned poles of robot and diva and their two effects: (1) catatonia (robot) and (2) hallucination (performance—being watched and recorded). These same two effects can be seen as the virus that has infected Disney World. The driving force behind Disney World, Walt Disney's intellect, operated from a belief system that was clearly congruent with high modernism: exultant, expansive, sincere, filled with master narratives (Enlightenment, Progress, Imagination, etc.). But with the passage of time, Disney, himself, has become a logo, a brand name, even a simulacrum.

With the passage of time (metonymy: inescapable, after all), Disney World has become decorative on the side of ornament rather than on the side of the engineer. All those tableaux in the air-conditioned darkness of the various Houses produce the catatonia of robotics, while the visitors who view them provide the hallucination of performance, of being watched and recorded. Wollen cites Warhol: "The more you look and it's exactly the same, the better and emptier you feel" (sic) (27). I am quite sure this is *not* the response Disney had in mind when he first created Disneyland.

Nor did he have in mind Thomas More's notions of utopia (Marin's context) when he conceived of Disneyland. I think he had in mind an environmental prototype, an extension of his film studio into the urban landscape of Southern California, a construct that would exist in competitive contrast with both Hollywood (more "real" and more accessible than Hollywood) and Los Angeles (less "real" and less afflicted with urban problems than LA). The vitality and vicissitudes of Los Angeles (the unchecked sprawl of the city, its smog, drugs, gangs, racial tensions, economic woes) have conspired to "age" both Hollywood and Disneyland. This lesson learned, the Disney people did not repeat their mistake when they expanded to Florida. Orlando provides no such threat to Disney World, and Hollywood, in the form of MGM and Universal, has followed Disney to Florida. What is true about both locations is the availability of preexistent tourist flows, the good weather all-year around, and the proximity of oceans. It is difficult to imagine Disney World in gray wet northern climates like Atlantic City or Seattle (or Tokyo and Paris, for that matter).

Yet every effort is expended to make us forgetful of climate and nearby oceans, as though these prerequisites at the blueprint stage become rivals at the operational stage. We are made forgetful of beaches by all the water contained *within* Disney World, forgetful of the Kennedy Space Center by Space Mountain and Big Thunder, forgetful of the oppressive heat by all the air-conditioned

Houses, whatever the ideology therein. I see a parallel here with the postcasino build-up of Atlantic City. The beaches and boardwalk, trademarks of the precasino era, were ignored, as people turned inward, turned their backs to the beaches, seduced by gambling, neon, floor shows, and prepaid packaged trips. And I think the accelerated erosion of the beach and various dumping scandals can be dated to coincide with the coming of the casino era.

I am not implying that Disney World has ruined the landscape of Florida. What I am saying is that the theme parks make us forgetful of ecology. The theme music for the History of Motion is "Fun to be Free," as though (1) machinery could be synonymous with freedom and (2) fun could make us forgetful of the down side of technology (energy exhaustion, pollution, destruction of the ozone layer, job layoffs, etc.).

Baudrillard insists that "Disneyland is presented as imaginary in order to make us believe that the rest is real" ("Precession" 262). Marin collapses the two terms: "Thus, the visitor who has left reality outside finds it again, but as a real 'IMAGINAIRE'" (56). I disagree with Baudrillard's assertion, because going in and coming out are quite different: the entrance may offer contrast and opposition, but the exit blurs distinctions, collapsing the terms, as Marin suggests. And what mediates the experience is the myth of technology, whose importance is insufficiently noted in both Baudrillard and Marin. Disney World is presented as imaginary, yes, but repressing a transcendental metaphysics, repressing a "real" not unlike Hegel's hoped-for end of history, made harmonious in this case through technology. Disney World is presented as imaginary in order to make us disbelieve that the rest is real. History can be evaded. Death can be deferred. What Disney had in mind, I contend, was a monument that would survive the century in which he lived, and then finally he wished to survive that century as well. Marin notes that "a myth is a narration which fantastically 'resolves' a fundamental contradiction in a given society" (65).

The given society is the United States. The fundamental contradiction is that death still occurs. We can create machines, simulacra, doubles, which then have a life of their own, an immortal life, while we prime movers and creators still die. The fantastic resolution, if one tries to evade history and disbelieve in death, is to believe that eventually we can master the technology of life expectancy. This is the myth of technology played out so powerfully, not only inside Disney World, but outside as well and by the same multinational corporations that built the "history" Houses at EPCOT.

The narcissism of the body as a kind of "control screen" (thus, forgetful of aging and dying) is an adjunct of the myth of technology, just as the disappearance of nature or landscape is a prerequisite to the emergent myth. Baudrillard defines obscenity this way: "no longer of what is hidden, repressed, forbidden or obscure; on the contrary, it is the obscenity of the visible" ("Ecstasy" 131). In such an excess of the visible, the commodity becomes "readable, gives up its secret, has only its price" ("Ecstasy" 132). Yet, while this definition serves to describe the surface effect of Disney World, it cannot account for the possibility of reading a coherent ideology of technology engineered by Disney (my exposition), and it is as though this exposure had been anticipated, expected, accounted for. The purveyors of this ideology seem secure in the knowledge that people will still come either way. Naive or informed, people keep coming, Baudrillard and Marin among them, indistinguishable from the hordes of school children, high school marching bands, retirees, and movie stars.

The unthinkable (to stay away altogether) is never thought. In this regard Disney is aligned with his detractors, in that both Baudrillard/Marin and the Disney people depend upon the continued arrival of visitors, and both conspire to keep the unthinkable repressed. The essays of Marin and Baudrillard lose currency if Disneyland were suddenly to become a ghost town. Imagine, in the case of Baudrillard, the hypothetical situation in which a reading of "The Precession of Simulacra" preempted a visit, dissuaded a visitor from coming, served instead as "stand-in" for the actual trip. The article would then literally become, itself, the map that precedes the territory, the simulacrum replacing direct experience, theory replacing experience by cautioning readers away from the experience. To preclude such a possibility, the detractors have unwittingly made themselves complicit in the ideology they attack.

It is my contention that what is finally repressed in metaphor is metonymy itself: the endlessness of desire, always effectively concealed because the one is atemporal, the other is not. Metonymy reciprocates metaphor (as though anticipating a remedy for lack), but not through repression.

I have already shown in my study how Disney World was built as metaphor (the atemporal grid, the repression of shame and lack, the various namings, from Space Mountain to Spaceship Earth). And perhaps in its ideal state (that is, with no people there, before the gates have opened or after they're closed), this metaphoric operation succeeds, for machinery feels no endlessness of desire. But, as soon as people are admitted to the park, they bring metonymy along with them. They bring their mortal bodies and their lived time, their spatial contiguity, their knowledge gained by passing through, their side-by-side contrasts, their sexual and cultural differences. And here is where I find myself inserted into the analysis, for I am the one who experiences the excess of metaphor metonymically.

I experience Marin and Baudrillard in a similar way. Cultural difference may account for the fact that these foreign critics approach American culture through metaphor first, much the same way that metaphor colors and limits my experience of French culture. But we also differ in the way we deploy these tropes as strategies of writing. In Marin's article, Thomas More's utopia becomes the 3D glasses through which we see Disneyland as "degenerative utopia," ending in myth or collective fantasy. There is no direct access to Disneyland, separate from the prologue metaphor of utopia. The metonymic walk-through is reduced to a straight-line trajectory on a map, Main Street USA leading directly to Fantasyland, with noted "eccentric centers" to the right and left. We never get the feeling that Marin ever rode a single ride or entered a single exhibit, because experience is always abstracted in terms of the various maps in his article, the result of which is an avoidance of temporality and a transformation of the connotative into the denotative.

With Baudrillard the abstraction of metaphor is more complex. I always feel when reading him that he has witnessed the explosion of some unmentioned bomb that I have failed to see: maybe a neutron bomb, which has destroyed, or at least deadened, all the people, while leaving all the simulacra lively and intact. We are already in the "desert of the real," left to wonder at what hypothetical past moment the real was irretrievably lost to us without our notice. He describes this landscape as "nuclear and genetic, no longer specular and discursive" ("Precession" 253), and I have to disagree, in terms of Disney World and my study, in which the specular and discursive are very much alive. Even if I concede that his remarks on Disneyland are passing remarks, one example among many to support his major thesis, I still want to note the atemporal and metaphoric way he equates Disneyland with Watergate and Watergate with the Loud family, positing as associative editing, if I can borrow from film language here, what is in reality a series of jump cuts. He writes, in fact, like Eisenstein: full of quick brushstrokes, provocative impressions, skaterly glances and seductive loops, with no long take or depth-of-field.

The failure of Euro Disney to catch on makes sense to me. Transplanted to France, the country that coined the word chauvinism, Disney World must seem an eyesore of greedy capitalism, forced Americana. America has always thrived on a culture of a fast present tense, disrespectful of, or inattentive to, history, while Europeans have always been steeped in history. Some of my French friends have told me privately that the French react negatively to the enforced uniforms, the protocol, the caricaturish aspects of Disney.

Still, the Disney people may yet prevail. Saudi Prince Waleed bin Talal bin Abdulaziz will spend up to $500 million and buy as much as 24% of a new $1.04 billion stock offering from Euro Disney as part of Euro Disney's deal with banks to restructure its $3.7 billion debt (Moore 1).

Even as it tries to evade history inside its theme parks, Disney is an active player in contemporary history in the way it changes the landscape wherever the parks are built and the ways local economies and ecologies are affected. My analysis here has been given some urgency by Disney's plans to build a $650 million U.S. history theme park (complete with housing developments, hotels, shops, golf courses, and RV parks) in Virginia, with a projected opening in 1998.

Blueprints for the park include the following: (1) Crossroads USA (antique steam trains); (2) President's Square (audiovisual presentation of the American Revolution; (3) Native America (raft ride recreating the Lewis and Clark expedition); (4) Civil War Fort (circlevision theater, reenactments of battle episodes from the Civil

War); (5) We The People (multimedia, replica of Ellis Island, looks at the U.S. immigrant history); (6) Enterprise (high-speed ride through a turn-of-the-century mill); (7) Victory Field (parachute rides and military equipment of World War II); (8) State Fair (Ferris wheel, roller coaster, small town America, with exhibition all-star game of baseball legends); and (9) Family Farm (country wedding, barn dance, and buffet).

Historians have founded an opposition group: Protect Historic America. Their argument: "Who needs Disneyized history within a few miles of 13 historic towns, 12 Civil War battle sites and 17 historic districts?" (Moss and Puente 1, 2).

My position on the proposed history theme park should be clear from this study. It is one thing to tolerate Disneyland and Disney World with their competing posthistories repressing the shame, vitality, and all traces of race-class-gender-sexuality of a more accurate history. It is quite another thing to contemplate the Disney people assimilating/swallowing/cannibalizing Virginia and its many historical markers for a playground to make money. One example, to embody all of my objections: the Civil War, our country's most shameful moment, was never amusing and should never be carnivalized (or trivialized) into circlevision theater.

My boys are older now, have studied the Civil War in school, and agree with me that a Disney history park in Virginia would be a big mistake.[4] No one should make money off the suffering of that war, they feel. Disney's amusement parks should be about escape, they tell me. I agree. There is no such thing as posthistory, because history cannot be escaped.

Notes

1. Unfortunately, the history of translations in this country works like this. We have the arrogance to assume foreign texts were written in our native English, bypassing all the problems of translation.

2. I note here that one of my students came to class recently dressed in an EPCOT T-shirt for Italy: Mickey Mouse with outstretched hands toward the leaning tower of Pisa. Possible readings of this image are: (1) Mickey will catch the tower if it falls, thus lending a superior helping hand to an inferior country with bad architects; or (2) Mickey will keep the tower from falling, meaning EPCOT props up Italy.

3. Wollen gave this information in a keynote speech at the Florida State Con-

ference on Film and Literature. The theme of his talk was the uses of looting and purloining in Warhol, Burroughs, and Godard, material which then became a book entitled *Raiding the Icebox.*

4. The Disney people have abandoned the idea of building their history theme park at this particular site. They have stated that they are looking at other sites in Virginia and elsewhere.

Works Cited

Apple, Max. *The Propheteers.* New York: Harper, 1987.

Baudrillard, Jean. "The Ecstasy of Communication." *The Anti-Aesthetic: Essays on Postmodern Culture.* Ed. Hal Foster. Port Townsend: Bay Press, 1983. 127–34.

———. "The Precession of Simulacra." *Art After Realism: Rethinking Representation.* Ed. Brian Wallis. New York: Godine, 1984. 253–83. Orig. in *Art and Text* 11 (Sept. 1983): 3–47. Also rpt. in *Simulations.* By Baudrillard. New York: Semiotext(e), 1983.

Jameson, Fredric. *The Political Unconscious: Narrative as a Socially Symbolic Act.* Ithaca: Cornell UP, 1981.

Marin, Louis. "Disneyland: A Degenerate Utopia." *Glyph* 1. Baltimore: Johns Hopkins UP, 1977.

Moore, Martha T. "Saudi Prince Buying Into Euro Disney." *USA Today* 2 June 1994: 1.

Moss, Desda, and Maria Puente. "Uncivil War Over Disney." *USA Today* 2 June 1994: 1, 2.

Rose, Jacqueline. *Sexuality in the Field of Vision.* London: Verso, 1986.

Singer, Alan. "Desire's Desire: Toward an Historical Formalism." *Enclitic* VIII.1–2 (Spring/Fall 1984): 57–67.

South Atlantic Quarterly 92.1 (Winter 1993). This entire issue is devoted to Disney. Rpt. as a book by Duke UP titled "Inside the Mouse: Work and Play at Disney World," 1995.

Wollen, Peter. *Raiding the Icebox.* Bloomington: Indiana UP, 1993.

BOOKS RECEIVED

Abelman, Nancy, and John Lie. *Blue Dreams: Korean Americans and the Los Angeles Riots.* Cambridge: Harvard UP, 1995.

Abraham, Nicolas. *Rhythms: On the Work, Translation, and Psychoanalysis.* Trans. Benjamin Thigpen and Nicholas T. Rand. Stanford: Stanford UP, 1995.

Acland, Charles R. *Youth, Murder, Spectacle: The Cultural Politics of "Youth in Crisis."* Boulder: Westview, 1995.

Affron, Charles, and Mirella Jona Affron. *Sets in Motion: Art Direction and Film Narrative.* New Brunswick: Rutgers UP, 1995.

Airhihenbuwa, Collins O. *Health and Culture: Beyond the Western Paradigm.* Thousand Oaks: Sage, 1995.

Aldgate, Anthony. *Censorship and the Permissive Society: British Cinema and Theatre, 1955–1965.* Oxford: Clarendon, 1995.

Arteaga, Alfred, ed. *An Other Tongue: Nation and Ethnicity in the Linguistic Borderlands.* Durham: Duke UP, 1994.

Ashcroft, Bill, Gareth Griffiths, and Helen Tiffin, eds. *The Post-Colonial Studies Reader.* New York: Routledge, 1995.

Awkward, Michael. *Negotiating Difference: Race, Gender, and the Politics of Positionality.* Chicago: U of Chicago P, 1995.

Baudrillard, Jean. *The Illusion of the End.* Trans. Chris Turner. Stanford: Stanford UP, 1994.

Bauer, Dale M. *Edith Wharton's Brave New Politics.* Madison: U of Wisconsin P, 1995.

Beck, Ulrich, Anthony Giddens, and Scott Lash. *Reflexive Modernization: Politics, Tradition, and Aesthetics in the Modern Social Order.* Stanford: Stanford UP, 1994.

Bederman, Gail. *Manliness and Civilization.* Chicago: Chicago UP, 1995.

Behdad, Ali. *Belated Travelers: Orientalism in the Age of Colonial Dissolution.* Durham: Duke UP, 1994.

Bersani, Leo. *Homos.* Cambridge: Harvard UP, 1995.

Bertens, Hans. *The Idea of the Postmodern: A History.* New York: Routledge, 1995.

Beverley, John, José Oviedo, and Michael Aronna, eds. *The Postmodern Debate in Latin America.* Durham: Duke UP, 1995.

Blanchot, Maurice. *The Work of Fire.* Trans. Charlotte Mandell. Stanford: Stanford UP, 1995.

Boggs, Carl. *The Socialist Tradition: From Crisis to Decline.* New York: Routledge, 1995.

Booker, M. Keith, and Dubravka Juraga. *Bakhtin, Stalin, and Modern Russian Fiction: Carnival, Dialogism, and History.* Westport: Greenwood, 1995.

Bosworth, R. J. B. *Explaining Auschwitz and Hiroshima: History Writing and the Second World War, 1945–1990.* New York: Routledge, 1993.

Bourdieu, Pierre, and Hans Haacke. *The Exchange.* Stanford: Stanford UP, 1995.

Brady, Jeanne. *Schooling Young Children: A Feminist Pedagogy for Liberatory Learning.* Albany: State U of New York P, 1995.

Brahm, Gabriel, Jr., and Mark Driscoll. *Prosthetic Territories: Politics and Hypertechnologies.* Boulder: Westview, 1995.

Brettle, Jane, and Sally Rice, eds. *Public Bodies, Private States: New Views on Photography, Representation and Gender.* Manchester: Manchester UP, 1994.

Brinker-Gabler, Gisela, ed. *Encountering the Other(s): Studies in Literature, History, and Culture.* Albany: State U of New York P, 1995.

Brown, Stewart, ed. *The Pressures of the Text: Orality, Texts and the Telling of Tales.* U of Birmingham African Studies Series. Birmingham: U of Birmingham P, 1995.

Brownell, Susan. *Training the Body for China: Sports in the Moral Order of the People's Republic.* Chicago: U of Chicago P, 1995.

Burnham, Clint. *The Jamesonian Unconscious: The Aesthetics of Marxist Theory.* Durham: Duke UP, 1995.

Caudwell, John Thornton. *Televisuality: Style, Crisis, and Authority in American Television.* New York: Rutgers UP, 1995.

Chanan, Michael. *Repeated Takes: A Short History of Recording and Its Effects on Music.* New York: Verso, 1995.

Classen, Constance, David Howes, and Anthony Synnott. *Aroma: The Cultural History of Smell.* New York: Routledge, 1994.

Colas, Santiago. *Postmodernity in Latin America: The Argentine Paradigm.* Durham: Duke UP, 1995.

Cooper, Carolyn. *Noises in the Blood: Orality, Gender, and the "Vulgar" Body of Jamaican Popular Culture.* Durham: Duke UP, 1995.

Corner, John. *Television Form and Public Address.* London: Edward Arnold, 1995.

Creekmur, Corey K., and Alexander Doty, eds. *Gay, Lesbian, and Queer Essays on Popular Culture.* Durham: Duke UP, 1995.

Davies, Carole Boyce. *Black Women, Writing and Identity*. New York: Routledge, 1994.

———, ed. *Black Women's Diasporas*. New York: New York UP, 1995.

———, ed. *International Dimensions of Black Women's Writing*. New York: New York UP, 1995.

De Graef, Ortwin. *Titanic Light: Paul De Man's Post-Romanticism, 1960–1969*. Lincoln: U of Nebraska P, 1995.

De La Campa, Roman, E. Ann Kaplan, and Michael Sprinker, eds. *Late Imperial Culture*. New York: Verso, 1995.

Delumeau, Jean. *History of Paradise: The Garden of Eden in Myth and Tradition*. New York: Continuum, 1995.

Dentith, Simon. *Bakhtinian Thought: An Introductory Reader*. New York: Routledge, 1995.

Derrida, Jacques. *The Gift of Death*. Trans. David Wills. Chicago: U of Chicago P, 1995.

———. *On the Name*. Ed. Thomas Dutoit. Trans. David Wook, John P. Leavey, Jr., and Ian McLeod. Stanford: Stanford UP, 1995.

———. *Points . . . Interviews, 1974–1994*. Ed. Elisabeth Weber. Trans. Peggy Kamuf and others. Stanford: Stanford UP, 1995.

Devi, Mahasweta. *Imaginary Maps*. Trans. Gayatri Chakravorty Spivak. New York: Routledge, 1995.

Duff, Anthony, Sandra Marshall, Rebecca Emerson Dobash, and Russell P. Dobash, eds. *Penal Theory and Practice: Tradition and Innovation in Criminal Justice*. Fulbright Papers 14. Manchester: Manchester UP, 1994.

Dutton, Kenneth R. *The Perfectible Body: The Western Ideal of Male Physical Development*. New York: Continuum, 1995.

Eagleton, Terry. *Heathcliff and the Great Hunger: Studies in Irish Culture*. New York: Verso, 1995.

Earl, James W. *Thinking About "Beowulf."* Stanford: Stanford UP, 1995.

Edmunds, Susan. *Out of Line: History, Psychoanalysis and Montage in H.D.'s Long Poems*. Stanford: Stanford UP, 1995.

Epstein, Julia. *Altered Conditions: Disease, Medicine, and Storytelling*. New York: Routledge, 1995.

Gabbard, Krin, ed. *Jazz Among the Discourses*. Durham: Duke UP, 1995.

———, ed. *Representing Jazz*. Durham: Duke UP, 1995.

Gartman, David. *Auto Opium: A Social History of American Automobile Design*. New York: Routledge, 1994.

Gay, Penny. *As She Likes It: Shakespeare's Unruly Women*. New York: Routledge, 1994.

Geertz, Clifford. *After the Fact: Two Countries, Four Decades, One Anthropologist*. Cambridge: Harvard UP, 1995.

Gevisser, Mark, and Edwin Cameron, eds. *Defiant Desire: Gay and Lesbian Lives in South Africa.* New York: Routledge, 1995.

Glass, James M. *Psychosis and Power: Threats to Democracy in the Self and the Group.* Ithaca: Cornell UP, 1995.

Goellner, Ellen W., and Jacqueline Shea Murphy, eds. *Bodies of the Text: Dance as Theory, Literature as Dance.* New Brunswick: Rutgers UP, 1995.

GoGwilt, Christopher. *The Invention of the West: Joseph Conrad and the Double-Mapping of Europe and Empire.* Stanford: Stanford UP, 1995.

Gordon, Lewis R. *Bad Faith and Antiblack Racism.* Atlantic Highlands: Humanities P, 1995.

Guillory, John. *Cultural Capital: The Problem of Literary Canon Formation.* Chicago: U of Chicago P, 1993.

Feenberg, Andrew, and Alastair Hannay. *Technology and the Politics of Knowledge.* Bloomington: Indiana UP, 1995.

Felski, Rita. *The Gender of Modernity.* Cambridge: Harvard UP, 1995.

Fox, Pamela. *Class Fictions: Shame and Resistance in the British Working Class Novel, 1890–1945.* Durham: Duke UP, 1995.

Frow, John. *Cultural Studies and Cultural Vale.* Oxford: Clarendon, 1995.

Fry, Paul H. *A Defense of Poetry: Reflections on the Occasion of Writing.* Stanford: Stanford UP, 1995.

Haggerty, George E., and Bonnie Zimmerman, eds. *Professions of Desire: Lesbian and Gay Studies in Literature.* New York: MLA, 1995.

Halkin, Ariela. *The Enemy Reviewed: German Popular Literature through British Eyes between the Two World Wars.* Westport: Praeger, 1995.

Halton, Eugene. *Bereft of Reason: On the Decline of Social Thought and Prospects for Its Renewal.* Chicago: U of Chicago P, 1995.

Hanne, Michael. *The Power of the Story: Fiction and Political Change.* Providence: Berghahn, 1994.

Heide, Margaret J. *Television Culture: "Thirtysomething" and the Contradictions of Gender.* Philadelphia: U of Pennsylvania P, 1995.

Holloway, Karla F. C. *Codes of Conduct: Race, Ethics, and the Color of Our Character.* New Brunswick: Rutgers UP, 1995.

Horowitz, Daniel, ed. *American Social Classes in the 1950s: Selections from Vance Packard's "The Status Seekers."* New York: St. Martin's, 1995.

Hutcheon, Linda. *Irony's Edge: The Theory and Politics of Irony.* New York: Routledge, 1994.

Huyssen, Andreas. *Twilight Memories: Marking Time in a Culture of Amnesia.* New York: Routledge, 1995.

Ikegami, Eiko. *The Taming of the Samurai: Honorific Individualism and the Making of Modern Japan.* Cambridge: Harvard UP, 1995.

Jackson, Jr., Earl. *Strategies of Deviance: Studies in Gay Male Representation.* Bloomington: Indiana UP, 1995.
Jackson, Michael. *At Home in the World.* Durham: Duke UP, 1995.
Jagose, Annamarie. *Lesbian Utopics.* New York: Routledge, 1994.
Jenks, Chris, ed. *Visual Culture.* New York: Routledge, 1995.
Johnson, Claudia Durst. *Understanding "The Scarlet Letter": A Student Casebook to Issues, Sources, and Historical Documents.* Westport: Greenwood, 1995.
Karcher, Carolyn L. *The First Woman in the Republic: A Cultural Biography of Lydia Maria Child.* Durham: Duke UP, 1995.
Kemble, Frances A., and Frances A. Butler Leigh. *Principles and Privilege: Two Women's Lives on a Georgia Plantation.* Ann Arbor: U of Michigan P, 1995.
King, Katie. *Theory in Its Feminist Travels: Conversations in U.S. Women's Movements.* Bloomington: Indiana UP, 1994.
Konstan, David. *Greek Comedy and Ideology.* New York: Oxford UP, 1995.
Kracauer, Siegfried. *The Mass Ornament: Weimar Essays.* Trans. and ed. Thomas Y. Levin. Cambridge: Harvard UP, 1995.
Kritzman, Lawrence D. *Auschwitz and After: Race, Culture, and "the Jewish Question" in France.* New York: Routledge, 1995.
Kroeber, Karl, ed. *American Indian Persistence and Resurgence.* Durham: Duke UP, 1994.
Lacoue-Labarthe, Philippe. *Musica Ficta: Figures of Wagner.* Trans. Felicia McCarren. Stanford: Stanford UP, 1995.
Larson, Kerry C. *Whitman's Drama of Consensus.* Chicago: U of Chicago P, 1988.
Laudet, Claire, and Richard Cox, eds. *Le Peuple de France Aujourd'hui.* Manchester: Manchester UP, 1995.
Lauret, Maria. *Liberating Literature: Feminist Fiction in America.* New York: Routledge, 1994.
Lemelle, Sidney J., and Robin D. G. Kelley. *Imagining Home: Class, Culture and Nationalism in the African Diaspora.* New York: Verso, 1994.
Lentricchia, Frank, and Thomas McLaughlin, eds. *Critical Terms for Literary Study.* 1990. Chicago: U of Chicago P, 1995.
Leonard, James S., Christine E. Wharton, Robert Murray Davis, and Jeanette Harris, eds. *Authority and Textuality: Current Views of Collaborative Writing.* West Cornwall: Locust, 1994.
Leonard, Jerry, ed. *Legal Studies as Cultural Studies: A Reader in (Post) Modern Critical Theory.* Albany: State U of New York P, 1995.
Limon, Jose E. *Dancing with the Devil: Society and Cultural Poetics in Mexican-American South Texas.* Madison: U of Wisconsin P, 1994.

Lionnet, Françoise. *Postcolonial Representations: Women, Literature, Identity.* Ithaca: Cornell UP, 1995.

Loshitzky, Yosefa. *The Radical Faces of Godard and Bertolucci.* Detroit: Wayne State UP, 1995.

Lowith, Karl. *Martin Heidegger and European Nihilism.* Ed. Richard Wolin. New York: Columbia UP, 1995.

Malkki, Liisa H. *Purity and Exile: Violence, Memory, and National Cosmology Among Hutu Refugees in Tanzania.* Chicago: U of Chicago P, 1995.

Marcus, George E., ed. *Technoscientific Imaginaries: Conversations, Profiles, and Memoirs.* Chicago: U of Chicago P, 1995.

Marissen, Michael. *The Social and Religious Designs of J. S. Bach's Brandenburg Concertos.* Princeton: Princeton UP, 1995.

Marshall, Margaret J. *Contesting Cultural Rhetorics: Public Discourse and Education, 1890–1900.* Ann Arbor: U of Michigan P, 1995.

McLaren, Peter L. *Critical Pedagogy and Predatory Culture: Oppositional Politics in a Postmodern Era.* New York: Routledge, 1995.

McLaren, Peter L., and James M. Giarelli, eds. *Critical Theory and Educational Research.* Albany: State U of New York P, 1995.

McRobbie, Angela. *Postmodernism and Popular Culture.* New York: Routledge, 1994.

Miller, J. Hillis. *Topographies.* Stanford: Stanford UP, 1995.

Miller, Nancy K. *French Dressing: Women, Men and Ancien Regime Fiction.* New York: Routledge, 1995.

Moon, Michael, and Cathy N. Davidson, eds. *Subjects and Citizens: Nation, Race, and Gender from "Oroonoko" to Anita Hill.* Durham: Duke UP, 1995.

Mumford, Laura Stempel. *Love and Ideology in the Afternoon: Soap Opera, Women, and Television Genre.* Bloomington: Indiana UP, 1995.

Musser, Charles. *Thomas A. Edison and His Kinetographic Motion Pictures.* New Brunswick: Rutgers UP, 1995.

Nichols, Bill. *Blurred Boundaries: Questions of Meaning in Contemporary Culture.* Bloomington: Indiana UP, 1994.

Nietzsche, Friedrich. *Unfashionable Observations.* Trans. Richard T. Gray. Vol. 2 of *The Complete Works of Friedrich Nietzsche.* Stanford: Stanford UP, 1995.

Oboler, Suzanne. *Ethnic Labels, Latino Lives: Identity and the Politics of (Re)-Presentation in the United States.* Minneapolis: U of Minnesota P, 1995.

Olaniyan, Tejumola. *Scars of Conquest/Masks of Resistance.* New York: Oxford UP, 1995.

Ortiz, Fernando. *Cuban Counterpoint: Tobacco and Sugar.* 1947. Durham: Duke UP, 1995.

Otis, Laura. *Organic Memory: History and the Body in the Late Nineteenth and Early Twentieth Centuries.* Lincoln: U of Nebraska P, 1994.

Outhwaite, William. *Habermas: A Critical Introduction*. Stanford: Stanford UP, 1994.

Perniola, Mario. *Enigmas: The Egyptian Moment in Society and Art*. New York: Verso, 1995.

Peters, Michael, ed. *Education and the Postmodern Condition*. Westport: Bergin and Garvey, 1995.

Petro, Patrice, ed. *Fugitive Images: From Photography to Video*. Bloomington: Indiana UP, 1995.

Pfeil, Fred. *White Guys: Studies in Postmodern Domination and Difference*. New York: Verso, 1995.

Phelan, Shane. *Getting Specific: Postmodern Lesbian Politics*. Minneapolis: U of Minnesota P, 1994.

Pickering, Andrew. *The Mangle of Practice: Time, Agency, and Science*. Chicago: U of Chicago P, 1995.

Pieterse, Jan Nederveen. *White on Black: Images of Africa and Blacks in Western Popular Culture*. New Haven: Yale UP, 1995.

Pietropaolo, Laura, and Ada Testaferi, eds. *Feminisms in the Cinema*. Bloomington: Indiana UP, 1995.

Price, Richard, and Sally Price. *Enigma Variations*. Cambridge: Harvard UP, 1995.

Ragussis, Michael. *Figures of Conversion: "The Jewish Question" and English National Identity*. Durham: Duke UP, 1995.

Redhead, Steve. *Unpopular Cultures: The Birth of Law and Popular Culture*. Manchester: U of Manchester P, 1995.

Reynolds, Simon, and Joy Press. *The Sex Revolts: Gender, Rebellion and Rock 'n' Roll*. Cambridge: Harvard UP, 1995.

Riddel, Joseph N. *Purloined Letters: Originality and Repetition in American Literature*. Ed. Mark Bauerlein. Baton Rouge: Louisiana State UP, 1995.

Robertson, George, Melinda Mash, Lisa Tickner, Jon Bird, Barry Curtis, and Tim Putnam, eds. *Travellers' Tales: Narratives of Home and Displacement*. New York: Routledge, 1994.

Rubinstein, Ruth P. *Dress Codes: Meanings and Messages in American Culture*. Boulder: Westview, 1995.

Russ, Joanna. *To Write Like a Woman: Essays in Feminism and Science Fiction*. Bloomington: Indiana UP, 1995.

Sadoff, Dianne F., and William E. Cain, eds. *Teaching Contemporary Theory to Undergraduates*. New York: MLA, 1994.

San Juan, Jr., E. *Hegemony and Strategies of Transgression: Essays in Cultural Studies and Comparative Literature*. Albany: State U of New York P, 1995.

Savigliano, Marta E. *Tango and the Political Economy of Passion*. Boulder: Westview, 1995.

Schefer, Jean Louis. *The Deluge, the Plague: Paolo Uccello.* Trans. Tom Conley. Ann Arbor: U of Michigan P, 1995.

Seitz, Brian. *The Trace of Political Representation.* Albany: State U of New York P, 1995.

Serres, Michel. *Genesis.* Trans. Genevieve James and James Nielson. Ann Arbor: U of Michigan P, 1995.

———. *The Natural Contract.* Trans. Elizabeth MacArthur and William Paulson. Ann Arbor: U of Michigan P, 1995.

Serres, Michel, with Bruno Latour. *Conversations on Science, Culture, and Time.* Trans. Roxanne Lapidus. Ann Arbor: U of Michigan P, 1995.

Shamdasani, Sonu, and Michael Munchow, eds. *Speculations after Freud: Psychoanalysis, Philosophy and Culture.* New York: Routledge, 1994.

Shershow, Scott Cutler. *Puppets and "Popular" Culture.* Ithaca: Cornell UP, 1995.

Shohat, Ella, and Robert Stam. *Unthinking Eurocentrism: Multiculturalism and the Media.* New York: Routledge, 1994.

Sletter, Christine E., and Peter L. McLaren, eds. *Multicultural Education, Critical Pedagogy, and the Politics of Difference.* Albany: State U of New York P, 1995.

Spanos, William V. *The Errant Art of Moby-Dick: The Canon, the Cold War, and the Struggle for American Studies.* Durham: Duke UP, 1995.

Starn, Orin, Carolos Ivan Degregori, and Robin Kirk, eds. *The Peru Reader: History, Culture, Politics.* Durham: Duke UP, 1995.

Stave, Shirley A. *The Decline of the Goddess: Nature, Culture, and Women in Thomas Hardy's Fiction.* Westport: Westview, 1995.

Taylor, Diana, and Juan Villegas, eds. *Negotiating Performance: Gender, Sexuality, and Theatricality in Latin/o America.* Durham: Duke UP, 1994.

Tester, Keith. *Media, Culture and Morality.* New York: Routledge, 1994.

Thomas, Helen, ed. *Dance, Gender and Culture.* New York: St. Martin's, 1993.

Tonglin, Lu. *Misogyny, Cultural Nihilism, and Oppositional Politics: Contemporary Chinese Experimental Fiction.* Stanford: Stanford UP, 1995.

Umland, Samuel J., ed. *Philip K. Dick: Contemporary Critical Interpretations.* Westport: Greenwood, 1995.

Visker, Rudi. *Michel Foucault: Genealogy as Critique.* New York: Verso, 1995.

Vrettos, Athena. *Somatic Fictions: Imagining Illness in Victorian Culture.* Stanford: Stanford UP, 1995.

Wald, Priscilla. *Constituting Americans: Cultural Anxiety and Narrative Form.* Durham: Duke UP, 1995.

Wei-ming, Tu, ed. *The Living Tree: The Changing Meaning of Being Chinese Today.* Stanford: Stanford Up, 1994.

Wiegman, Robyn. *American Anatomies: Theorizing Race and Gender.* Durham: Duke UP, 1995.

Wiley, Norbert. *The Semiotic Self.* Chicago: U of Chicago P, 1994.

Williams, Jeffrey, ed. *PC Wars: Politics and Theory in the Academy.* New York: Routledge, 1995.

Wills, David. *Prosthesis.* Stanford: Stanford UP, 1995.

Wojciehowski, Dolora A. *Old Masters, New Subjects: Early Modern and Poststructuralist Theories of Will.* Stanford: Stanford UP, 1995.

Wolff, Janet. *Resident Alien: Feminist Cultural Criticism.* New Haven: Yale UP, 1995.

Young, Robert J. C. *Colonial Desire: Hybridity in Theory, Culture and Race.* New York: Routledge, 1995.

Zimmermann, Patricia R. *Real Families: A Social History of Amateur Film.* Bloomington: Indiana UP, 1995.

Zwarg, Christina. *Feminist Conversations: Fuller, Emerson and the Play of Reading.* Ithaca: Cornell UP, 1995.

CONTRIBUTORS

Inge E. Boer is an associate professor at the Belle van Zuylen Institute of the Amsterdam Graduate Center for Multicultural and Comparative Gender Studies, at the University of Amsterdam, The Netherlands. Recently, she co-edited with Mieke Bal *The Point of Theory: Practices of Cultural Analysis* (New York/Amsterdam: Continuum/Amsterdam University Press, 1994). Her book *Rereading the Harem and the Despot: Changes in French Cultural Representations of the Orient in the Late Eighteenth and Early Nineteenth Centuries* is forthcoming.

Celeste Fraser Delgado is an assistant professor in the English department at Penn State University, specializing in transnational cultural studies. Her publications include articles on Argentinian detective fiction in the *Latin American Literary Review* and on feminist revisions of "traditional family values" in anthologies on African and African-American women writers. Her current research project, "Global Housekeeping: The Structural Adjustment of Gender in the U.S., Argentina, and Kenya," explores the conflicting images of tradition, family, and home deployed in each context in local struggles over the imposition of the global neoliberal economy.

David Golumbia has published articles on science fiction, subaltern cultural theory, feminist philosophy and theory, philosophy of mind, and analytic metaphysics. Author of a forthcoming book, *Against Universality: Founding Cultural Studies*, he is currently working on a critique of contemporary philosophical realism as well as a study of whiteness in recent U.S. literature and culture.

Charles Hersch is an assistant professor of political science at Cleveland State University. He is currently completing a book about the role of the arts in political education in the United States in the 1950s and 1960s.

David Kellogg is a senior fellow at the University of North Carolina at Chapel Hill, completing a work entitled *Deploying the Poetic: The Discursive Construction of Contemporary American Verse Culture.*

Anouar Majid teaches literature, cultural theory, and writing at the University of New England in Maine. He has worked on American radical

literature and is now examining the impact of Islam on Afro-Arab literature within the larger context of Third World intellectual discourses and
transnational capitalism.

William F. Van Wert teaches film, creative writing, theory, and contemporary fiction at Temple University. He has authored two books on film,
two short story collections, a novella, and numerous articles, short stories,
poems, and essays. His forthcoming book, *Memory Links,* will be published
by the University of Georgia Press.

the review of

Education Pedagogy Cultural Studies

Editors
Patrick Shannon and Henry A. Giroux
Pennsylvania State University, University Park, Pennsylvania USA

The *review of Education/ Pedagogy/ Cultural Studies* continues to expand the aims and scope of the previous journal, *The Review of Education*, by publishing extended essays concerning books and other texts about the field of education. By challenging the traditional boundaries which separate academic disciplines, the new journal creates a spark in which debates in education can be more broadly and realistically defined.

Because educational issues are debated, the journal features essays from a variety of theoretical, ideological, and political perspectives. Underlying these debates is the issue of pedagogy — a view of how people within any context specify a particular vision of what knowledge is of most value, what it means to know something, and how we might construct representations of ourselves, others and our physical and social environment. *Education/Pedagogy/Cultural Studies* publishes essays on "texts" which address these contructions, connecting the field of education with cultural practices, artifacts, and institutions.

4 issues per volume • ISSN: 1071-4413 • Current Subscription: Volume 18 (1996)
Base List Rate*: $79

Special Society Rate for individual members of the American Educational Research Association, the Association for Supervision and Curriculum Development, and the American Educational Studies Association: $48

*Base List Rate available only to individuals. This rate includes postage and handling charges. Institutions should contact their agent or the publisher for separate rates. The US dollar rate applies in North America only. All prices are subject to change without notice.

Gordon and Breach Publishers

North/South America: c/o International Publishers Distributor Order Department:
P.O. Box 27542, Newark, NJ 07101-8742, USA • Tel: (800) 545-8398/ Fax: (215) 750-6343
Europe: P.O. Box 90, Reading, Berkshire, RG1 8JL, UK • Tel: +44 (0)173-456-8316/ Fax: (0)173-456-8211
Australia/Asia: PO Box 1180, Singapore 9111 • Tel: +65 741 6933 / Fax: +65 741 6922

STANFORD HUMANITIES REVIEW

SHR engages current cultural issues in an ongoing, interdisciplinary dialogue. Each issue is organized around a current intellectual debate and includes contributions from a range of disciplines with a multinational perspective.

issue 5:1 contested politics

religious disciplines & structures of modernity

How has modern secular power reconstituted and polemicized religious and ethnic difference through nationalist politics? This issue examines how religious traditions have shaped historical and cultural experiences of modernity. Contrary to much recent scholarship that has made the West its focus, essays in this volume discuss such questions in the context of the Middle East and South Asia. Contributors include Talal Asad, Joel Beinin, Suad Joseph, Barbara Metcalf, Aron Rodrigue, and Gauri Viswanathan.

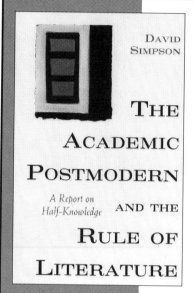